Combined 3D Rendering Series
3D Rendering in Windows®
3D Models in Motion
3D Articulation

by D. James Benton

Copyright © 2016-2021 by D. James Benton, all rights reserved.

Windows is a trademark of the Microsoft Corporation.
Excel and Visual Studio are also trademarked by Microsoft.
OpenGL is a trademark of Silicon Graphics, Inc.
GLUT (OpenGL Utilities Library) is copyright by Mark Kilgard.

3D Studio is a trademark of AutoDesk, the makers of AutoCAD.
Tecplot is a trademark of Tecplot, Inc.

Preface

This is a combination of three books: *3D Rendering in Windows®*, *3D Models in Motion*, and *3D Articulation*. This is a how-to guide on rendering three-dimensional objects. The target operating system is Windows®, but these same principles and techniques could be used in other contexts. The primary implementation is based on OpenGL™, but alternate rendering systems are also presented. In this text we will cover the finer details of code and object development. We will also explore how to implement advanced features and controls. We will assume the reader is familiar with C programming. Many references are available on that subject, including my book, *Version Independent Programming*. As in that text, we will require that <u>all</u> code function properly on <u>any</u> version and configuration of Windows®. All of the software described herein is available free online.

All of the examples contained in this book,
(as well as a lot of free programs) are available at:
https://www.dudleybenton.altervista.org/software/index.html

All of the color figures can be found here (click on cover):
https://djamesbenton.altervista.org/

Figure 1. Molten Salt Reactor Model

Table of Contents

	page
Preface	i
Chapter 1. Introduction	1
Chapter 2. Basic Concepts	3
Chapter 3. The View	5
Chapter 4. The Math	6
Chapter 5. The Objects	12
Chapter 6. The Lighting	15
Chapter 7. Shading, Scattering, and Texture	16
Chapter 8. Shadows, Reflections, and Stenciling	18
Chapter 9. Rendering	20
Chapter 10. Painting	21
Chapter 11. 3D Rendering with OpenGL	22
Chapter 12. The OpenGL™ Examples	24
Chapter 13. Stonehenge 1-2-3	30
Chapter 14. The 3D Studio® Model Viewer	33
Chapter 15. 3D Rendering without OpenGL	36
Chapter 16. Simple Sort and Paint	47
Chapter 17. The Generic 3D Model Viewer	51
Chapter 18. Virtual Reality Markup Language	53
Chapter 19. Sky Fly	63
Chapter 20. The Knight's Tour	78
Chapter 21. Displaying Three-Dimensional Data	89
Chapter 22. Geometric Shapes	93
Chapter 23. Meshes	99
Chapter 24. Complex Objects	103
Chapter 25. Textured Objects	107
Chapter 26. Viewpoint	112
Chapter 27. Lighting	114
Chapter 28. Simple Motion	116
Chapter 29. Linkage Motion	120
Chapter 30. Track Motion	132
Chapter 31. Reflecting Motion	138
Chapter 32. Bouncing Motion	140
Chapter 33. Sliding Motion	142
Chapter 34. Combining Simple Motions	148
Chapter 35. Swimming Motion	158
Chapter 36. Stretching Motion	162
Chapter 37. Exploding Motion	166
Chapter 38. Soaring Motion	170
Chapter 39. Reciprocating Motion	176
Chapter 40. Simple Leg Motion	185
Chapter 41. Walking Motion	188
Chapter 42. Skeletal Motion	203
Chapter 43. Rigid Wing Articulation	214
Chapter 44. Flexed Wing Articulation	220
Chapter 45. Undulating Articulation	225
Chapter 46. Modeling Hair	227
Appendix A: Example Details & Setup	249

Appendix B. Working with Pixel Contexts 253
Appendix C. Working with Textures 257
Appendix D. Working with Resources.. 259
Appendix E. Working with Lists... 261
Appendix F. Working with Collections 265
Appendix G. Working with Topography... 267
Appendix H. Selection of Objects 269
Appendix I. OpenGL™ Stenciling... 270
Appendix J. Rendering: How Long Does It Take? 272
Appendix K. Splitting a Model Mathematically 274
Appendix L. Texture-Linked Models.. 280
Appendix M. Element Orientation 282
Appendix N: Painting without Flicker 283
Appendix O: Spinning Cube 284
Appendix P: Random Numbers... 286
Appendix Q. Hot Key Rotation... 289
Appendix R: GLUT® & Windows® 292
Appendix S. Format Conversions Using TP2 294
Appendix T: Compilers 297
Appendix U. Win3D by Leendert Ammeraal.. 298

Figure 2. Manhattan Project Virtual Museum

Chapter 1. Introduction

There are many books and articles on rendering 3D objects using OpenGL™. This is intended as a supplement to, not a replacement for, such texts. There are eight basic considerations in creating and displaying a three-dimensional scene:

1) The relationship between the viewer and the scene (the view).
2) The coordinate transformations (the math).
3) The geometric representation of the scene (the objects).
4) The type and position of the light sources (the lighting).
5) How the surface of the objects reacts to lighting (shading, scattering, & reflecting).
6) Modifying light/object interactions (shadows & stenciling).
7) Combining the elements above to create the scene (rendering).
8) Displaying the rendered scene (painting).

There are also eight steps to implement these in a Windows® program:

1) Load the resources (bitmaps, icons, meshes, etc.).
2) Register the classes[1] (the main window plus any special controls).
3) Create the windows (the main window plus any special controls).
4) Establish the context[2] for rendering.
5) Gather user inputs (angles and distance between viewer and objects, determine which objects will be included, position of light source, etc.).
6) Render the scene.
7) Paint the rendering onto the display.
8) Check for user input and return to step 5.

We will cover each of these in the subsequent chapters.

Figure 3. Molten Salt Reactor Model

---

[1] Note that Windows® classes have nothing to do with classes in C++.
[2] Device contexts and pixel formats will be discussed later.

Before we dive into the material, I should comment on two things: 1) programming languages and 2) long sections of code appearing in this text. First, there is nothing in the world of coding like the C language. C has no equal nor any significant competition. Python, Ruby, and Pearl are superfluous. Don't waste your time on them. Second, the code contained herein (though some sections are admittedly long) is clear and concise—something you will rarely find online. Most of the code available online is sloppy and absurdly verbose. Carefully read and learn from the code supplied herein, not only for specific content but also for succinctness. I have been writing code for almost five decades and began at a time when each byte, instruction, and millisecond mattered.

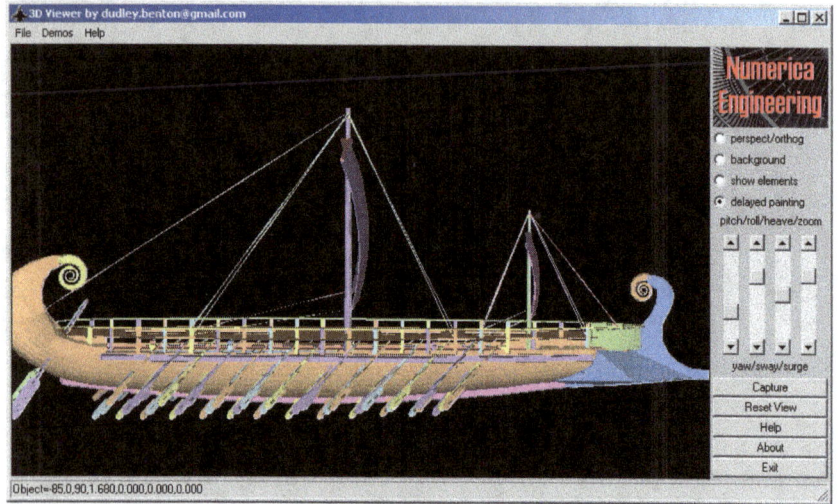

Figure 4. 3D Viewer

Chapter 2. Basic Concepts

We will first consider rendering with the OpenGL™ system and then with an alternate one. OpenGL™ is very powerful, but it has certain limitations. There are two reasons you might want to render 3D objects without this powerful library: 1) it isn't compatible with your system and 2) you don't want to be locked into 24-bit color depth. OpenGL™ and 24-bits/pixel are inseparable: you don't get one without the other. Several methods for rendering 3D images are presented in this book. Fully functioning codes and libraries are provided on line for every example, including the T-Rex depicted on the cover.

3D rendering is an important part of graphical user interface design, data analysis and presentation, game design, prototype design, and marketing. There are many tools available for 3D rendering–ranging from free to very expensive. Such tools can be used to build static content that can be played back through your application. Live rendering in response to user input is far preferable and can be built into your application with a reasonable level of effort. There are over fifty complete examples provided with this book that will help you do just that.

There are four essential parts of an interactive 3D model are:

1) Graphical User Interface (GUI)
2) Pixel Rendering Context (PRC)
3) Three-Dimensional Objects (3DO)
4) Rendering Instruction Set (RIS)

We must also have the operating system (in this case Windows®) and the rendering engine (in this case OpenGL). These combine to produce the final result—an interactive 3D model.

Graphical User Interface

This part of the whole is much like any other application. It performs the basic tasks of program loading, memory allocation, and file I/O.

Pixel Rendering Context

The OpenGL™ rendering engine requires a *pixel context* in order to deliver the result. An image is created within this context and then painted into a window that is a part of the GUI. The pixel context must have certain characteristics in order to implement the desired model building. See Appendix B for more on pixel contexts. Once the model is rendered into the pixel context, it can be displayed within the GUI.

3D Objects

Other than lines, all 3D objects are flat surfaces. There are no *solid* or *smooth* objects. All surfaces are composed of triangles or quadrangles. Even spheres, cylinders, and rolling hills are combinations of simpler polygons: triangles or quadrangles. While the rendering engine will accept a hexagon, this will ultimately be painted as six triangles.

All surfaces are either colored based on the vertices or draped with an image. A polygon may have a single color or this may vary linearly between the vertices using simple 2D interpolation for each of the color components. Draping images are called *textures* and have four components, abbreviated RGBA (red, green, blue, additional). The fourth parameter (given the symbol A) can be used in several ways to produce different visual effects. Windows® 24 bit images are ordered BGR (blue, green, red) and must be reordered before passing them to the OpenGL™ rendering engine as a bound texture.

Rendering Instructions

The way OpenGL™ works is very simple (though not easy or trivial)... You first clear the pixel context, set up the lighting, and define the viewpoint (which might be thought of as the camera position). You then send all of the 3D objects to the rendering engine. After this is complete, you paint the result onto a window within the GUI. While you can change some things inside the pixel context after building it and also add more items, the normal procedure is to clear and then rebuild everything. This process eliminates ambiguities and also determines the rate of animation, which is limited by the time required to clear and rebuild.

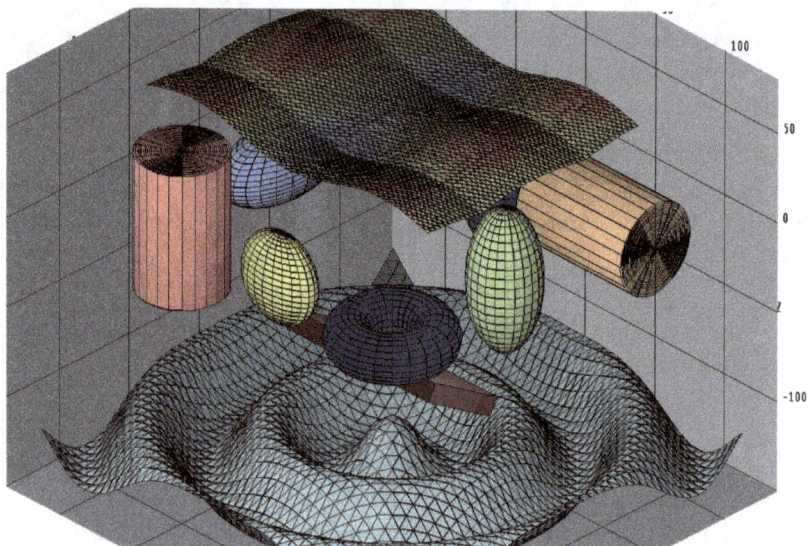

Figure 5. 3D Shapes

Chapter 3. The View

The relationship between the viewer and the scene is illustrated in the following figure:

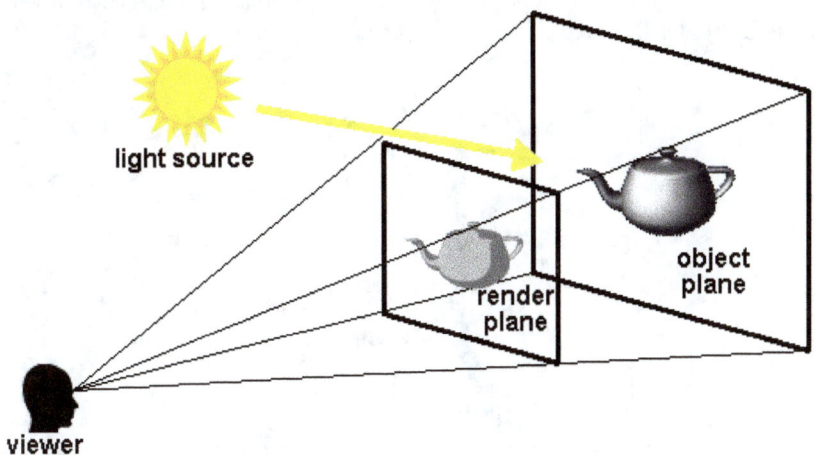

Figure 6. Object and Rendering Planes

The light shines from the source onto the object. The surface of the object reacts to the light. Modified light then travels from the object to the viewer, passing through the render plane. Our goal is to construct what would appear in the render plane and paint this on the display.

If the render plane is closer to the viewer than to the object, there will be no perception of depth. When this distance goes to zero, the orthographic projection results. As the render plane gets closer to the object than to the viewer, the perception of depth will be exaggerated. A rendering that preserves the perception of depth as illustrated above is called perspective.

Chapter 4. The Math

In 3D rendering, all of the spatial relationships between the viewer, light source, object, and planes are represented as vectors. A vector is group of coordinates, in this case, representing three-dimensional space. The following figure illustrates the three principal coordinates: x, y, and z:

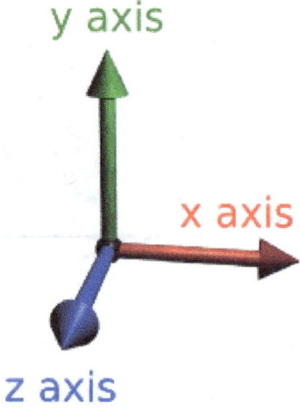

Figure 7. 3D Axis Vectors

These three axes are orthogonal, that is, mutually perpendicular (forming right angles with each other). The property of orthogonality is very important in the transformations that will be used in rendering. These three axes also conform to the right hand rule or convention, as illustrated in the following figure:

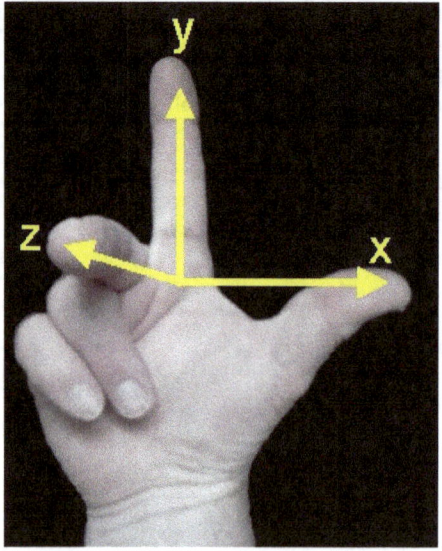

Figure 8. Right-Hand Orientation

It is most efficient to handle the coordinates as a group or vector. This also simplifies the notation and facilitates calculations, as there are conventions for describing and rules for performing operations on vectors. The first of these is the unit vector. A vector along the x-axis, having length 1, is given the symbol, *i*. A vector along the y-axis, having length 1, is given the symbol, *j*. A vector along the z-axis, having length 1, is given the symbol, *k*. The vector formed by a line starting at the origin (x=0, y=0, z=0) out to some point (x,y,z) can be written $v = x\mathbf{i} + y\mathbf{j} + z\mathbf{k}$. This vector can also be represented by the matrix: [x,y,z].

There are three basic operations with vectors that are foundational to 3D rendering. These are addition, dot (or scalar) product, and cross (or vector) product. The addition of two vectors can be visualized by placing the tail of the second on the head of the first and then drawing a line from the tail of the first to the head of the second, as illustrated below in 2D:

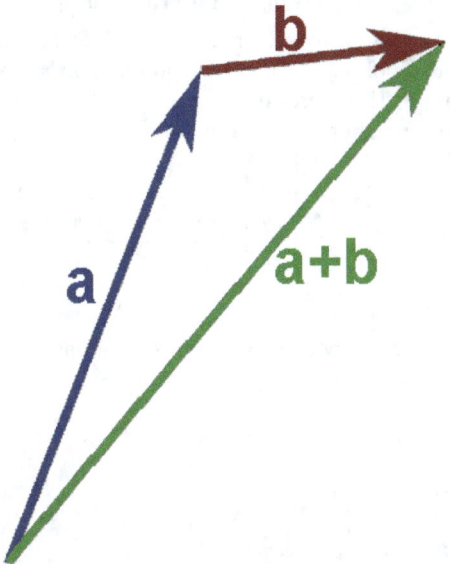

Figure 9. Vector Sum

This operation can be represented by the following matrices:

$$\begin{bmatrix} ax \\ ay \\ az \end{bmatrix} + \begin{bmatrix} bx \\ by \\ bz \end{bmatrix} = \begin{bmatrix} ax+bx \\ ay+by \\ az+bz \end{bmatrix}$$

The dot product of two vectors produces a scalar (or single value) and is illustrated in 2D by the following figure:

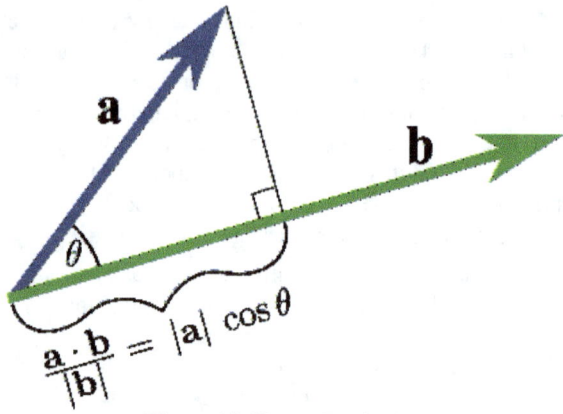

Figure 10. Vector Projection

The angle between the two vectors is θ and |a| denotes the length of vector a. Another way of looking at the dot product, $a \cdot b = |a| \times |b| \times \cos(\theta)$, is the projection of a onto b. If a were to cast a shadow on b, how long would that shadow be? In matrix notation this operation is:

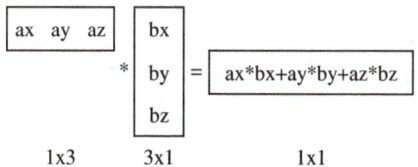

The following code snippet performs this operation:

```
double DotProduct(double*A,double*B,int n)
{
int i;
double d;
for(d=i=0;i<n;i++)
d+=A[i]*B[i];
return(d);
}
```

The cross product is where the right hand rule comes in. Where the dot product combines two vectors to produce a scalar, the cross product combines two vectors to produce a third vector. The most basic relationships are presented in terms of the unit vectors, i, j, and k. First, the dot product:

$$i \cdot j = j \cdot k = k \cdot i = 0$$

The above relationships arise from the fact that $\cos(90°)=0$ and the unit vectors form right angles with each other. The cross products are:

$$i \times j = k \quad j \times k = i \quad k \times i = j$$

The order of these operations, along with the right hand rule, determines the sign of the resultant vector. With a dot product, the order doesn't matter, but with a cross product it does. Reversing the order of the vectors above changes the sign of the resultant:

$$j \times i = -k \quad k \times j = -i \quad i \times k = -j$$

The cross product can be represented in matrix form by:

$$a \times b = \begin{vmatrix} i & j & k \\ ax & ay & az \\ bx & by & bz \end{vmatrix} = \begin{matrix} (ay*bz-az*by)i \\ (az*bx-ax*bz)j \\ (ax*by-ay*bx)k \end{matrix}$$

The center expression enclosed in || indicates the determinant. The following code snippet performs this operation:

```
void CrossProduct(double*A,double*B,double*C)
{
C[0]=A[1]*B[2]-A[2]*B[1];
C[1]=A[2]*B[0]-A[0]*B[2];
C[2]=A[0]*B[1]-A[1]*B[0];
}
```

Various transformations can be represented by matrix operations, for instance, scaling. A vector can be made three times as long by the following transformation:

$$\begin{vmatrix} 3 & 0 & 0 \\ 0 & 3 & 0 \\ 0 & 0 & 3 \end{vmatrix} \begin{vmatrix} x \\ y \\ z \end{vmatrix} = \begin{vmatrix} 3x \\ 3y \\ 3z \end{vmatrix}$$

That is, a 3x3 matrix times a 3x1 matrix equals a 3x1 matrix. By convention, the first is the number of rows and the second is the number of columns. When multiplying two matrices, one of size LxM by MxN, the result will be size LxN. The number of columns in the first matrix (M) must equal the number of rows in the second (also M). Matrix multiplication, [A]x[B]=[C], can be expressed by the following formula:

$$C_{l,n} = \sum_{m=1}^{M} A_{l,m} B_{m,n} \qquad (4.1)$$

This is implemented by the following code snippet:

```
void MatrixMultiply(double*A,double*B,double*C, int
    L,int M,int N)
{
int l,m,n;
for(l=0;l<L;l++)
for(n=0;n<N;n++)
  for(C[N*l+n]=m=0;m<M;m++)
  C[N*l+n]+=A[M*l+m]*B[N*m+n];
}
```

A more general scaling, x*Sx, y*Sy, z*Sz, would be performed by the following matrix operation:

$$\begin{vmatrix} Sx & 0 & 0 \\ 0 & Sy & 0 \\ 0 & 0 & Sz \end{vmatrix} * \begin{vmatrix} x \\ y \\ z \end{vmatrix} = \begin{vmatrix} x*Sx \\ y*Sy \\ z*Sz \end{vmatrix}$$

Some transformations require adding a constant to the resultant (or right hand side) of the operation. This is accomplished by adding a fourth component or augmenting the vector and matrix, as in:

$$\begin{vmatrix} Sx & 0 & 0 & 0 \\ 0 & Sy & 0 & 0 \\ 0 & 0 & Sz & 0 \\ 0 & 0 & 0 & C \end{vmatrix} * \begin{vmatrix} x \\ y \\ z \\ 1 \end{vmatrix} = \begin{vmatrix} x*Sx \\ y*Sy \\ z*Sz \\ C \end{vmatrix}$$

Rotations are performed about one axis at a time. A rotation about the x-axis by an angle θ is performed by the following matrix operation:

$$\begin{vmatrix} 1 & 0 & 0 \\ 0 & \cos(\theta) & -\sin(\theta) \\ 0 & \sin(\theta) & \cos(\theta) \end{vmatrix}$$

A rotation about the y-axis by an angle φ is performed by the following matrix operation:

$$\begin{vmatrix} \cos(\phi) & 0 & \sin(\phi) \\ 0 & 1 & 0 \\ -\sin(\phi) & 0 & \cos(\phi) \end{vmatrix}$$

A rotation about the z-axis by an angle ψ is performed by the following matrix operation:

$$\begin{vmatrix} \cos(\psi) & -\sin(\psi) & 0 \\ \sin(\psi) & \cos(\psi) & 0 \\ 0 & 0 & 1 \end{vmatrix}$$

These operations are performed by the following code snippet:

```
void RotateX(double*V,double*U,double theta)
{
double R[3*3];
R[0]=1.;R[1]=0.   ;R[2]=0.;
R[3]=0.;R[4]=cos(theta);R[5]=-sin(theta);
R[6]=0.;R[7]=sin(theta);R[8]= cos(theta);
MatrixMultiply(R,V,U,3,3,1);
}
```

```
void RotateY(double*V,double*U,double phi)
  {
  double R[3*3];
  R[0]= cos(phi);R[1]=0.;R[2]=sin(phi);
  R[3]=0.   ;R[4]=1.;R[5]=0.;
  R[6]=-sin(phi);R[7]=0.;R[8]=cos(phi);
  MatrixMultiply(R,V,U,3,3,1);
  }
void RotateZ(double*V,double*U,double psi)
  {
  double R[3*3];
  R[0]=cos(psi);R[1]=-sin(psi);R[2]=0.;
  R[3]=sin(psi);R[4]= cos(psi);R[5]=0.;
  R[6]=0.   ;R[7]=0.   ;R[8]=1.;
  MatrixMultiply(R,V,U,3,3,1);
  }
```

OpenGL™ performs these operations for you, but it is important to understand what it's doing so that you can direct the library to do what intend. More transformations and vector operations will be presented in Chapter 15, rendering without OpenGL™.

Figure 11. 3D Letters

Chapter 5. The Objects

By computational necessity, the geometric representation of a 3D scene is composed of individual objects. Each of these objects must be broken down into polygons, as illustrated below:

Figure 12. Triangular Elements

The most basic polygon would be a line, but reflecting light requires a surface. The simplest polygon that defines a surface is a triangle. The surface of the teapot above has been described by an assemblage of triangles. Pairs of triangles in some regions could be combined, as illustrated below:

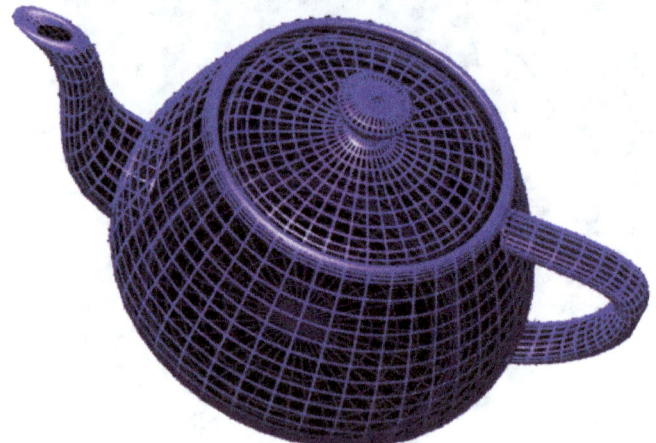

Figure 13. Quadrangular Elements

There is no spatial ambiguity in a polygon having only three distinct vertices, as the three points define a unique plane. There is, however, spatial ambiguity in any polygon having more than three vertices, as illustrated below:

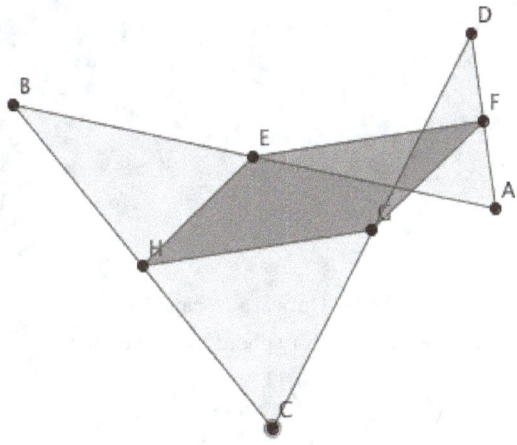

Figure 14. Non-Coplanar Elements

as any combination of three may define a different plane. There is also an orientation that is associated with polygons, as it is important to know whether you are looking at the front or the back side of something. The convention for polygon orientation follows from the right hand rule for vectors. This orientation is illustrated in the following figure:

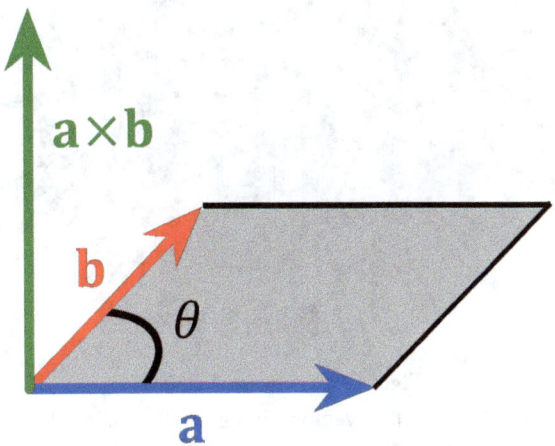

Figure 15. Planar Projection

The cross product of the two vectors, *a* and *b*, lying in the plane forms the outward normal area vector *a×b*. Each polygon on the surface has an associated outward normal vector, as illustrated in this next figure:

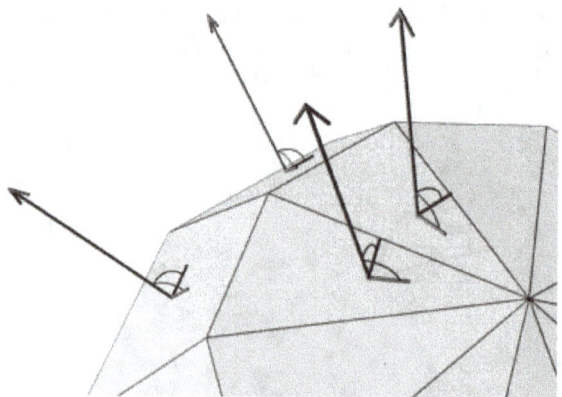

Figure 16. Outward Normal Vectors

Outward normal area vectors for sphere look like this:

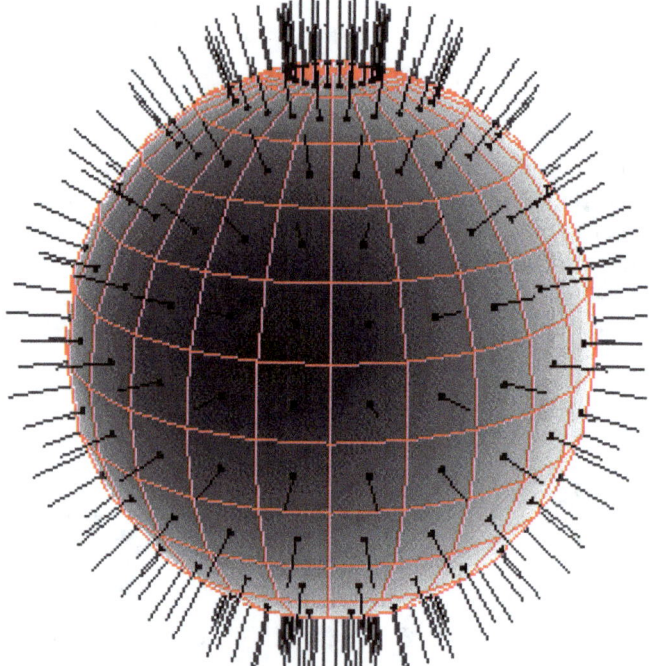

Figure 17. Outward Normals

    The cross product of the vectors lying in the plane form the outward normal, which determines the relationship between that part of the surface and the light source.

Chapter 6. The Lighting

There are different types of light sources, including point and spot lights:

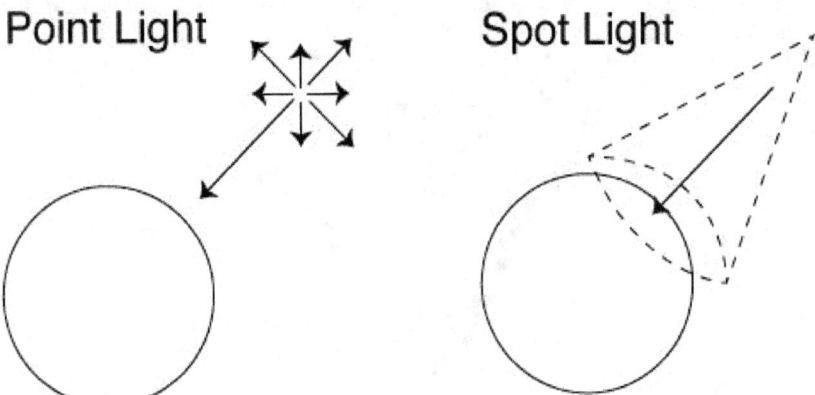

Figure 18. Light Sources

Light is also classified as being either directional or ambient: as if coming from a particular source or as if coming from everywhere:

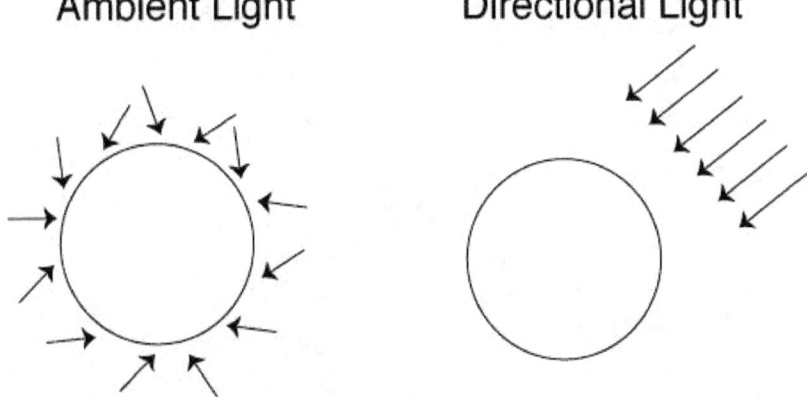

Figure 19. Light Destinations

The light source may be white (containing all colors) or contain only some colors. The position of the light source relative to the objects and viewer is also important. Defining the light source (or sources) is one of the first steps in rendering the 3D scene.

Of the examples contained in the online archive, the OpenGL™ Move Light and Mesa Teapot examples are the best illustrations of light source positioning.

Chapter 7. Shading, Scattering, and Texture

One of the most important aspects of 3D rendering is modeling how the surface of the objects reacts to lighting. The simplest model of light is illustrated in the following figure:

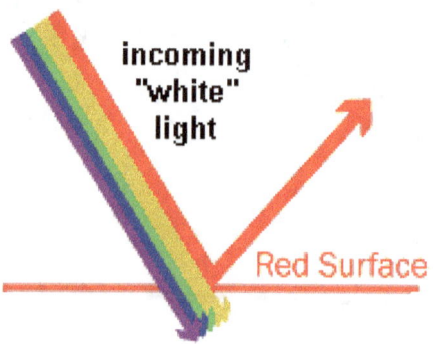

Figure 20. Incident Light

This next figure illustrates what this looks like for a familiar object:

Figure 21. Reflected Light

The interaction between real light and actual surfaces is more complex than this, as illustrated below:

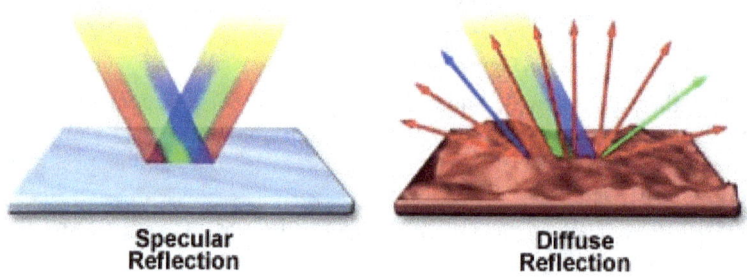

Figure 22. Surface Roughness

A shiny surface will produce a specular reflection and a rough surface will produce a diffuse reflection. A surface may even change the color of the light, as illustrated in this next figure:

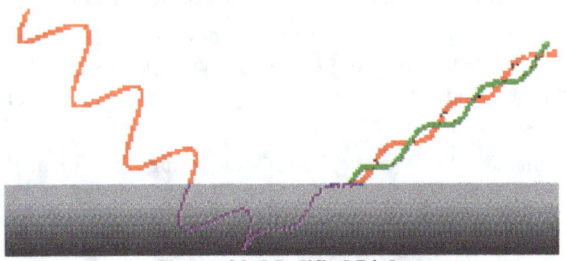

Figure 23. Modified Light

The more realistic you want objects to appear, the more effort you will have to put into the light/surface interactions. The OpenGL™ library can handle several levels of complexity, but it does have limitations that will be discussed later. The various options in lighting and surfaces provided by OpenGL™ are illustrated in the teapots example that is included in the SDK:

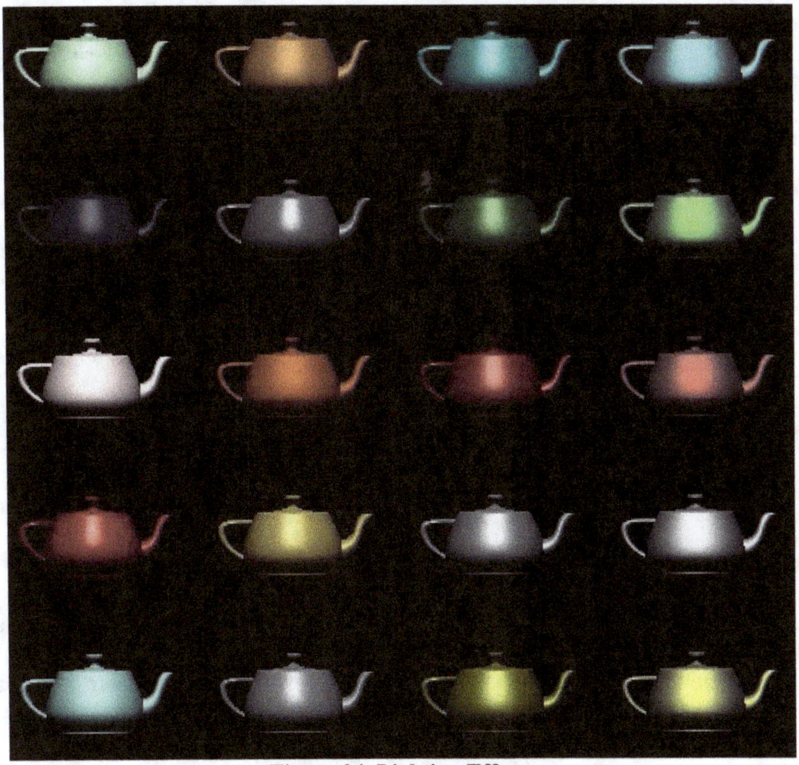

Figure 24. Lighting Effects

Some of the combinations above look like plastic, while others look metallic or ceramic. The polygons defining the teapot are the same in each case.

Chapter 8. Shadows, Reflections, and Stenciling

Shadows, reflections, and other similar scene enhancements are implemented using stenciling and multiple drawing passes. Dino shade is a good example of this. Consider the following explanation by the developer, Mark J. Kilgard:

> We can eliminate the visual "artifact" of seeing the "flipped" dinosaur underneath the floor by using stencil. The idea is to draw the floor without color or depth. Update but so that a stencil value of one is where the floor will be. Later when rendering the dinosaur reflection, only update pixels with a stencil value of 1 to make sure the reflection is only on the floor, not below the floor.
>
> Back face culling will be used to only draw either the top or the bottom floor. This produces a floor with two distinct appearances. The top floor surface is dark red and reflective. The bottom floor surface is dark blue and not reflective.
>
> Draw the floor with stencil value 3. This assures that the shadow will only be drawn once per floor pixel (and only on the floor pixels).
>
> Only render where stencil is set above 2 (i.e., 3 where the top floor is). Update stencil with 2 where the shadow gets drawn so we don't redraw the shadow.

The following section of code from this example that illustrates how this is implemented:

```
if((stencilReflection&&renderReflection)||
   (stencilShadow&&renderShadow))
  glClear(GL_COLOR_BUFFER_BIT|GL_DEPTH_BUFFER_BIT|
    GL_STENCIL_BUFFER_BIT);
else
  glClear(GL_COLOR_BUFFER_BIT|GL_DEPTH_BUFFER_BIT);
glDisable(GL_DEPTH_TEST);
glColorMask(GL_FALSE,GL_FALSE,GL_FALSE,GL_FALSE);
glEnable(GL_STENCIL_TEST);
glStencilOp(GL_REPLACE,GL_REPLACE,GL_REPLACE);
glStencilFunc(GL_ALWAYS,1,0xFFFFFFFF);
drawFloor();
glColorMask(GL_TRUE,GL_TRUE,GL_TRUE,GL_TRUE);
glEnable(GL_DEPTH_TEST);
glStencilFunc(GL_EQUAL,1,0xFFFFFFFF);
glStencilOp(GL_KEEP,GL_KEEP,GL_KEEP);
```

The examples that use stenciling to produce visual effects include: Chess, Dino Draw, Dino Shade, Reflect Dino, Reflect 2, and Shapes. The Knight's Tour, Stonehenge 2, and View3DS examples use stenciling to identify objects but not for visual effects.[3]

The reflect example appears to be a reflection, but is actually a clever painting and does not use stenciling. Instead, this example uses mipmaps to

---

[3] See Appendix G for details.

define the relationship between the flat image of a tree and the curved surface of the torus, as in the following code snippet:

```
gluBuild2DMipmaps(GL_TEXTURE_2D,format,w,h,GL_RGB,
    GL_UNSIGNED_BYTE,image);
glTexParameterfv(GL_TEXTURE_2D,GL_TEXTURE_WRAP_S,
    GL_REPEAT);
glTexParameterfv(GL_TEXTURE_2D,GL_TEXTURE_WRAP_T,
    GL_REPEAT);
glTexEnvfv(GL_TEXTURE_ENV,GL_TEXTURE_ENV_MODE,
    GL_MODULATE);
cube=glGenLists(1);
BuildCube();
cage=glGenLists(2);
BuildCage();
cylinder=glGenLists(3);
BuildCylinder(60);
torus=glGenLists(4);
BuildTorus(0.65,20,.85,65);
genericObject=torus;
```

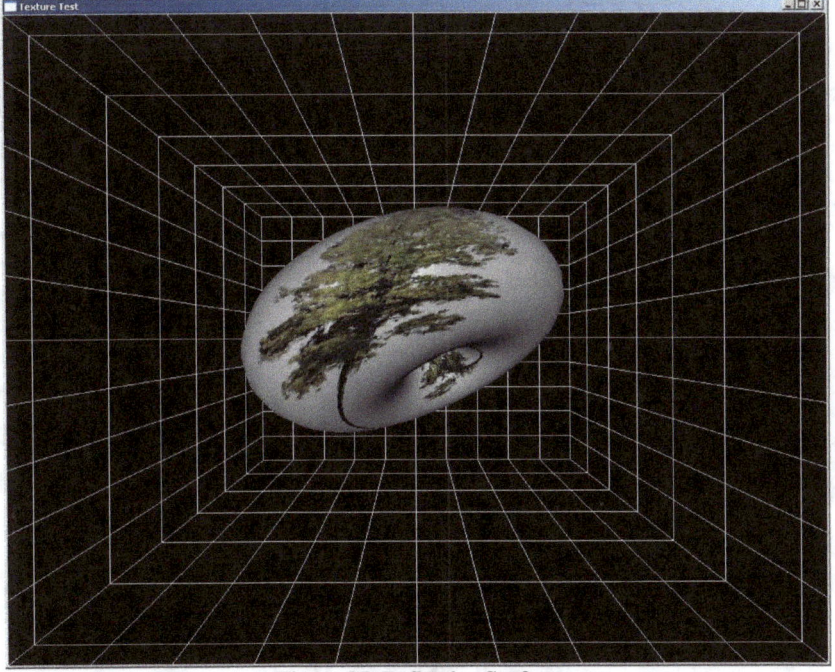

Figure 25. Reflective Surface

The maps and textures are prepared before allocating the rendering lists and building the objects. This is more elaborate in appearance than the Earth & Moon example, but the method is the same.

Chapter 9. Rendering

Methods for rendering 3D objects can be divided into two categories: 1) ray tracing and 2) everything else. Ray tracing is like particle tracking for photons, only more computationally intensive. Ray tracing produces the most realistic results, but is entirely impractical for anything that is interactive. Ray tracing requires a server farm and a budget the size of most countries' GDP. OpenGL™ doesn't use ray tracing and we're not going to cover it in this book.

The two most common rendering methods that don't involve ray tracing are: 1) hidden surface and 2) Z-buffering. The hidden surface method is also much too computationally intensive to be practical in this context. The Z-buffering method of rendering is called by several names, including rasterization and shading, but these are misnomers. The Z-buffering method is by far the fastest method and can produce acceptable results with reasonable effort.

The concept of Z-buffering is quite simple: Draw the projection of each element of each object one pixel at a time. If you carry along all of the terms, each pixel will have a depth associated with it (i.e., a distance from the viewer). If the latest pixel is closer to the observer than the one previous one, replace it; otherwise discard it.

Z-buffering requires a depth plane as well as a color plane. OpenGL™ most often uses a single-precision (32-bit) floating-point Z-buffer, although there are several other options. All of the OpenGL™ calls that pass floating-point values use single-precision (32-bit) types. This choice of Z-buffer depth achieves good quality and speed.[4]

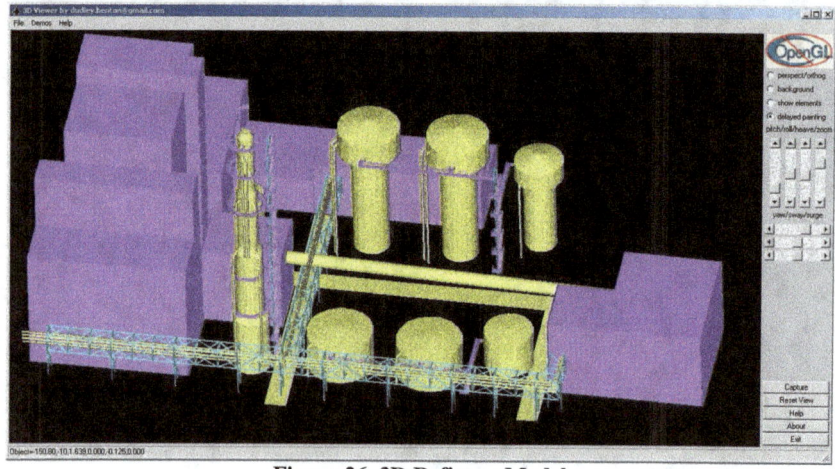

Figure 26. 3D Refinery Model

---

[4] For more options see Appendix C.

Chapter 10. Painting

Whether you're using OpenGL™ or some other library, the scene is rendered in memory and then painted onto the display after it is complete. With OpenGL™ the painting step is performed by calling SwapBuffers(). Call glutSwapBuffers() when using the OpenGL™ GLUT® library.

The long ago 2 and spin cube examples use BitBlt() to paint the image from memory onto the display. The long ago 1, Stonehenge 3, and View3D examples use InvalidateRect() or RedrawWindow() to force the graphics window to repaint (i.e., receive the WM_PAINT message) and then SetDIBitsToDevice() to paint the bitmap from memory onto the display. The difference between these last two groups is necessitated by the pixel depth. The long ago 2 and spin cube images can be created in the same depth as the display using WinAPI function calls and bitmap handles; whereas, the long ago 1, Stonehenge 3, and View3D images are always 8 bits/pixel–regardless of the display color depth–and are created by direct manipulation of each pixel (i.e., each byte in the bitmap).

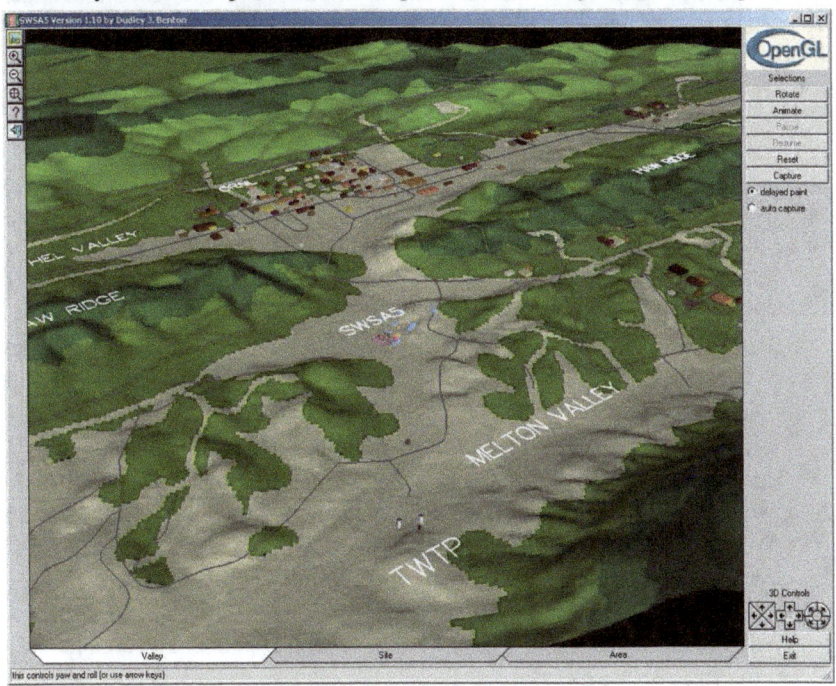

Figure 27. Landfill Site 3D Model

Chapter 11. 3D Rendering with OpenGL

There are many books and articles on rendering 3D objects using OpenGL™. This book is a supplement to, not a replacement for, such texts. There are at least two reasons for this book. First, OpenGL™ was developed on and for the Unix® O/S. Most of the available examples assume you will be building and running these on either Unix® or Linux®.

Microsoft® supported OpenGL™ before it established their proprietary product, DirectX®, but has since dismissed OpenGL™ and made various changes to the Visual Studio® C compiler so that it will no longer compile the original examples. Second, there are essential aspects of working with OpenGL™ that are not well explained within the context of the Windows® O/S. There are also essential aspects of 3D rendering that are assumed to be common knowledge in the OpenGL™ literature that are truly arcane outside of Unix®.

For example, OpenGL™ texture files are problematic in Windows®. The RGB, BW, and TEX file formats are unknown outside of Unix®. Granted, the BMP file format is unique to Windows® and not recognized on the WWW, but the GIF, PNG, JPG, and TIF file formats are universally recognized. It requires a special image editing tool, endless format conversions, or rewriting the texture code in order to work with these non-Unix formats. I have done the latter for you.

Some C compilers will recognize a forward or backslash as a path separator, but others will not. The OpenGL™ examples do not follow other conventions, for instance, the use of <header.h> to indicate a file located in a common folder vs. "header.h" to indicate a local file in the current folder. These and other differences result in an explosion of compiler errors that can be daunting.

The OpenGL™ examples assume both a console and a graphic application window. The examples originally came with the following main program statement:

```
int main(int argc,char**argv,char**envp)
```

This is the standard main program for a console application.[5] While this does work with recent versions, the expected main program statement for a Windows® program is the following:

```
int WINAPI WinMain(HINSTANCE hInstance,HINSTANCE
    hPrev,char*lpszLine,int nShow)
```

In this case, the parsed command line is available, but not as an argument:

```
extern int __argc;
extern char**__argv;
extern char**_environ;
```

---

[5] Users familiar with Windows® and unfamiliar with Unix® or Linux® mistakenly refer to a console application as a DOS box. The more accurate Windows® term for such is a command prompt.

Some of the OpenGL™ examples include keyboard input, but it is handled entirely different from the standard for Windows® programs. Getting OpenGL™ to work seamlessly within the context of Windows® is not burdensome or overly complicated, but it isn't well documented. That is the object of this book.

All of the modified examples accompanying this book will compile with the latest version of Visual Studio® and are available on the web free of charge. They are all contained in a single ZIP file, separated into individual folders. This archive includes an Excel® spreadsheet that lists each example and can be sorted by category.

The essential parts of the Visual Studio® C compiler are available free of charge on the Microsoft® web site. Download the W7.1 SDK and the W7 DDK. After you install these, combine all of the bin, lib, and include folders for the x86 platform into a single location: C:\VC32. That and these examples are all you need to get started.

Getting Started

I recommend that you start with the simplest examples, for instance, ACCNOT or SCENE, which have simple lighting and basic shapes. Use GLUT®, the OpenGL™ Utility Toolkit, and GLAUX, the OpenGL™ Auxiliary Library, to do most of the work for you. Familiarize yourself with the lighting and point-of-view. When you are comfortable with one, move on to another example and then up to a higher level, for instance PLANETUP, which has a large and small wireframe sphere (Earth & Moon) that you can rotate and orbit by pressing the arrow keys.

Figure 28. Cannon Chess

Chapter 12. The OpenGL™ Examples

The over fifty examples contained in the online archive (see Appendix A) cover most aspects of 3D rendering. They also vary considerably in complexity. I suggest starting with the simplest examples and working your way up to the more complex.

The Simplest Examples

The simplest examples are accnot, Planet Up, scclrlt, scene, Tea Amb, and T-Prim. I suggest you start with accnot to get the basics of shape generation. Then move on to scene and scclrlt to get the basics of lighting. Accnot is shown below:

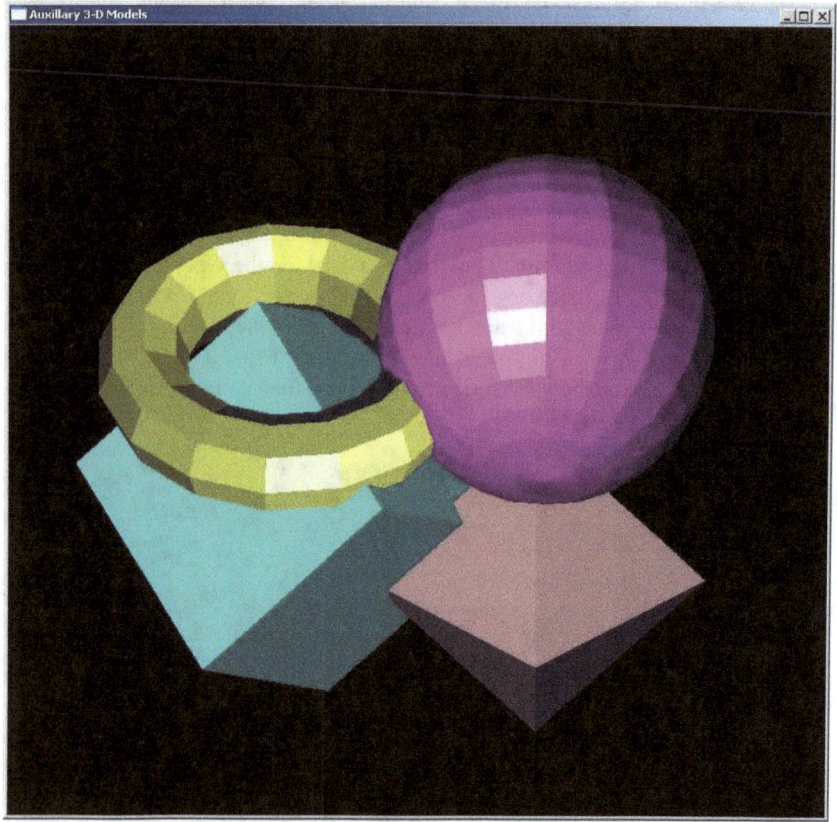

Figure 29. Geometric Shapes

Animated Examples

Animation is one of the main reasons for 3D rendering. The elements of animation included in these examples can be separated into three categories: 1) rotations and translations, 2) objects that change in shape, 3) user-controlled motions. The examples that fall into this first category include: Atlantis,

Blender, Bounce, Chess, Cube Map, Dino Ball, Dino Draw, Dino Shade, Dino Spin, Earth & Moon, Gears, Gear Train, Ideas, Lorenz, Occlude, Olympic Rings, Planet Up, Point Burst, Puzzle, Reflect, Reflect Dino, Reflect 2, and Roller Coaster. The examples that fall into the second category include: Blue Pony, Morph3D, and Origami. The examples that fall into the third category include: Knight's Tour, Move Light, Shapes, Sky Fly, Stonehenge 1, Stonehenge 2, Stonehenge 3, T-Select, View3D, and View3DS.

I suggest you start with Planet Up, then Bounce, then Olympic Rings and Atlantis. After you have mastered these, move on to Morph3D and Blue Pony. When you have mastered these, move on to Origami. The Ideas and Sky Fly examples are quite complex. The dinosaur examples are between these last two groups in complexity. I would recommend them next.

Dinosaurs

Five of the examples from the OpenGL™ Software Development Kit that involve drawing a simple dinosaur have been included in the online archive. These illustrate many important concepts and steps in the development of a complete three-dimensional rendering system. These are listed below in order of increasing complexity: 1) Dino Ball, 2) Dino Draw, 3) Dino Spin, 4) Reflect Dino, and 5) Dino Shade.

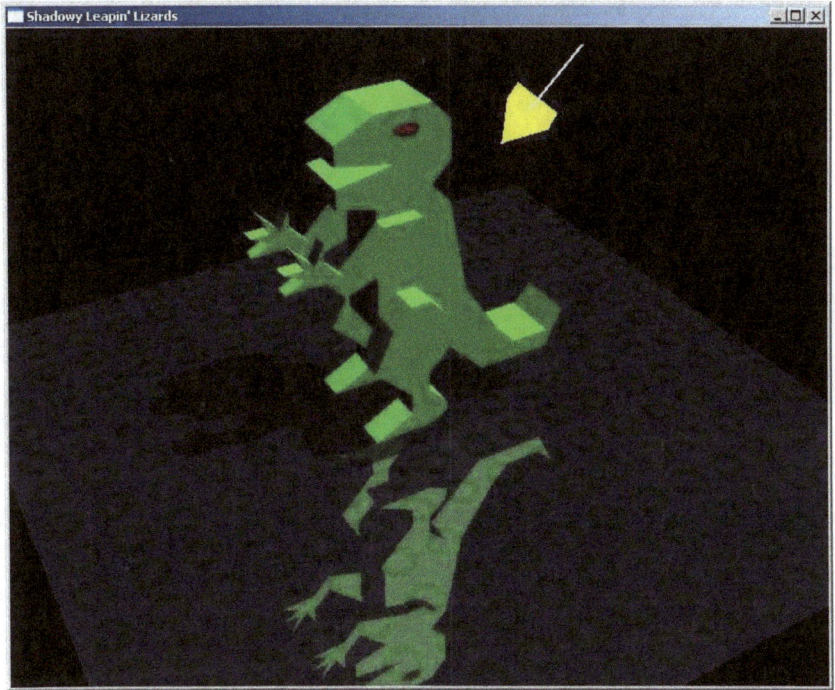

Figure 30. Bouncing Dinosaur with Reflection

The first three illustrate creating and drawing the dinosaur object. The fourth illustrates creating a reflection. The fifth illustrates shadow, reflection, and a moving light source. The combined result is shown in the preceding figure. The variable rate of bounce in the dinosaur examples is realistic. Bouncing is a case of sinusoidal motion. These illustrate more complex motion than simple rotation. I suggest that you go through each of these examples, changing a few things (colors, lighting, size), and recompile.

Blue Pony

Brian Paul's Blue Pony example is a classic. It's simple, compact, entertaining, and illustrates several important concepts. The entire source code is less than 500 lines long and includes painting the OpenGL™ logo on a billboard, creating the pony, articulating the legs, and prancing it around.

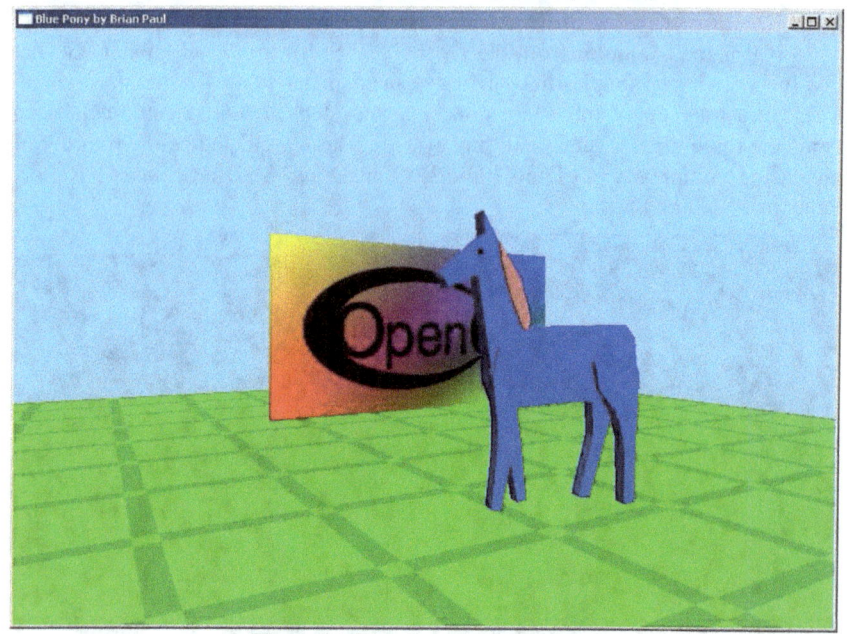

Figure 31. Blue Pony by Brian Paul

The structure of this program is simple and straightforward. The section of code that paints the logo is less than 20 lines long. It would be a good exercise to add grass to the ground and then a realistic coat of hair to the pony. Refer to the Earth & Moon example on how to add these two textures as resources in a RC file. The extra step to compile the resource file is in _compile.bat in the Earth & Moon folder. Remember that the height and width of the textures must be a power of 2.

Earth & Moon

This example is the simplest example of shape rendering (a single call to draw a sphere), the simplest animation (rotation), and the simplest draping a texture over a surface. The size of the Moon relative to the Earth is correct, but the distance between them is greatly reduced. The rotation is in the correct direction, but the Moon orbital period is much shorter than actual.

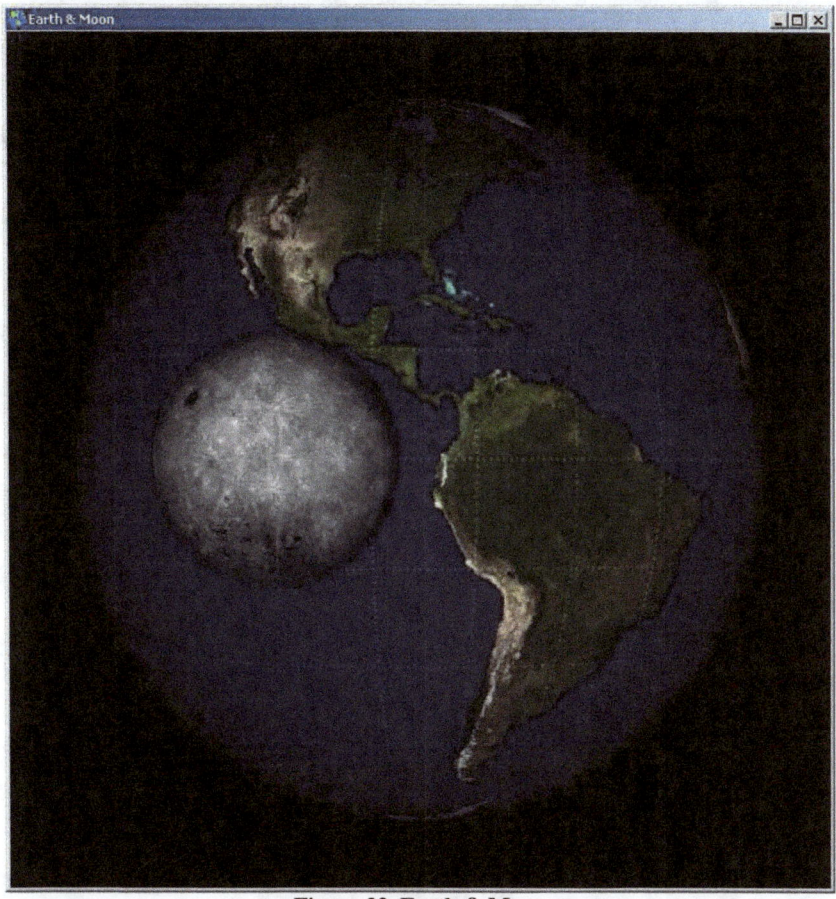

Figure 32. Earth & Moon

This example uses gluSphere(), which is in the GLUT® library. This library contains similar functions to create a cone, cylinder, disk, and partial disk. These are defined in glu.h. Use of these functions facilitates draping the texture over the shape through the use of quadrics. A quadric is a second order surface. I suggest you try this same thing with the other shapes and other textures. Remember that the height and width of the textures must be a power of 2.

The GLAUX library has more functions to create a variety of geometric objects, including:

auxSolidBox()	auxWireBox()
auxSolidCone()	auxWireCone()
auxSolidCube()	auxWireCube()
auxSolidCylinder()	auxWireCylinder()
auxSolidDodecahedron()	auxWireDodecahedron()
auxSolidIcosahedron()	auxWireIcosahedron()
auxSolidOctahedron()	auxWireOctahedron()
auxSolidSphere()	auxWireSphere()
auxSolidTeapot()	auxWireTeapot()
auxSolidTetrahedron()	auxWireTetrahedron()
auxSolidTorus()	auxWireTorus()

If you use the aux function calls you will need to use glBindTexture() and glTexCoord2d() or one of its variants to map the textures onto the objectss. The examples that include calls to auxSolid() include: accnot, alpha3d, dofnot, Fog, Material, Move Light, scclrlt, Scene, Tea Amb, Teapots, TexGen. The examples that include calls to glTexCoor() include: Blue Pony, Chess, Cube Map, Dino Shade, Knight's Tour, Perf Draw, Point Burst, Reflect 2, Teapot, View3DS. I suggest you first try replacing the call to gluSphere() with auxSolidSphere() and then add the calls to glTexCoord().

Surfaces & Lighting Examples

In addition to the dinosaurs, there are ten examples that primarily illustrate surfaces and lighting. These are: alpha3d, dof not, fog, ideas, material, reflect, scclrlt, scene, teapot, and teapots. As you have already mastered scclrlt and scene, I suggest starting with teapots and material. Teapot is quite complex and I suggest you not work with this until after you have mastered most of the other examples. The teapots were shown in the chapter on shading, scattering, & reflecting.

The material example is shown below:

Figure 33. Materials and Lighting
Examples of Surface Material Effects

Images draped over an object are called textures. OpenGL™ requires that textures be 24-bit (red-green-blue). Textures must also have a width and height that are a power of 2. Several of the examples use files with extension RGB or BW. These are not recognized by any Windows® program, but you can read them and convert them to BMP using the code in readtex.c, which can be found in the Blue Pony, Iso-Surf, Reflect, Reflect 2, and Teapot folders.

You will find code to read and write BMP, GIF, and JPG files in the spin cube folder. You will also find code that uses Windows® API calls to change the bits/pixel and dimensions of an image in the View3DS folder. You can read the textures after the application begins, as in the Reflect and Teapot examples, or load them as resources, as in the Blue Pony and Earth & Moon examples.

You can use quadrics and the GLUT® library or calls to glTexCoord() to associate the textures with the locations on the surface of your objects. I suggest starting with the former and moving to the latter. I recommend Earth & Moon, Knight's Tour, Reflect, and Stonehenge 2 as examples of more complex texture mappings. You should also find the View3DS example quite helpful.

Chapter 13. Stonehenge 1-2-3

There are three examples included in the online archive representing Stonehenge: 1) the original one that came with the OpenGL™ Software Development Kit, 2) one that is a little more complicated and has three-dimensional controls, and 3) this one that doesn't use OpenGL™. This last example contains all the code necessary to render 3D objects, including the primitive calculations. These three examples illustrate many different things.

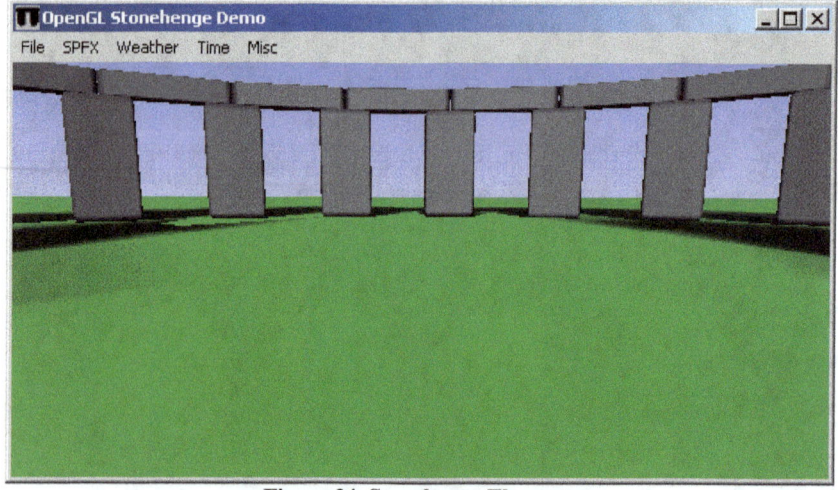

Figure 34. Stonehenge Elements

The first example illustrates several basic effects, including: lighting, shadows, fog, telescope view, and anti-aliasing. It also illustrates simulated weather conditions, including: clear, foggy, very foggy, and rainy. The orientation and position of the light source is supposed to account for the position of the sun, but doesn't work very well. The OpenGL™ Move Light and Mesa Teapot examples are much better examples of light source positioning. The OpenGL™ Dino Shade example is also helpful. The Stonehenge demo mode shows how to build complex animations.

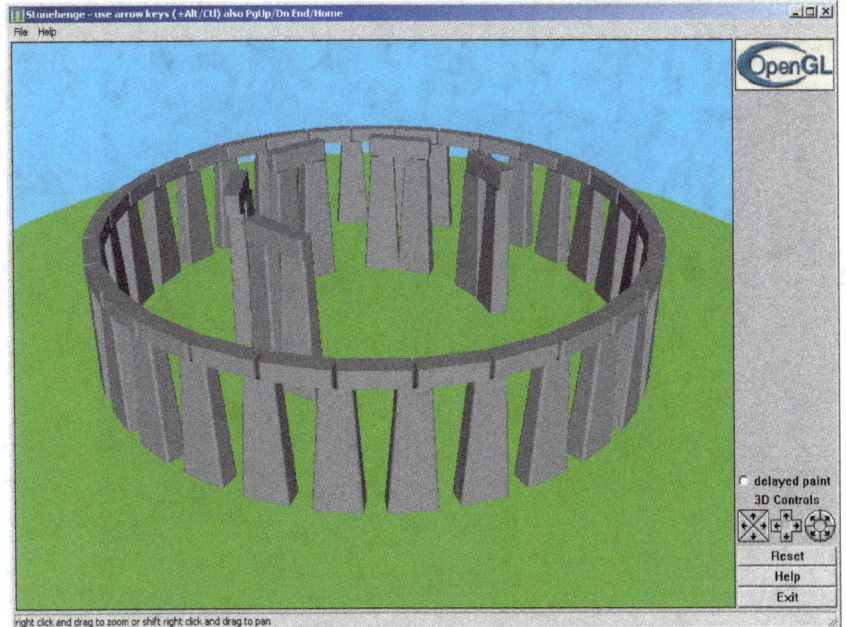

Figure 35. Stonehenge with OpenGL™

The second example is a more complete Windows® program, with buttons and greater control over where the rendering is painted. It has custom controls for three-dimensional rotation and translation and accepts input from the keyboard, including the arrow keys, coupled with the alt and control keys.

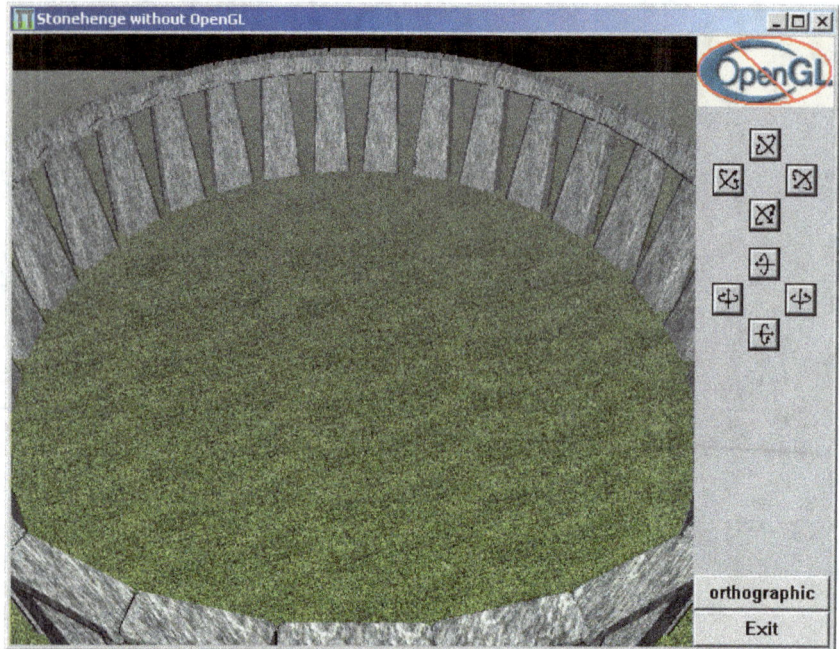

Figure 36. Stonehenge without OpenGL™

The third example is also a complete Windows® program with a different set of custom buttons to control rotation and view. This example does not use OpenGL™, rather it includes all of the primitive rendering calculations necessary, including draping of textures (or bitmaps) over objects.

Chapter 14. The 3D Studio® Model Viewer

This example illustrates many features of 3D rendering with OpenGL™ as well as Windows® applications. It includes: menus, keyboard input, custom controls, reading textures, reading a binary file, selecting a pixel format, painting in a child window, constructing complex objects from geometric primitives, lighting, perspective, and texture mapping.

This program loads and displays a 3D Studio® model. Three models are included (T-Rex, elephant, and sheep). Countless models are available free online. One good source is TurboSquid:

https://www.turbosquid.com/Search/3D-Models/free

The T-Rex model is shown here:

Figure 37. T-Rex Model

These models often come as a ZIP file with the textures embedded. A good exercise would be to add the code to open the zip file and read the model and textures. I have provided code elsewhere to read and write ZIP files from the disk or from memory. The latter allows you to include a ZIP file as a binary resource inside a Windows® application.

This example is a good illustration of how to create and display complex models that are defined by a mesh and one or more textures. The basic structures are elements and nodes. These are defined as:

```
typedef struct{int i,j,k,m;DWORD color;}ELEM;
typedef struct{float u,v,x,y,z;}NODE;
```

Each element has three or more nodes, whose indices are identified by i, j, and k. Each element also has a color and possibly a material (or texture (or bitmap)) identified by m. Each node has a coordinate in three-dimensional space defined by x, y, and z. The additional variables u and v identify the corresponding location within the material (or texture) m. The lower left corner of the texture is (0,0) and the upper right corner is (1,1). These coordinates are regardless of the width and height of the texture in pixels. As OpenGL™ uses single precision floats, there is no point defining these as double precision. The following code snippet illustrates how to render such a mesh.

```
for(l=0;l<elems;l++)
{
i=elem[l].i;
j=elem[l].j;
k=elem[l].k;
m=elem[l].m;
v1[0]=(node[i].x-xc)/s;
v1[1]=(node[i].y-yc)/s;
v1[2]=(node[i].z-zc)/s;
v2[0]=(node[j].x-xc)/s;
v2[1]=(node[j].y-yc)/s;
v2[2]=(node[j].z-zc)/s;
v3[0]=(node[k].x-xc)/s;
v3[1]=(node[k].y-yc)/s;
v3[2]=(node[k].z-zc)/s;
p[0]=v2[0]-v1[0];
p[1]=v2[1]-v1[1];
p[2]=v2[2]-v1[2];
q[0]=v3[0]-v1[0];
q[1]=v3[1]-v1[1];
q[2]=v3[2]-v1[2];
CrossProduct(p,q,n);
if(textures&&fill_polygons&&m>=0)
 {
 glColor(WHITE);
 glEnable(GL_TEXTURE_2D);
 glBindTexture(GL_TEXTURE_2D,texture[m]);
 glBegin(GL_TRIANGLES);
 glNormal3fv(n);
 glTexCoord2d(node[i].u,node[i].v);
 glVertex3fv(v1);
 glTexCoord2d(node[j].u,node[j].v);
 glVertex3fv(v2);
 glTexCoord2d(node[k].u,node[k].v);
 glVertex3fv(v3);
 glEnd();
 }
else
 {
 glDisable(GL_TEXTURE_2D);
 glColor(elem.color);
 glBegin(GL_TRIANGLES);
 glNormal3fv(n);
 glVertex3fv(v1);
 glVertex3fv(v2);
```

```
    glVertex3fv(v3);
    glEnd();
}
```

The material can change from one element to the other, so this is inside the loop. It doesn't take long to enable or disable textures or to bind a particular texture. In this case, binding is simply setting an index. The more computationally intensive task has already been done and stored in the coordinates u and v.

In order to properly manage the relationship between lighting and surfaces–whether or not they have a texture–you must define the outward normal of each element. This is accomplished above by creating two vectors: one from nodes i to j and another from i to k. The cross product of these two vectors is the outward normal.

You must scale and center the objects. This is accomplished above by subtracting the coordinates from the centroid (xc, yc, zc) and dividing by the scaling factor, s. The value of s depends on the scaling of the model as well as the view setup.

Chapter 15. 3D Rendering without OpenGL

There are two reasons I can think of that you might want to render 3D objects without this powerful system: 1) OpenGL™ it isn't compatible with your system and 2) you don't want to be locked into 24-bit color depth. Perhaps the most compelling reason for not wanting to be locked into 24-bit color depth is to produce animated GIFs.

Since the dawn of the World Wide Web, the standard for animations has been the GIF–not the ASF, AVI, MOV, MPG, SWF, or WMV. GIFs are limited to 256 colors. The JPG and similar formats based on lossy compression are fine for pictures, but not for graphs, line drawings, or anything else that has clear boundaries. Creating an animation in 24 bits/pixel color and then reducing it to 8 bits/pixel produces undesirable results in both quality and compression.

Rather than using 24 bits/pixel color, it is possible to produce quality renderings using only 42 colors: black, white, blue, brown, cyan, green, magenta, orange, purple, red, yellow, and 31 shades of gray. As this is less than 64, the resulting images require only 6 bits and can be adequately compressed without loss of information. Gradations of shade are created by dithering the primary color with the range of black to gray to white.

This same shading scheme was used by Tecplot® through Version 8. Tecplot® switched to OpenGL™ and 24-bit colors with Version 9. The earlier versions of Tecplot® produced animations using the Raster Meta File format (RM), which could be easily converted to GIF[6]. More recent versions of Tecplot® produce Audio Visual Interleave (AVI) files, which don't compress nearly as well and add nothing in the way of quality.

To end up with a clean, compact animation using only 8 bits/pixel you must render it with this goal in mind.

The scene is stored in a bitmap plus a depth buffer. A stencil buffer is optional. Unless you implement special mixed floating-point and integer calculations, as is the case with OpenGL™, you might as well use double-precision floating-point numbers for the depth buffer. I use 8-bit color so that there is one byte per pixel in the bitmap. This also simplifies addressing. Windows® requires the width of the bitmap to be a multiple of 4.

The basic steps in rendering are: 1) clear the bitmap and Z-buffer, 2) render the objects, and 3) paint the bitmap onto the display. To clear the bitmap, set all values to the background color with memset(). To clear the Z-buffer, set all the values to DBL_MAX (i.e., infinitely far from the observer).

All objects must be broken down into lines or triangles and rendered one at a time. These 2 or 3 points are transformed using the rotations, translations, and scalings defined in Chapter 4. Three distinct points (i.e., a triangle) define a plane in three-dimensional space. This plane can be described mathematically

---

[6] A free RM to GIF conversion tool with source code is available on my web site.

by a*x+b*y+c*z=1, where a, b, and c are constants. In the case of a line, either a or b is zero. Replace every pixel along the line (or within the triangle) if the value of z is less than the previous value, in which case, replacing the value of z as well.

The index of the color (or shade of gray) that goes into the bitmap depends on the color of the surface (or the color of the texture mapped onto the surface) and the angle of the surface with respect to the light source(s). If the sum of x+y is odd, an appropriate shade of gray is selected. If the sum of x+y is even, the base color is selected.

Different algorithms for light and surface interaction can be used to produce various effects. The simplest would be either 0 (black) or 1 (white), depending on whether the surface is toward or away from the light source(s). The next level of complexity would be $\rho=(1-\cos(\varsigma))/2$, where ς is the angle between the outward normal of the surface and the light source. When $\varsigma=0°$, $\rho=0$ (black) and when $\varsigma=180°$, $\rho=1$ (white).

The outward normal is calculated using the cross product as described in Chapter 4. Don't paint the back side of surfaces, as these point away from the observer. The back side of objects can be identified by the angle between the outward normal and the viewer (i.e., $\varsigma<90°$ pointing away from the viewer and $\varsigma>90°$ pointing toward the viewer).

The following structures facilitate these operations:
```
typedef struct tagCOLOR{
   BYTE b;
   BYTE g;
   BYTE r;
   }COLOR;
typedef struct tagVECTOR{
   double x;
   double y;
   double z;
   double w;
   }VECTOR;
typedef struct tagVERTEX{
   COLOR c;
   VECTOR p;
   VECTOR n;
   }VERTEX;
typedef struct tagMATRIX{
   VECTOR x;
   VECTOR y;
   VECTOR z;
   VECTOR w;
   }MATRIX;
MATRIX Identity={{1,0,0,0},{0,1,0,0},
    {0,0,1,0},{0,0,0,1}};
```
The following functions perform the necessary matrix operations:

```
VECTOR Vector(double x,double y,double z,double w)
  {
  static VECTOR P;
  P.x=x;
  P.y=y;
  P.z=z;
  P.w=w;
  return(P);
  }
MATRIX Matrix(VECTOR Vx,VECTOR Vy,VECTOR Vz,VECTOR Vw)
  {
  static MATRIX M;
  M.x=Vx;
  M.y=Vy;
  M.z=Vz;
  M.w=Vw;
  return(M);
  }
VERTEX Vertex(VECTOR p,COLOR c)
  {
  static VERTEX V;
  V.c=c;
  V.p=p;
  return(V);
  }
double Euclidean(VECTOR P)
  {
  return(sqrt(P.x*P.x+P.y*P.y+P.z*P.z+P.w*P.w));
  }
double DotProduct(VECTOR P,VECTOR Q)
  {
  return(P.x*Q.x+P.y*Q.y+P.z*Q.z+P.w*Q.w);
  }
VECTOR CrossProduct(VECTOR P,VECTOR Q)
  {
  static VECTOR R;
  R.x=P.y*Q.z-P.z*Q.y;
  R.y=P.z*Q.x-P.x*Q.z;
  R.z=P.x*Q.y-P.y*Q.x;
  R.w=P.w*Q.w;
  return(R);
  }
VECTOR Direction(VECTOR P,VECTOR Q)
  {
  static VECTOR R;
  R.x=Q.x-P.x;
  R.y=Q.y-P.y;
  R.z=Q.z-P.z;
  R.w=Q.w-P.w;
  return(R);
```

```
    }
VECTOR Normalize(VECTOR P)
    {
    static VECTOR N;
    double d=Euclidean(P);
    if(d>0.)
        {
        N.x=P.x/d;
        N.y=P.y/d;
        N.z=P.z/d;
        N.w=P.w/d;
        }
    else
        {
        N.x=P.x;
        N.y=P.y;
        N.z=P.z;
        N.w=P.w;
        }
    return(N);
    }
void MatrixMultiply(double*A,double*B,double*C,int l,
    int n,int m)
    {
    int i,j,k;
    for(i=0;i<l;i++)
        for(j=0;j<m;j++)
            for(C[m*i+j]=k=0;k<n;k++)
                C[m*i+j]+=A[n*i+k]*B[m*k+j];
    }
```

The following functions perform rotations, translations, and scaling of points:

```
void TranslateObjective(double x,double y,double z)
    {
    MATRIX Q=Transform[matrix_stack];
    MATRIX P=Identity;
    P.x.w=x;
    P.y.w=y;
    P.z.w=z;
    MatrixMultiply((double*)&Q,(double*)&P,
        (double*)(Transform+matrix_stack),4,4,4);
    }
void ScaleObjective(double x,double y,double z)
    {
    MATRIX Q=Transform[matrix_stack];
    MATRIX P=Identity;
    P.x.x=x;
    P.y.y=y;
    P.z.z=z;
```

```
    MatrixMultiply((double*)&Q,(double*)&P,
      (double*)(Transform+matrix_stack),4,4,4);
  }
void RotateObjective(double a,double b,double c)
  {
  MATRIX P,Q;
  Q=Transform[matrix_stack];
  P=Identity;
  P.y.y=cos(a);P.y.z=-sin(a);
  P.z.y=sin(a);P.z.z= cos(a);
  MatrixMultiply((double*)&Q,(double*)&P,
    (double*)(Transform+matrix_stack),4,4,4);
  Q=Transform[matrix_stack];
  P=Identity;
  P.x.x=cos(b);P.x.z=-sin(b);
  P.z.x=sin(b);P.z.z= cos(b);
  MatrixMultiply((double*)&Q,(double*)&P,
    (double*)(Transform+matrix_stack),4,4,4);
  Q=Transform[matrix_stack];
  P=Identity;
  P.x.x=cos(c);P.x.y=-sin(c);
  P.y.x=sin(c);P.y.y= cos(c);
  MatrixMultiply((double*)&Q,(double*)&P,
    (double*)(Transform+matrix_stack),4,4,4);
  }
```

The following functions manipulate a stack of transforms that can be stored and retrieved in the same way as glPushMatrix() and glPopMatrix():

```
MATRIX Transform[8];
int matrix_stack;
void PushTransform()
  {
  if(++matrix_stack>=sizeof(Transform)/sizeof(MATRIX))
    Abort(__LINE__,"objective matrix stack overflow");
  Transform[matrix_stack]=Transform[matrix_stack-1];
  }
void PopTransform()
  {
  if(--matrix_stack<0)
    Abort(__LINE__,"objective matrix stack underflow");
  }
```

The following functions render a line and triangle, respectively:

```
void RenderLine(int x1,int y1,int x2,int y2,BYTE c)
  {
  int dx,dy,x,y;
  if(abs(x2-x1)>abs(y2-y1))
    {
    if(x1>x2)
      {
      x=x2;
```

```
      x2=x1;
      x1=x;
      y=y2;
      y2=y1;
      y1=y;
      }
   dx=x2-x1;
   dy=y2-y1;
   if(dx!=0)
      {
      for(x=x1;x<=x2;x++)
         {
         if(x<0)
            continue;
         if(x>=Scene.w)
            break;
         y=y1+dy*(x-x1)/dx;
         if(y<0)
            continue;
         if(y>=Scene.h)
            continue;
         Scene.c[Scene.w*y+x]=c;
         }
      }
   else
      {
      if(y1>=0&&y1<Scene.h)
         {
         for(x=x1;x<=x2;x++)
            {
            if(x<0)
               continue;
            if(x>=Scene.w)
               break;
            Scene.c[Scene.w*y1+x]=c;
            }
         }
      }
   }
else
   {
   if(y1>y2)
      {
      y=y2;
      y2=y1;
      y1=y;
      x=x2;
      x2=x1;
      x1=x;
      }
```

```
            dx=x2-x1;
            dy=y2-y1;
            if(dy!=0)
               {
              for(y=y1;y<=y2;y++)
                 {
                 if(y<0)
                    continue;
                 if(y>=Scene.h)
                    break;
                 x=x1+dx*(y-y1)/dy;
                 if(x<0)
                    continue;
                 if(x>=Scene.w)
                    continue;
                 Scene.c[Scene.w*y+x]=c;
                 }
               }
            else
               {
              if(x1>=0&&x1<Scene.w)
                 {
                 for(y=y1;y<=y2;y++)
                    {
                    if(y<0)
                       continue;
                    if(y>=Scene.h)
                       break;
                    Scene.c[Scene.w*y+x1]=c;
                    }
                 }
               }
         }
      }

void OutlineTriangle(NODE*n1,NODE*n2,NODE*n3,BYTE c)
   {
   int x1,x2,x3,y1,y2,y3;
   x1=nint(n1->x);
   y1=nint(n1->y);
   x2=nint(n2->x);
   y2=nint(n2->y);
   x3=nint(n3->x);
   y3=nint(n3->y);
   RenderLine(x1,y1,x2,y2,c);
   RenderLine(x2,y2,x3,y3,c);
   RenderLine(x3,y3,x1,y1,c);
   }

void RenderTriangle(NODE*n1,NODE*n2,NODE*n3,BYTE c)
```

```
{
int i,x,x1,x2,x3,xa,xb,y,y1,y2,y3,ya,yb;
double
  Det,D11,D12,D13,D21,D22,D23,D31,D32,D33,Z,Zo,Zx,Zy;
BYTE g,s;
NODE w1,w2,w3;

/* determine equation of projected plane of element */

Det=(n2->x-n1->x)*(n3->y-n2->y)-(n3->x-n2->x)*(n2->y-
   n1->y);
if(fabs(Det)>10.)
    {
    D11=(n2->x*n3->y-n3->x*n2->y)/Det;
    D12=(n3->x*n1->y-n1->x*n3->y)/Det;
    D13=(n1->x*n2->y-n2->x*n1->y)/Det;
    D21=(n2->y-n3->y)/Det;
    D22=(n3->y-n1->y)/Det;
    D23=(n1->y-n2->y)/Det;
    D31=(n3->x-n2->x)/Det;
    D32=(n1->x-n3->x)/Det;
    D33=(n2->x-n1->x)/Det;
    Zo=n1->z*D11+n2->z*D12+n3->z*D13;
    Zx=n1->z*D21+n2->z*D22+n3->z*D23;
    Zy=n1->z*D31+n2->z*D32+n3->z*D33;
    }
  else
    {
    Zo=(n1->z+n2->z+n3->z)/3.;
    Zx=Zy=0.;
    }

/* project light source onto plane of element */

if(!(Light.a|Light.s))
    Abort(__LINE__,"you must call SetSpotLight() or
    SetAmbientLighting() before rendering");
w1.x=n2->x-n1->x;
w1.y=n2->y-n1->y;
w1.z=n2->z-n1->z;
w2.x=n3->x-n1->x;
w2.y=n3->y-n1->y;
w2.z=n3->z-n1->z;
w3.x=w1.y*w2.z-w1.z*w2.y;
w3.y=w1.z*w2.x-w1.x*w2.z;
w3.z=w1.x*w2.y-w1.y*w2.x;
Z=sqrt(w3.x*w3.x+w3.y*w3.y+w3.z*w3.z);
if(Z>DBL_EPSILON)
    {
    w3.x/=Z;
```

```
      w3.y/=Z;
      w3.z/=Z;
      }
    else
      {
      w3.x=0.;
      w3.y=0.;
      w3.z=0.;
      }
    Z=w3.x*Light.n.x+w3.y*Light.n.y+w3.z*Light.n.z;
    Z=max(0.,min(1.,fabs(Z)));
    g=max(0,min(32,(BYTE)nint(32.*Z)));
    s=background?black:white;

/* paint element */

    x1=nint(n1->x);
    y1=nint(n1->y);
    x2=nint(n2->x);
    y2=nint(n2->y);
    x3=nint(n3->x);
    y3=nint(n3->y);

    while(1)
      {
      if(y1>y2)
        {
        y=y1;
        y1=y2;
        y2=y;
        x=x1;
        x1=x2;
        x2=x;
        }
      else if(y2>y3)
        {
        y=y2;
        y2=y3;
        y3=y;
        x=x2;
        x2=x3;
        x3=x;
        }
      else
        break;
      }
    ya=max(0,y1);
    yb=min(y2,Scene.h);
    for(y=ya;y<yb;y++)
      {
```

```
    if(y1==y2||x1==x2)
      xa=x1;
    else
      xa=(x1*(y2-y)+x2*(y-y1))/(y2-y1);
    if(y1==y3||x1==x3)
      xb=x3;
    else
    xb=(x1*(y3-y)+x3*(y-y1))/(y3-y1);
    if(xa>xb)
      {
      x=xa;
      xa=xb;
      xb=x;
      }
    xa=max(0,xa);
    xb=min(xb,Scene.w-1);
    i=Scene.w*y+xa;
    Z=Zo+Zx*xa+Zy*y;
    for(x=xa;x<=xb;x++,i++,Z+=Zx)
      {
      if(Z<=Scene.z[i])
        continue;
      Scene.z[i]=Z;
      if(show_elements&&(x==xa||x==xb))
        Scene.c[i]=s;
      else if((x+y)%2)
        Scene.c[i]=g;
      else
        Scene.c[i]=c;
      }
    }
  ya=max(0,y2);
  yb=min(y3,Scene.h-1);
  for(y=ya;y<=yb;y++)
    {
    if(y2==y3||x2==x3)
      xa=x2;
    else
      xa=(x2*(y3-y)+x3*(y-y2))/(y3-y2);
    if(y1==y3||x1==x3)
      xb=x3;
    else
      xb=(x1*(y3-y)+x3*(y-y1))/(y3-y1);
    if(xa>xb)
      {
      x=xa;
      xa=xb;
      xb=x;
      }
    xa=max(0,xa);
```

```
      xb=min(xb,Scene.w-1);
      i=Scene.w*y+xa;
      Z=Zo+Zx*xa+Zy*y;
      for(x=xa;x<=xb;x++,i++,Z+=Zx)
        {
        if(Z<=Scene.z[i])
          continue;
        Scene.z[i]=Z;
        if(show_elements&&(x==xa||x==xb))
          Scene.c[i]=s;
        else if((x+y)%2)
          Scene.c[i]=g;
        else
          Scene.c[i]=c;
        }
      }
    }
```

Figure 38. OpenGL™ Stonehenge Model

Chapter 16. Simple Sort and Paint

A simple way to render 3D objects is to sort them by their distance from the viewer and paint them back to front. The flange example illustrates this technique. It can be fast and can produce acceptable results in many cases, but is rather limited in quality, as illustrated in the following figure:

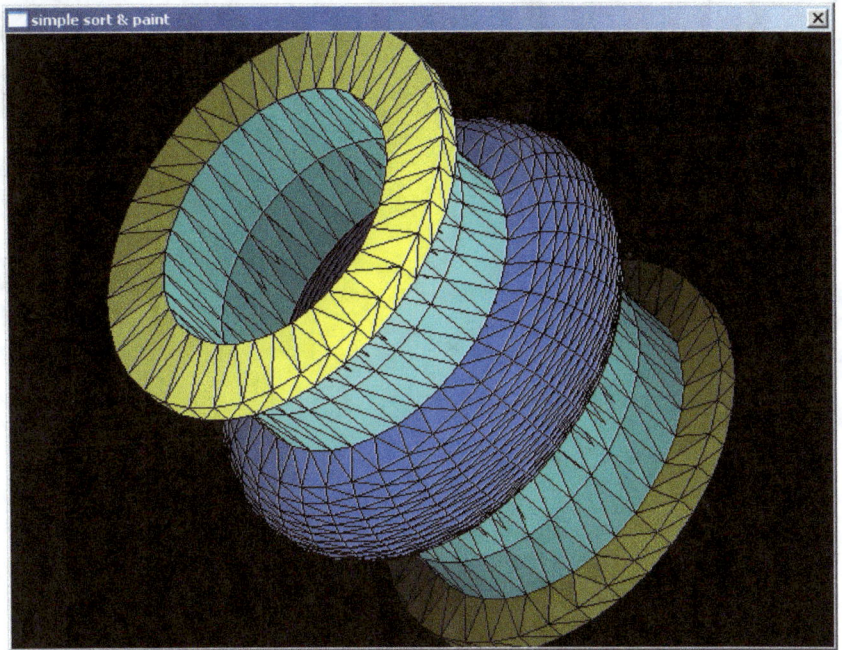

Figure 39. Sort-and-Paint

In this example the object is constructed from 3D triangular elements, each with a basic color. When rendering, the three nodes defining each element are rotated, scaled, and centered. The x and y location of each node is converted to an integer, where it will be painted into the display buffer in memory. The base color of each element is modified in brightness, based on the depth (i.e., z location), to enhance the perception of depth.

In this example, all of the drawing and painting is implemented using Windows® API calls. The final result is painted onto the display using BitBlt() to eliminate flicker. This simple orthographic projection could be improved to show perspective.

Note that some of the lines overlap in the figure above. This is due to the fact that all of the elements are painted, regardless of their position, only the order of painting is sorted so that the closer elements are painted last. You could add a check for the orientation of each element and only draw the ones facing the observer.

The sort and paint process is very simple. The sorting process requires only a few lines of code:

```
int CompareDepth(const void*v1,const void*v2)
   {
   return(Elem[*(int*)v1].z-Elem[*(int*)v2].z);
   }
...
   depth=calloc(Ne,sizeof(int));
   for(n=0;n<Ne;n++)
      depth[n]=n;
   qsort(depth,Ne,sizeof(int),CompareDepth);
   for(n=0;n<Ne;n++)
      {
      i=depth[n];
      rgb=Shade(Elem[i].rgb,Elem[i].z);
      hbr=CreateSolidBrush(rgb);
      hbr=SelectObject(buffer.dc,hbr);
      Polygon(buffer.dc,Elem[i].p,3);
      hbr=SelectObject(buffer.dc,hbr);
      DeleteObject(hbr);
      }
   free(depth);
```

The depth index is first filled with the default order, depth[n]=n, then qsort() is used with CompareDepth() to rearrange the order. Finally, the polygons are drawn in the sorted order. The depth index is only needed for these few steps.

The flange example rotates based on a timer. The surface example is quite similar, only it uses a rainbow of colors from blue to red based on elevation. The surface example also accepts keyboard input to control rotation and zoom. Three different surfaces are included. The following is an example:

Figure 40. 3D Surface Example

The keyboard input is handled by the following simple section of code:

```
if(wMsg==WM_KEYDOWN)
  {
  if(LOWORD(wParam)==VK_RIGHT)
    angle.x+=5;
  else if(LOWORD(wParam)==VK_LEFT)
    angle.x-=5;
  else if(LOWORD(wParam)==VK_DOWN)
    angle.y+=5;
  else if(LOWORD(wParam)==VK_UP)
    angle.y-=5;
  else if(LOWORD(wParam)==VK_END)
    angle.z+=5;
  else if(LOWORD(wParam)==VK_HOME)
    angle.z-=5;
  else if(LOWORD(wParam)==VK_PRIOR)
    scale.S*=1.05;
  else if(LOWORD(wParam)==VK_NEXT)
    scale.S/=1.05;
  else
    return(FALSE);
  RenderObjects();
  return(FALSE);
  }
```

The sombrero surface is included with this example:

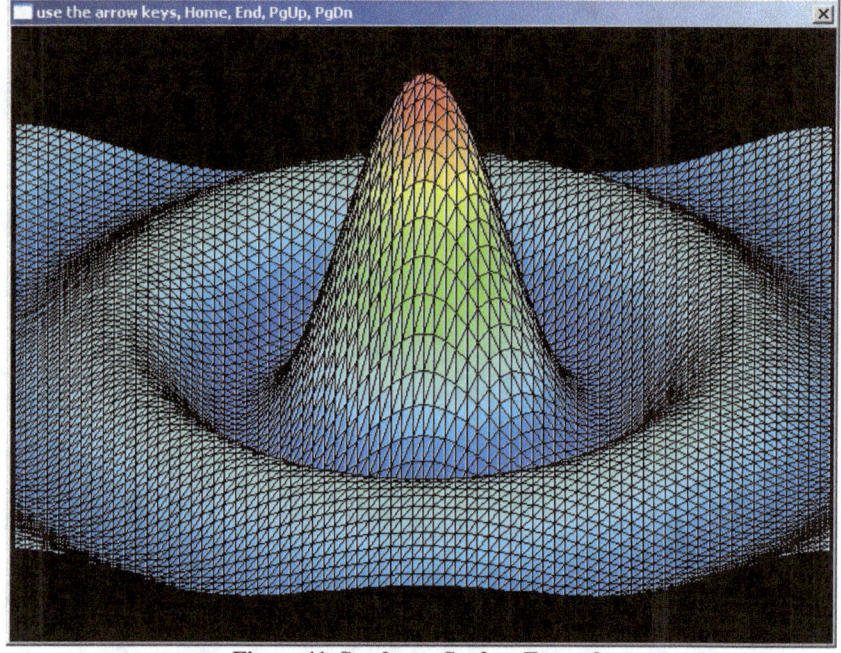

Figure 41. Sombrero Surface Example

Chapter 17. The Generic 3D Model Viewer

The View3D example illustrates how to import, export, and render general 3D objects without using OpenGL™. It works with 8-bit color and will create animated GIFs. It contains everything you need to accomplish these functions and doesn't depend on any third-party drivers or libraries. The following is typical rendering of a familiar object:

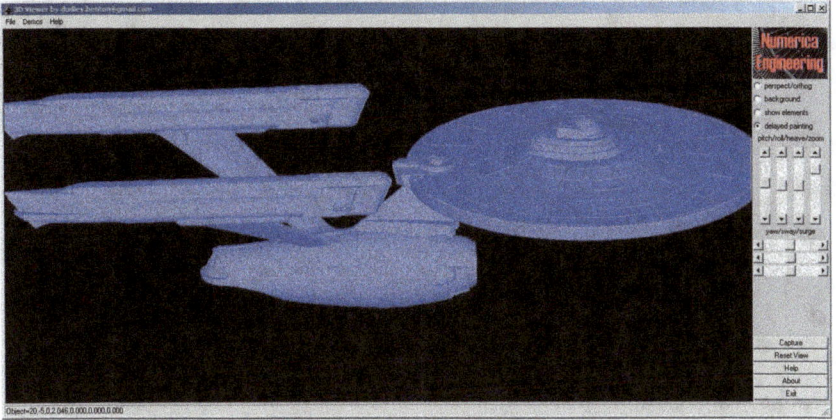

Figure 42. Spaceship Example

This application also includes the functions to build several geometric shapes, including: chess king, coil, cone, cylinder, disk, dodecahedron, ellipsoid, hexahedron, icosahedron, Klein bottle, octahedron, pipe (or tube), polygon, rectangle, ring, rotoid (meandering tube of varying radius, such as the handle and spout of the teapot), sea shell, sombrero, sphere, teapot, tetrahedron, and torus.

The sea shell is shown below:

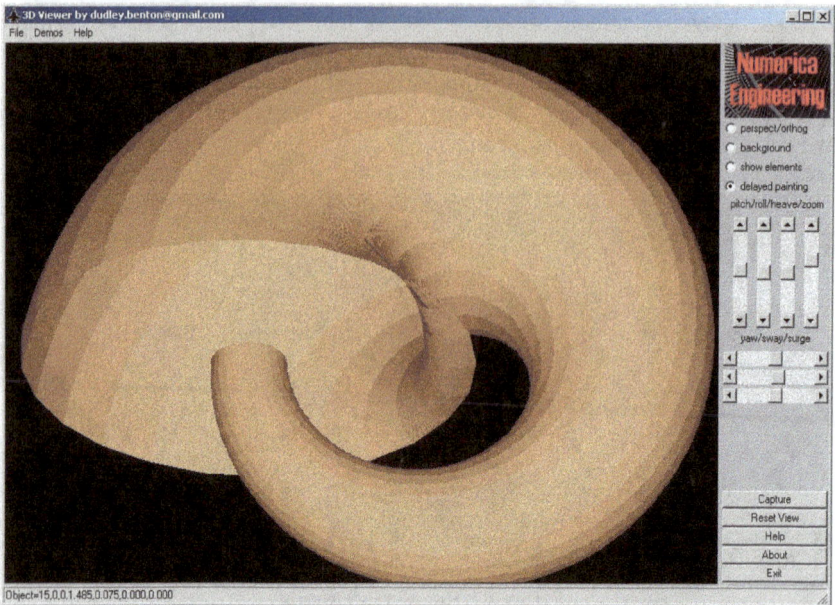

Figure 43. Seashell Example

Chapter 18. Virtual Reality Markup Language

Virtual Reality Markup Language (VRML) is used throughout the Internet for creating 3D models and many are available free on-line. I have included a VRML viewer and 9 models of familiar Star Trek® and Star Wars® objects. This 669 line program will read VRML and display the model. It also accepts keyboard input to control rotation and zoom.

The display quality is rather poor, as the simple sort and paint method is used, but you could replace this simple implementation with one of the more complex ones, such as OpenGL™. The most useful part of this code is reading the VRLM. You could also add this section to either View3DS (that uses OpenGL™) or View3D (which uses an 8-bit painting scheme). The short-comings of the sort and paint implementation can be clearly seen in this figure:

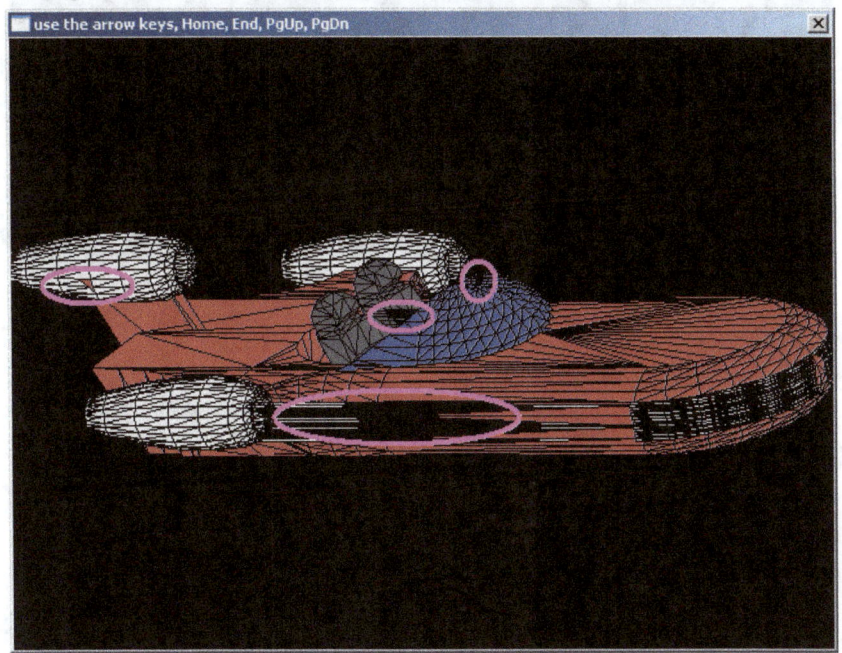

Figure 44. Landspeeder Example

If this model had been rendered with a Z-buffer, the flaws highlighted in the above figure would not be present. Use of perspective and surface texturing (as in the other applications contained herein) would also greatly enhance the appearance, especially of this next model:

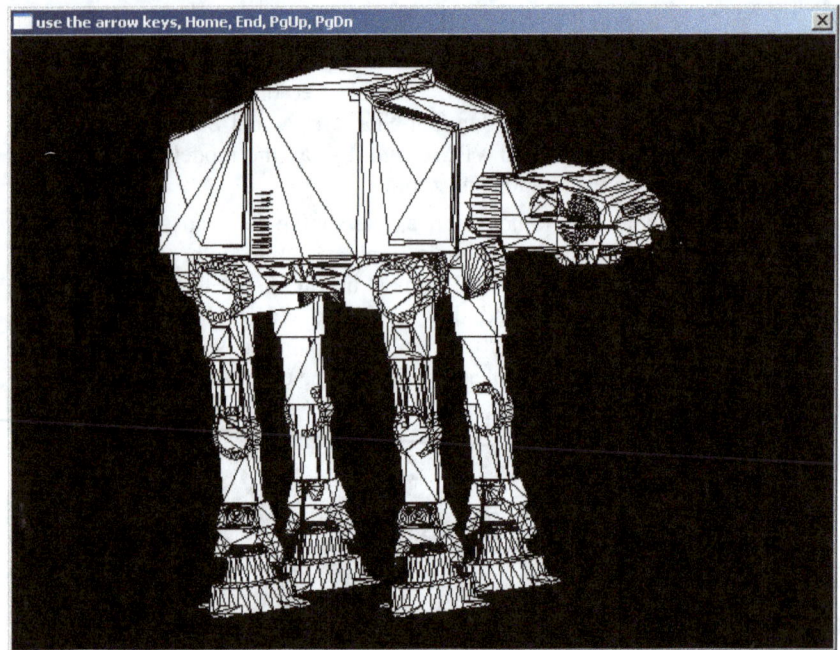

Figure 45. Imperial Walker Example

While the 3D Studio® file format is binary, the VRML format is plain ASCII text. There are many documents available on-line describing the VRML format, so the presentation here will be brief. VRML script includes comments, beginning with # and consists of sections, set off by opening and closing braces. The following snippet illustrates transforms, lighting, and material properties:

```
#VRML V1.0 ascii
# Pioneer (tm) was used to create this VRML file.
Separator {
 Background {
  fields [ MFColor skyColors ]
  skyColors    0.502 0.502 0.502
  }
 TransformSeparator {
  MatrixTransform {
   matrix
     1.000 0.000 0.000 0
     0.000 -0.000 -1.000 0
     0.000 1.000 -0.000 0
     4.827 4.089 1.121 1
   }
  }
 Separator {
  MaterialBinding {
   value OVERALL
```

```
    }
  Material {
    ambientColor [
       0.300 0.300 0.300,
    ]
    diffuseColor [
       0.604 0.604 0.604,
    ]
    specularColor [
       0.300 0.300 0.300,
    ]
    emissiveColor [
       0.000 0.000 0.000,
    ]
    shininess [
       0.340,
    ]
    transparency [
       0.000,
    ]
  }
  ...
}
```

The model may be broken up into several sections, each with a different transformation and colors. The vertices are defined in a section marked as "coordinates" and the polygons are defined in a section marked as "indices." The orientation of the polygons is also provided, as this is essential for determining the outward normal of the surfaces. The following snippet illustrates the vertices and polygons:

```
Coordinate3 {
  point     [
    -0.578 -0.248  3.625,
    -0.402 -0.248  3.813,
    -0.402 -0.018  3.813,
    -0.578 -0.018  3.625,
    -0.459 -0.248  3.514,
    -0.283 -0.248  3.702,
    -0.283 -0.018  3.702,
    -0.459 -0.018  3.514,
    -0.720 -0.538  3.687,
     0.796 -0.538  3.687,
     0.796 -0.224  3.687,
    -0.720 -0.224  3.687,
    -0.720 -0.538  3.651,
     0.796 -0.538  3.651,
     0.796 -0.224  3.651,
    -0.720 -0.224  3.651,
    -0.351  0.601  3.655,
  ]
```

```
  }
  ShapeHints {
    creaseAngle 0.698
    vertexOrdering CLOCKWISE
    shapeType SOLID
    faceType UNKNOWN_FACE_TYPE
  }
  DEF City IndexedFaceSet {
    coordIndex [
      2, 1, 0, -1,
      3, 2, 0, -1,
      5, 4, 0, -1,
      1, 5, 0, -1,
      6, 5, 1, -1,
      2, 6, 1, -1,
      7, 6, 2, -1,
      3, 7, 2, -1,
      4, 7, 3, -1,
      0, 4, 3, -1,
      6, 7, 4, -1,
      5, 6, 4, -1,
    ]
  }
}
```

The model structure inherent in the VRML format is one that I have found to be most efficient. The VRML View application uses a list of triangles, as this is easily rendered using the Windows® API calls. This is simple to encode, but less efficient. In general, there will be far more elements than nodes in a model. The node transformations may also be more computationally intensive, depending on the speed of the Floating-Point-Unit (FPU). It is, therefore, more efficient to keep the nodes and polygons separate. In the rendering process, first transform all of the nodes in a loop, and then draw all of the polygons, which are simply lists of nodes. In VRML parts of the model may be described separately and you may want to keep this distinction, rather than combining all of the parts.

As illustrated in the preceding script snippets, the structure of VRML is simple and straightforward, making it relatively easy to understand and read. The following code performs this task:

```
char*getwrl(char*bufr,FILE*fp)
{
int i,l=0;
while(1)
  {
  i=fgetc(fp);
  if(i==EOF)
    {
    if(l)
      {
      bufr[l]=0;
```

```c
            return(bufr);
          }
        else
          return(NULL);
      }
    else if(i<=' '||i==',')
      {
      if(l)
        {
        bufr[l]=0;
        return(bufr);
        }
      }
    else if(strchr("{[]}",i))
      {
      if(l)
        {
        ungetc(i,fp);
        bufr[l]=0;
        return(bufr);
        }
      else
        {
        bufr[0]=i;
        bufr[1]=0;
        return(bufr);
        }
      }
    else
      bufr[l++]=i;
    }
  }

struct{int*index,m,n;}poly;
struct{DWORD*rgb;int m,n;}matl;
typedef struct{double X,Y,Z;}XYZ;
struct{XYZ*xyz;int m,n;}node;

void AddPoly(int i,int j,int k,DWORD rgb)
  {
  XYZ p,q,r;
  p=node.xyz[poly.index[i]];
  q=node.xyz[poly.index[j]];
  r=node.xyz[poly.index[k]];
  AddTriangle(p.X,-p.Z,-p.Y,q.X,-q.Z,-q.Y,r.X,-r.Z,-
    r.Y,rgb);
  }

void ReadVRML(char*fname)
  {
```

```
char bufr[128],*ptr;
int ccw=TRUE,MaterialBinding=FALSE;
int b,g,i,j,m,n,r;
double B,G,R,X,Y,Z;
FILE*fp;

if((fp=fopen(fname,"rt"))==NULL)
  Abort(__LINE__,"can't open file %s",fname);

matl.m=100;
matl.n=0;
matl.rgb=allocate(__LINE__,matl.m,sizeof(DWORD));
matl.rgb[0]=0xFF0000;

node.m=1000;
node.n=0;
node.xyz=allocate(__LINE__,node.m,sizeof(XYZ));

poly.m=1000;
poly.n=0;
poly.index=allocate(__LINE__,poly.m,sizeof(int));

while((ptr=getwrl(bufr,fp))!=NULL)
  {
  if(!_stricmp(ptr,"ccw"))
    {
    if((ptr=getwrl(bufr,fp))==NULL)
      Abort(__LINE__,"unexpected EOF");
    if(!_stricmp(ptr,"FALSE"))
      ccw=FALSE;
    else if(!_stricmp(ptr,"TRUE"))
      ccw=TRUE;
    else if(_stricmp(ptr,"UNKNOWN"))
      Abort(__LINE__,"expected ccw to be TRUE or
  FALSE");
    }
  else if(!_stricmp(ptr,"colorIndex"))
    Abort(__LINE__,"can't handle colorIndex yet");//
  else if(!_stricmp(ptr,"coordIndex"))
    {
    if(node.n==0)
      Abort(__LINE__,"points expected before
  coordIndex");
    if((ptr=getwrl(bufr,fp))==NULL)
      Abort(__LINE__,"unexpected EOF");
    if(strcmp(ptr,"\x5B"))
      Abort(__LINE__,"expected \x5B to follow
  coordIndex");
    poly.n=0;
    while(1)
```

```
        {
        if((ptr=getwrl(bufr,fp))==NULL)
           Abort(__LINE__,"unexpected EOF");
        if(!strcmp(ptr,"\x5D"))
           break;
        if(sscanf(ptr,"%li",&n)!=1)
           Abort(__LINE__,"scan error");
        if(n>=node.n)
           Abort(__LINE__,"no such point %li",n);
        if(poly.n>=poly.m)
           {
           poly.m+=1000;
           poly.index=reallocate(__LINE__,poly.index,
poly.n,poly.m,sizeof(int));
           }
        poly.index[poly.n++]=n;
        }
     if(MaterialBinding)
        continue;
     i=0;
     while(i<poly.n)
        {
        n=0;
        while(poly.index[i+n]>=0)
           n++;
        if(ccw)
           for(j=2;j<n;j++)
              AddPoly(i+j-2,i+j-1,i+j,matl.rgb[0]);
        else
           for(j=2;j<n;j++)
              AddPoly(i+j,i+j-1,i+j-2,matl.rgb[0]);
        i+=n+1;
        }
     poly.n=0;
     }
  else if(!_stricmp(ptr,"diffuseColor"))
     {
     if((ptr=getwrl(bufr,fp))==NULL)
        Abort(__LINE__,"unexpected EOF");
     matl.n=n=0;
     matl.rgb[0]=0xFF0000;
     if(strcmp(ptr,"\x5B"))
        n=1;
     while(1)
        {
        if(n==0)
           {
           if((ptr=getwrl(bufr,fp))==NULL)
              Abort(__LINE__,"unexpected EOF");
           if(!strcmp(ptr,"\x5D"))
```

```
            break;
        }
        if(sscanf(ptr,"%lf",&R)!=1)
          Abort(__LINE__,"scan error");
        if((ptr=getwrl(bufr,fp))==NULL)
          Abort(__LINE__,"unexpected EOF");
        if(sscanf(ptr,"%lf",&G)!=1)
          Abort(__LINE__,"scan error");
        if((ptr=getwrl(bufr,fp))==NULL)
          Abort(__LINE__,"unexpected EOF");
        if(sscanf(ptr,"%lf",&B)!=1)
          Abort(__LINE__,"scan error");
        if(matl.n>=matl.m)
        {
          matl.m+=100;
          matl.rgb=reallocate(__LINE__,matl.rgb,matl.n,
matl.m,sizeof(DWORD));
        }
        r=(BYTE)max(0,min(255,255*R));
        g=(BYTE)max(0,min(255,255*G));
        b=(BYTE)max(0,min(255,255*B));
        matl.rgb[matl.n++]=RGB(r,g,b);
        if(n!=0)
          break;
      }
    }
    else if(!_stricmp(ptr,"MaterialBinding"))
    {
      if((ptr=getwrl(bufr,fp))==NULL)
        Abort(__LINE__,"unexpected EOF");
      if(strcmp(ptr,"\x7B"))
        Abort(__LINE__,"expected \x7B to follow
MaterialBinding");
      if((ptr=getwrl(bufr,fp))==NULL)
        Abort(__LINE__,"unexpected EOF");
      if(_stricmp(ptr,"value"))
        Abort(__LINE__,"expected value to follow
MaterialBinding");
      if((ptr=getwrl(bufr,fp))==NULL)
        Abort(__LINE__,"unexpected EOF");
      if(!_stricmp(ptr,"OVERALL"))
        MaterialBinding=FALSE;
      else if(stristr(ptr,"PER_FACE_INDEXED"))
        MaterialBinding=TRUE;
      else if(!_stricmp(ptr,"PER_FACE"))
        MaterialBinding=TRUE;
      else
        Abort(__LINE__,"expected OVERALL, PER_FACE, or
PER_FACE_INDEXED MaterialBinding");
      if((ptr=getwrl(bufr,fp))==NULL)
```

```
      Abort(__LINE__,"unexpected EOF");
    if(strcmp(ptr,"\x7D"))
      Abort(__LINE__,"expected \x7D to follow
MaterialBinding");
    }
  else if(!_stricmp(ptr,"materialIndex"))
    {
    if(poly.n==0)
      Abort(__LINE__,"coordIndex expected before
materialIndex");
    if((ptr=getwrl(bufr,fp))==NULL)
      Abort(__LINE__,"unexpected EOF");
    if(strcmp(ptr,"\x5B"))
      Abort(__LINE__,"expected \x5B to follow
materialIndex");
    i=0;
    while(1)
      {
      if((ptr=getwrl(bufr,fp))==NULL)
        Abort(__LINE__,"unexpected EOF");
      if(!strcmp(ptr,"\x5D"))
        break;
      if(sscanf(ptr,"%li",&m)!=1)
        Abort(__LINE__,"scan error");
      if(m<0||m>=matl.n)
        Abort(__LINE__,"no such material %li",m);
      if(i>=poly.n)
        Abort(__LINE__,"more material indices than
coordIndex groups");
      n=0;
      while(poly.index[i+n]>=0)
        n++;
      if(ccw)
        for(j=2;j<n;j++)
          AddPoly(i+j-2,i+j-1,i+j,matl.rgb[0]);
      else
        for(j=2;j<n;j++)
          AddPoly(i+j,i+j-1,i+j-2,matl.rgb[0]);
      i+=n+1;
      }
    if(i<poly.n)
      Abort(__LINE__,"fewer material indices than
coordIndex groups");
    poly.n=0;
    }
  else if(!_stricmp(ptr,"point"))
    {
    if((ptr=getwrl(bufr,fp))==NULL)
      Abort(__LINE__,"unexpected EOF");
    if(strcmp(ptr,"\x5B"))
```

```
            Abort(__LINE__,"expected \x5B to follow point");
         node.n=0;
         while(1)
            {
            if((ptr=getwrl(bufr,fp))==NULL)
               Abort(__LINE__,"unexpected EOF");
            if(!strcmp(ptr,"\x5D"))
               break;
            if(sscanf(ptr,"%lf",&X)!=1)
               Abort(__LINE__,"scan error");
            if((ptr=getwrl(bufr,fp))==NULL)
               Abort(__LINE__,"unexpected EOF");
            if(sscanf(ptr,"%lf",&Y)!=1)
               Abort(__LINE__,"scan error");
            if((ptr=getwrl(bufr,fp))==NULL)
               Abort(__LINE__,"unexpected EOF");
            if(sscanf(ptr,"%lf",&Z)!=1)
               Abort(__LINE__,"scan error");
            if(node.n>=node.m)
               {
               node.m+=1000;
               node.xyz=reallocate(__LINE__,node.xyz,node.n,
   node.m,sizeof(XYZ));
               }
            node.xyz[node.n].X=X;
            node.xyz[node.n].Y=Y;
            node.xyz[node.n].Z=Z;
            node.n++;
            }
         }
      else if(!_stricmp(ptr,"vertexOrdering"))
         {
         if((ptr=getwrl(bufr,fp))==NULL)
            Abort(__LINE__,"unexpected EOF");
         if(!_stricmp(ptr,"CLOCKWISE"))
            ccw=FALSE;
         else if(!_stricmp(ptr,"COUNTERCLOCKWISE"))
            ccw=TRUE;
         else if(_stricmp(ptr,"UNKNOWN_ORDERING"))
            Abort(__LINE__,"expected vertexOrdering to be
   CLOCKWISE or COUNTERCLOCKWISE");
         }
      }

fclose(fp);

free(poly.index);
free(matl.rgb);
free(node.xyz);
}
```

Chapter 19. Sky Fly

The Sky Fly example is perhaps the most complicated example included in the archive. It incorporates scene rendering (terrain and sky), a constantly changing viewer location, and complex mouse interaction. There are also "sprites" (little yellow paper airplanes) that fly about. The speed with which the scene is rendered is impressive. Mastering this example is a must for the advanced developer, especially if gaming is your objective.

Figure 46. SkyFly Example

The sprites are created with the following structures and functions:

```
/*This is the structure which contains the database. It
  is amalloc'ed
 *in shared memory so that forked processes can access
  it. Notice how
 *the flags and vertex data are separated to improve
  cacheing behavior.
```

```c
*/
typedef struct shared_data_struct {
  /* objects */
  perfobj_t paper_plane_obj;
  perfobj_t paper_plane_start_obj;
  perfobj_t paper_plane_2ndpass_obj;
  perfobj_t paper_plane_end_obj;
  perfobj_t terrain_texture_obj;
  perfobj_t*terrain_cells;
  perfobj_t clouds_texture_obj;
  perfobj_t clouds_obj;
  /* flags */
  unsigned int paper_plane_flags[2];
  unsigned int paper_plane_start_flags[3];
  unsigned int paper_plane_2ndpass_flags[3];
  unsigned int paper_plane_end_flags[3];
  unsigned int terrain_texture_flags[3];
  unsigned int**terrain_cell_flags;
  unsigned int clouds_texture_flags[3];
  unsigned int clouds_flags[2];
  /* data */
  perfobj_vert_t paper_plane_verts[22];
  perfobj_vert_t**terrain_cell_verts;
  perfobj_vert_t clouds_verts[4];
  }shared_data;

/* perfobj flags */
#define PD_TEXTURE_BIND       0
#define PD_DRAW_PAPER_PLANE   1
#define PD_DRAW_TERRAIN_CELL  2
#define PD_PAPER_PLANE_MODE   3
#define PD_PAPER_PLANE_POS    4
#define PD_VIEWER_POS         5
#define PD_DRAW_CLOUDS        6
#define PD_END                0x3fff
#define PLANES_START          0
#define PLANES_SECOND_PASS    1
#define PLANES_END            2

/* Offsets to data in perfobj_vert_t */
#define PD_V_POINT   0
#define PD_V_CPACK   3
#define PD_V_NORMAL  4
#define PD_V_COLOR   8
#define PD_V_TEX     12
#define PD_V_SIZE    16

void put_paper_plane(float*source,perfobj_t*pobj)
  {
  int j;
```

```
perfobj_vert_t*pdataptr=(perfobj_vert_t*)pobj->vdata;
unsigned int*flagsptr=pobj->flags;
float*sp=source;
*flagsptr++=PD_DRAW_PAPER_PLANE;
for(j=0;j<22;j++)
    {
    putn3fdata(sp+0,pdataptr);
    putv3fdata(sp+3,pdataptr);
    sp+=6;
    pdataptr++;
    }
*flagsptr++=PD_END;
}

void init_paper_planes(void)
    {
    perfobj_t*pobj;
    /* create various perf-objs for planes */
    pobj=&(SharedData->paper_plane_obj);
    pobj->flags=SharedData->paper_plane_flags;
    pobj->vdata=(float*)SharedData->paper_plane_verts;
    put_paper_plane(paper_plane_vertexes,pobj);
    pobj=&(SharedData->paper_plane_start_obj);
    pobj->flags=SharedData->paper_plane_start_flags;
    *(pobj->flags)=PD_PAPER_PLANE_MODE;
    *(pobj->flags+1)=PLANES_START;
    *(pobj->flags+2)=PD_END;
    pobj=&(SharedData->paper_plane_2ndpass_obj);
    pobj->flags=SharedData->paper_plane_2ndpass_flags;
    *(pobj->flags)=PD_PAPER_PLANE_MODE;
    *(pobj->flags+1)=PLANES_SECOND_PASS;
    *(pobj->flags+2)=PD_END;
    pobj=&(SharedData->paper_plane_end_obj);
    pobj->flags=SharedData->paper_plane_end_flags;
    *(pobj->flags)=PD_PAPER_PLANE_MODE;
    *(pobj->flags+1)=PLANES_END;
    *(pobj->flags+2)=PD_END;
    }

void fly_paper_planes(perfobj_t*paper_plane_pos)
    {
    int i;
    float speed=.08;
    float terrain_z;
    /* slow planes down in cyclops mode since frame rate
       is doubled */
    for(i=0;i<NUM_PLANES;i++)
        {
        /* If plane is not turning,one chance in 50 of
        starting a turn */
```

```c
      if(flock[i].Pcount==0 && IRND(50)==1)
        {
        /* initiate a roll */
        /* roll for a random period */
        flock[i].Pcount=IRND(100);
        /* random turn rate */
        flock[i].Pturn_rate=IRND(100)/10000.;
        flock[i].Pdirection=IRND(3)-1;
        }
      if(flock[i].Pcount>0)
        {
        /* continue rolling */
        flock[i].Proll+=flock[i].Pdirection*
   flock[i].Pturn_rate;
        flock[i].Pcount--;
        }
      else
        /* damp amount of roll when turn complete */
        flock[i].Proll*=.95;
      /* turn as a function of roll */
      flock[i].Pazimuth-=flock[i].Proll*.05;
      /* follow terrain elevation */
      terrain_z=terrain_height(flock[i].PX,flock[i].PY);
      /* use a "spring-mass-damp" system of terrain follow
   */
      flock[i].PZv=flock[i].PZv -
      .01*(flock[i].PZ-(max(terrain_z,0.) +
       2.*(float) i/NUM_PLANES+.3))-flock[i].PZv*.04;
      /* U-turn if fly off world!! */
      if(flock[i].PX<1||flock[i].PX>GRID_RANGE-
   2||flock[i].PY<1||flock[i].PY>GRID_RANGE-2)
         flock[i].Pazimuth+=M_PI;
      /* move planes */
      flock[i].PX+=cosf(flock[i].Pazimuth)*speed;
      flock[i].PY+=sinf(flock[i].Pazimuth)*speed;
      flock[i].PZ+=flock[i].PZv;
      }
   for(i=0;i<NUM_PLANES;i++)
      {
      *((float*)paper_plane_pos[i].vdata+0)=flock[i].PX;
      *((float*)paper_plane_pos[i].vdata+1)=flock[i].PY;
      *((float*)paper_plane_pos[i].vdata+2)=flock[i].PZ;
      *((float*)paper_plane_pos[i].vdata+3)
      =flock[i].Pazimuth*RAD_TO_DEG;
      *((float*)paper_plane_pos[i].vdata+4)
      =flock[i].PZv*(-500.);
      *((float*)paper_plane_pos[i].vdata+5)
      =flock[i].Proll*RAD_TO_DEG;
      }
   }
```

The terrain is created, eroded (to make it look more like rolling hills), and colored (to make it look like grass and dirt), by the following code:

```c
void create_terrain(void)
  {
  int r,c,i,x1,y1,x2,y2;
  int hillsize;
  hillsize=GRID_RANGE/12;
  A=(float*)calloc(GridDim*GridDim,sizeof(float));
  /* initialize elevation to zero,except band down
     middle where make a maximum height 'hill' that will
     later be inverted to
  *make the negative elevation 'canyon' */
  for(r=0;r<GridDim;r++)
    for(c=0;c<GridDim;c++)
      if(r>=(GridDim/2-2-IRND(2)) &&
  r<=(GridDim/2+2+IRND(2)))
        A[r*GridDim+c]=1.0;
      else
        A[r*GridDim+c]=0.0;
  /* create random sinusoidal hills that add on top of
     each other */
  for(i=1;i<=10*GridDim;i++)
    {
    /* randomly position hill */
    x1=IRND(GridDim-hillsize);
    x2=x1+hillsize/8+IRND(hillsize-hillsize/8);
    y1=IRND(GridDim-hillsize);
    y2=y1+hillsize/8+IRND(hillsize-hillsize/8);
    if((x1<=GridDim/2-4 && x2>=GridDim/2-4) ||
      (x1<=GridDim/2+4 && x2>=GridDim/2+4))
      {
      x1=IRND(2)-2+GridDim/2;
      x2=x1+IRND(GridDim/2-x1+2);
      }
    /* make a sinusoidal hill */
    for(r=x1;r<x2;r++)
      for(c=y1;c<y2;c++)
        {
        A[r*GridDim+c]+=.35 *
          (sinf(M_PI*(float)(r-x1)/(float)(x2-x1)) *
          (sinf(M_PI*(float)(c-y1)/(float)(y2-y1))));
        }
    }
  /* clamp the elevation of the terrain */
  for(r=1;r<GridDim;r++)
    for(c=1;c<GridDim;c++)
      {
      A[r*GridDim+c]=min(A[r*GridDim+c],.95);
      A[r*GridDim+c]=max(A[r*GridDim+c],0.);
      }
```

```c
    }

#define NUM_DROPS 80

void erode_terrain(void)
    {
    float x,y,xv,yv,dx,dy;
    float cut,min,take;
    int nm;
    static int t,xi,yi,xo,yo,done;
    int ii,jj,r,c;
    for(nm=1;nm<NUM_DROPS*GridDim;nm++)
        {
        /* find a random position to start the 'rain drop'
         */
        x=(float)(IRND(GridDim));
        y=(float)(IRND(GridDim));
        /* Clamp x and y to be inside grid */
        x=min(max(2.,x),(float) GridDim-2.);
        y=min(max(2.,y),(float) GridDim-2.);
        done=0;
        yv=xv=0.;
        t=0;
        cut=.3;
        while(!done)
          {
          xi=(int) x;
          yi=(int) y;
          min=90.;
          if(xi!=xo||yi!=yo)
            {
            cut*=.99;
            /* gradient */
            dx=(A[(xi+1)*GridDim+yi]-A[(xi-1)*GridDim+yi]);
            dy=(A[xi*GridDim+yi+1]-A[xi*GridDim+yi-1]);
            /* find lowest neighbor */
            for(ii=-1;ii<=1;ii++)
               for(jj=-1;jj<=1;jj++)
                  if(A[(xi+ii)*GridDim+yi+jj]<min)
                     min=A[(xi+ii)*GridDim+yi+jj];
            /* evaporate drop if sitting on my old location
         */
            if(M[xi][yi]==nm)
               done=1;
            M[xi][yi]=nm;
            /* cave in neighbors by .3 */
            for(ii=-1;ii<=1;ii++)
               for(jj=-1;jj<=1;jj++)
                  {
                  take=.3*cut*(A[(xi+ii)*GridDim+yi+jj]-min);
```

```
              A[(xi+ii)*GridDim+yi+jj]-=take;
              }
          /* take away from this cell by .7 */
          take=(A[xi*GridDim+yi]-min)*.7*cut;
          A[xi*GridDim+yi]-=take;
          }
      xo=xi;
      yo=yi;
      /* move drop using kinematic motion */
      xv=xv-dx-.8*xv;
      yv=yv-dy-.8*yv;
      x+=xv;
      y+=yv;
      /* make sure can't move by more that 1.0 in any
   direction */
      xv=max(xv,-1);
      yv=max(yv,-1);
      xv=min(xv,1);
      yv=min(yv,1);
      /* check to see if need a new drop */
      /* ie ran of world,got stuck,or at 'sea level' */
      if(x<1.||x>GridDim-1.||y<1.||y>GridDim-1.
      ||t++>2000
      ||cut<.01)
          done=1;
      if(A[xi*GridDim+yi]<0.0001)
          {
          A[xi*GridDim+yi]=0.;
          done=1;
          }
      } /* while(!done) with this drop */
    } /* next drop */
  /* invert the pseudo hill int the pseudo canyon */
  for(r=0;r<GridDim;r++)
    for(c=0;c<GridDim;c++)
      if(r>=GridDim/2-4 && r<=GridDim/2+4)
        A[r*GridDim+c]=max((-3.2*A[r*GridDim+c]),-1.8);
  }

void color_terrain(void)
  {
  float N[3],D,alt,maxelev=-1.;
  int x,y;
  for(x=0;x<GridDim;x++)
    for(y=0;y<GridDim;y++)
      maxelev=max(maxelev,A[x*GridDim+y]);
  for(x=1;x<GridDim-1;x++)
    for(y=1;y<GridDim-1;y++)
      {
      alt=A[x*GridDim+y]*1.5;
```

```c
        /* randomly perterb to get a mottling effect */
        alt+=IRND(100)/400.-.125;
        alt=min(alt,1.0);
        if(alt<-.11)
           {
           C[x][y][0]=0.6;/* soil/rock in canyon */
           C[x][y][1]=0.5;
           C[x][y][2]=0.2;
           }
        else if(alt<.000001)
           {
           C[x][y][0]=0.0;/* dark,jungle lowlands */
           C[x][y][1]=0.2;
           C[x][y][2]=0.05;
           }
        else if(alt<.90)
           {
           C[x][y][0]=alt*.25;/* green to redish hillsides
*/
           C[x][y][1]=(1.0-alt)*.4+.1;
           C[x][y][2]=0.1;
           }
        else
           {
           C[x][y][0]=alt;
           C[x][y][1]=alt;/* incresingly white snow */
           C[x][y][2]=alt;
           }
        /* compute normal to terrain */
        N[0]=A[(x-1)*GridDim+y]-A[(x+1)*GridDim+y];
        N[1]=A[x*GridDim+y-1]-A[x*GridDim+y+1];
        N[2]=2.0/ScaleZ;
        D=1.0/sqrtf(N[0]*N[0]+N[1]*N[1]+N[2]*N[2]);
        N[0]*=D;
        N[1]*=D;
        N[2]*=D;
        /* perform diffuse lighting of terrain */
        D=N[0]*LX+N[1]*LY+N[2]*LZ;
        D*=1.2;
        if(!IRND(4))
           D*=.5;
        D=max(D,0);
        /* darken terrain on shaded side */
        C[x][y][0]*=D;
        C[x][y][1]*=D;
        C[x][y][2]*=D;
        S[x][y]=(float)(x)/(float) CellDim;
        T[x][y]=(float)(y)/(float) CellDim;
        }
   }
```

The sky is created by the following functions:
```
void put_clouds_vert(float s,float t,float x,float
   y,float z,perfobj_vert_t*pdataptr)
   {
   float D[5];
   D[0]=s;
   D[1]=t;
   D[2]=x;
   D[3]=y;
   D[4]=z;
   putt2fdata(D,pdataptr);
   putv3fdata(D+2,pdataptr);
   }
void init_clouds(void)
   {
   perfobj_t*pobj;
   perfobj_vert_t*pdataptr;
   clouds=0;
   pobj=&(SharedData->clouds_texture_obj);
   pobj->flags=SharedData->clouds_texture_flags;
   put_texture_bind(2,pobj);
   pobj=&(SharedData->clouds_obj);
   pobj->flags=SharedData->clouds_flags;
   pobj->vdata=(float*)SharedData->clouds_verts;
   *(pobj->flags+0)=PD_DRAW_CLOUDS;
   *(pobj->flags+1)=PD_END;
   pdataptr=(perfobj_vert_t*)pobj->vdata;
   put_clouds_vert(0.,0.,-SKY,-SKY,SKY_HIGH,pdataptr);
   pdataptr++;
   put_clouds_vert(24.,0.,SKY+GRID_RANGE,-
      SKY,SKY_HIGH,pdataptr);
   pdataptr++;
   put_clouds_vert(24.,24.,SKY+GRID_RANGE,
      SKY+GRID_RANGE,SKY_HIGH,pdataptr);
   pdataptr++;
   put_clouds_vert(0.,24.,-
      SKY,SKY+GRID_RANGE,SKY_HIGH,pdataptr);
   }
```

The perception of flying is implemented with the following code:
```
void fly(perfobj_t*viewer_pos)
   {
   float terrain_z,xpos,ypos,xcntr,ycntr;
   float delta_speed=.003;
   xcntr=Wxsize/2;
   ycntr=Wysize/2;
   if(Xgetbutton(RKEY))
      init_positions();
   if(Xgetbutton(SPACEKEY))
      Keyboard_mode=!Keyboard_mode;
```

```c
if(Keyboard_mode)
  {
  /* step-at-a-time debugging mode */
  if(Keyboard_mode && Xgetbutton(LEFTARROWKEY))
     Azimuth-=0.025;
  if(Keyboard_mode && Xgetbutton(RIGHTARROWKEY))
     Azimuth+=0.025;
  if(Keyboard_mode && Xgetbutton(UPARROWKEY))
    {
    X+=cosf(-Azimuth+M_PI/2.)*0.025;
    Y+=sinf(-Azimuth+M_PI/2.)*0.025;
    }
  if(Keyboard_mode && Xgetbutton(DOWNARROWKEY))
    {
    X-=cosf(-Azimuth+M_PI/2.)*0.025;
    Y-=sinf(-Azimuth+M_PI/2.)*0.025;
    }
  if(Keyboard_mode && Xgetbutton(PAGEUPKEY))
     Z+=0.025;
  if(Keyboard_mode && Xgetbutton(PAGEDOWNKEY))
     Z-=0.025;
  }
else
  {
  /* simple,mouse-driven flight model */
  if(Xgetbutton(LEFTMOUSE) && Speed<.3)
     Speed+=delta_speed;
  if(Xgetbutton(RIGHTMOUSE) && Speed>-.3)
     Speed-=delta_speed;
  if(Xgetbutton(MIDDLEMOUSE))
     Speed=Speed*.8;
  xpos=(Xgetvaluator(MOUSEX)-xcntr)/((float)
  Wxsize*14.);
  ypos=(Xgetvaluator(MOUSEY)-ycntr)/((float)
  Wysize*.5);
  /* move in direction of view */
  Azimuth+=xpos;
  X+=cosf(-Azimuth+M_PI/2.)*Speed;
  Y+=sinf(-Azimuth+M_PI/2.)*Speed;
  Z-=ypos*Speed;
  }
/* keep from getting too close to terrain */
terrain_z=terrain_height(X,Y);
if(Z<terrain_z+.4)
   Z=terrain_z+.4;
X=max(X,1.);
X=min(X,GRID_RANGE);
Y=max(Y,1.);
Y=min(Y,GRID_RANGE);
Z=min(Z,20.);
```

```
    *((float*) viewer_pos->vdata+0)=X;
    *((float*)viewer_pos->vdata+1)=Y;
    *((float*)viewer_pos->vdata+2)=Z;
    *((float*)viewer_pos->vdata+3)=Azimuth;
    }
```

In this example the speed of rendering is greatly improved by eliminating the objects that aren't visible before passing them to OpenGL™, that is, culling. The following code accomplishes this:

```
void cull_proc(void)
  {
  static struct cull
    {
    perfobj_t**cells;
    perfobj_t viewer_pos_obj[2];
    unsigned int viewer_pos_flags[4];
    float viewer_position[2][4];
    float fovx,side,farr,epsilon,plane_epsilon;
    } cull;
  static int init=0;
  if(!init)
    {
    int x,y;
    cull.fovx=FOV*(float) Wxsize/(float) Wysize;
    cull.side=far_cull/cosf(cull.fovx/2.);
    cull.farr=2.*cull.side*sinf(cull.fovx/2.);
    cull.epsilon=sqrtf(2.)*CellSize/2.;
    cull.plane_epsilon=.5;
    cull.cells=(perfobj_t**)
     malloc(NumCells*NumCells*sizeof(perfobj_t *));
    for(x=0;x<NumCells;x++)
      for(y=0;y<NumCells;y++)
        cull.cells[x*NumCells+y] =
         &(SharedData->terrain_cells[x*NumCells+y]);
    ringbuffer.ring=malloc(RING_SIZE*sizeof(perfobj_t *));
    ringbuffer.head=ringbuffer.tail=0;
    cull.viewer_pos_obj[0].flags=cull.viewer_pos_flags;
    cull.viewer_pos_obj[0].vdata=
    cull.viewer_position[0];
    cull.viewer_pos_obj[1].flags=cull.viewer_pos_flags;
    cull.viewer_pos_obj[1].vdata=
    cull.viewer_position[1];
    *(cull.viewer_pos_flags)=PD_VIEWER_POS;
    *(cull.viewer_pos_flags+1)=PD_END;
    init=1;
    }
    {
    float*viewer;
    float vX,vY,vazimuth,px,py;
```

```
float left_area,right_area;
float left_dx,left_dy,right_dx,right_dy;
float ax,ay,bx,by,cx,cy;
float minx,maxx,miny,maxy;
int i,buffer=0;
int x,y,x0,y0,x1,y1;
perfobj_t*viewer_pos,*paper_plane_pos;
buffered_data*buffered;
perfobj_t*terrain_texture=&(SharedData-
>terrain_texture_obj);
perfobj_t*paper_plane=&(SharedData-
>paper_plane_obj);
perfobj_t*paper_plane_start=&(SharedData-
>paper_plane_start_obj);
perfobj_t*paper_plane_end=&(SharedData-
>paper_plane_end_obj);
perfobj_t*clouds_texture=&(SharedData-
>clouds_texture_obj);
perfobj_t*clouds=&(SharedData->clouds_obj);
buffered=gfxpipe->buffers[buffer];
viewer_pos=&(buffered->viewer_pos_obj);
paper_plane_pos=buffered->paper_plane_pos_obj;
vX=*((float*)viewer_pos->vdata+0);
vY=*((float*)viewer_pos->vdata+1);
vazimuth=*((float*)viewer_pos->vdata+3);
viewer=cull.viewer_position[buffer];
viewer[0]=vX;
viewer[1]=vY;
viewer[2]=*((float*)viewer_pos->vdata+2);
viewer[3]=vazimuth;
/* Begin cull to viewing frustrum */
ax=(vX-sinf(-vazimuth+cull.fovx*.5)*cull.side);
ay=(vY+cosf(-vazimuth+cull.fovx*.5)*cull.side);
bx=vX;
by=vY;
cx=(vX+sinf(vazimuth+cull.fovx*.5)*cull.side);
cy=(vY+cosf(vazimuth+cull.fovx*.5)*cull.side);
minx=min(min(ax,bx),cx);
miny=min(min(ay,by),cy);
maxx=max(max(ax,bx),cx);
maxy=max(max(ay,by),cy);
x0=max((int)(minx/CellSize),0);
x1=min((int)(maxx/CellSize)+1,NumCells);
y0=max((int)(miny/CellSize),0);
y1=min((int)(maxy/CellSize)+1,NumCells);
left_dx=ax-bx;
left_dy=ay-by;
right_dx=cx-bx;
right_dy=cy-by;
enter_in_ring(&cull.viewer_pos_obj[buffer]);
```

```
if(viewer[2]<SKY_HIGH)
   {
   /* draw clouds first */
   enter_in_ring(clouds_texture);
   enter_in_ring(clouds);
   }
enter_in_ring(terrain_texture);
/* Add visible cells to ring buffer */
for(x=x0;x<x1;x++)
   {
   for(y=y0;y<y1;y++)
      {
      float cntrx=(x+.5)*CellSize;
      float cntry=(y+.5)*CellSize;
      left_area=left_dx*(cntry-by)-left_dy*(cntrx-bx);
      right_area=right_dx*(cntry-by)-right_dy*(cntrx-bx);
      if((left_area<cull.epsilon*cull.side &&
right_area>-cull.epsilon*cull.side))
         {
         enter_in_ring(cull.cells[x*NumCells+y]);
         }
      }
   }
enter_in_ring(paper_plane_start);
/* Add visible planes to ring buffer */
for(i=0;i<NUM_PLANES;i++)
   {
   px=*((float*)paper_plane_pos[i].vdata+0);
   py=*((float*)paper_plane_pos[i].vdata+1);
   left_area=left_dx*(py-by)-left_dy*(px-bx);
   right_area=right_dx*(py-by)-right_dy*(px-bx);
   if(left_area<cull.plane_epsilon*cull.side &&
right_area>-cull.plane_epsilon*cull.side)
      {
      enter_in_ring(&paper_plane_pos[i]);
      enter_in_ring(paper_plane);
      }
   }
 enter_in_ring(paper_plane_end);
 if(viewer[2]>SKY_HIGH)
   {
   /* draw clouds after everything else */
   enter_in_ring(clouds_texture);
   enter_in_ring(clouds);
   }
 enter_in_ring((perfobj_t*)0);/* 0 indicates end of
frame */
 buffer=!buffer;
 }
```

```c
    }
void putv3fdata(float*v,perfobj_vert_t*ptr)
    {
    ptr->vert[0]=v[0];
    ptr->vert[1]=v[1];
    ptr->vert[2]=v[2];
    }

void putc3fdata(float*c,perfobj_vert_t*ptr)
    {
    ptr->color[0]=c[0];
    ptr->color[1]=c[1];
    ptr->color[2]=c[2];
    }

void putn3fdata(float*n,perfobj_vert_t*ptr)
    {
    ptr->normal[0]=n[0];
    ptr->normal[1]=n[1];
    ptr->normal[2]=n[2];
    }

void putt2fdata(float*t,perfobj_vert_t*ptr)
    {
    ptr->texture[0]=t[0];
    ptr->texture[1]=t[1];
    }

perfobj_t*get_from_ring(void)
    {
    static perfobj_t*pobj;
    while(ringbuffer.tail==ringbuffer.head)
        ;
    pobj=ringbuffer.ring[ringbuffer.tail%RING_SIZE];
    ringbuffer.tail++;
    return pobj;
    }

void draw_proc(void)
    {
    perfobj_t*too_draw;
    glClear(GL_COLOR_BUFFER_BIT|GL_DEPTH_BUFFER_BIT);
    while((too_draw=get_from_ring()))
        drawperfobj(too_draw);
    }

void draw(void)
    {
    int newCount;
    char buf[20];
```

```c
int i,len;
/* Draw the frame */
cull_proc();
draw_proc();
/* Update the frames per second count if we have gone
   past at least a quarter of a second since the last
   update. */
newCount=glutGet(GLUT_ELAPSED_TIME);
frameCount++;
if((newCount-lastCount)>1000)
  {
  fpsRate=(int)((10000.0F/(newCount-
  lastCount))*frameCount);
  lastCount=newCount;
  frameCount=0;
  }
if(show_timer)
  {
  sprintf(buf,"%3d.%d fps",fpsRate/10,fpsRate%10);
  glPushAttrib(GL_ENABLE_BIT|GL_CURRENT_BIT);
  glDisable(GL_LIGHTING);
  glDisable(GL_TEXTURE_2D);
  glDisable(GL_DEPTH_TEST);
  glDisable(GL_FOG);
  glDisable(GL_BLEND);
  glMatrixMode(GL_PROJECTION);
  glPushMatrix();
  glLoadIdentity();
  glOrtho(0,Wxsize,0,Wysize,-1,1);
  glMatrixMode(GL_MODELVIEW);
  glPushMatrix();
  glLoadIdentity();
  glColor3f(1.0F,1.0F,0.0F);
  glRasterPos2i(10,10);
  len=strlen(buf);
  for(i=0;i<len;i++)

  glutBitmapCharacter(GLUT_BITMAP_TIMES_ROMAN_24,buf[i]
  );
  glMatrixMode(GL_PROJECTION);
  glPopMatrix();
  glMatrixMode(GL_MODELVIEW);
  glPopMatrix();
  glPopAttrib();
  }
glutSwapBuffers();
}
```

Chapter 20. The Knight's Tour

The knight's tour example includes a lot of functionality, including rendering and moving pieces and the chessboard, 3D controls, user selection of materials, and chess move logic. The material selection dialog is shown below:

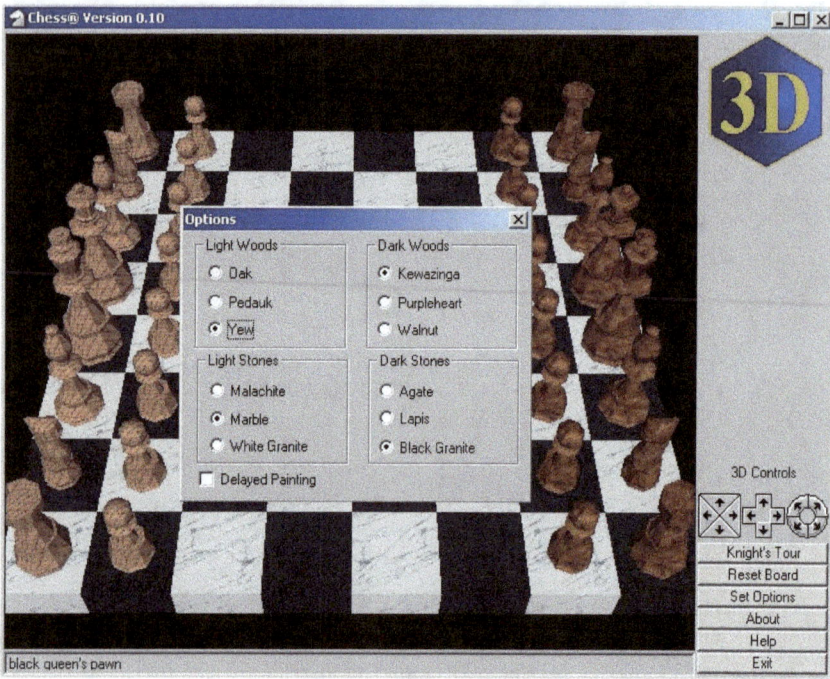

Figure 47. Chess Example

As the shape of the pieces is always the same, these are defined in data statements, such as the following:

```
typedef struct{short x1,y1,z1,x2,y2,z2,x3,y3,z3;}PIECE;

PIECE rook[]={
{ 1496,    229,      0, 1058,    229, 1058, 1579,     -5,      0},
{ 1117,     -5,   1117, 1579,     -5,    0, 1058,    229,   1058},
{ 1058,    229,   1058,    0,    229, 1496, 1117,     -5,   1117},
{    0,     -5,   1579, 1117,     -5, 1117,    0,    229,   1496},
{    0,    229,   1496,-1058,    229, 1058,    0,     -5,   1579},
{-1117,     -5,   1117,    0,     -5, 1579,-1058,    229,   1058},
{-1058,    229,   1058,-1496,    229,    0,-1117,     -5,   1117},
{-1579,     -5,      0,-1117,     -5, 1117,-1496,    229,      0},
{-1496,    229,      0,-1058,    229,-1058,-1579,     -5,      0},
{-1117,     -5,  -1117,-1579,     -5,    0,-1058,    229,  -1058},
{  etc,    etc,    etc,  etc,    etc,  etc,  etc,    etc,    etc},
{32767,  32767,  32767,32767,  32767,32767,32767,  32767,  32767}};
```

The last line containing 32767 indicates the end of data. Short integers are the smallest type and provide more than adequate resolution. The pieces are scaled as needed and assigned a texture by the following code:

```c
typedef struct{
  float v[9];
  float n[3];
  DWORD color;
  }MESH;

MESH*Bishop;
MESH*King;
MESH*Knight;
MESH*Pawn;
MESH*Queen;
MESH*Rook;

MESH*InitializePiece(PIECE*p)
  {
  int i;
  MESH*m;
  for(i=0;p[i].x1!=32767;i++)
    continue;
  m=calloc(i+1,sizeof(MESH));
  for(i=0;p[i].x1!=32767;i++)
    {
    m[i].v[0]=p[i].x1/10000.;
    m[i].v[1]=p[i].y1/10000.;
    m[i].v[2]=p[i].z1/10000.;
    m[i].v[3]=p[i].x2/10000.;
    m[i].v[4]=p[i].y2/10000.;
    m[i].v[5]=p[i].z2/10000.;
    m[i].v[6]=p[i].x3/10000.;
    m[i].v[7]=p[i].y3/10000.;
    m[i].v[8]=p[i].z3/10000.;
    m[i].color=0x0000FF;
    }
  m[i].color=-1;
  return(m);
  }

void SetPiece(int i,MESH*mesh,DWORD*wood,int col,int
    row,int rotation)
  {
  Piece[i].mesh=mesh;
  Piece[i].name=Object[i];
  Piece[i].wood=wood;
  Piece[i].col=col;
  Piece[i].row=row;
  Piece[i].rotation=rotation;
  }
```

```
void InitializePieces()
{
Bishop=InitializePiece(bishop);
King  =InitializePiece(king);
Knight=InitializePiece(knight);
Pawn  =InitializePiece(pawn);
Queen =InitializePiece(queen);
Rook  =InitializePiece(rook);
SetPiece(0x00,Rook  ,&light_wood,0,0,   0);
SetPiece(0x01,Knight,&light_wood,1,0,   0);
SetPiece(0x02,Bishop,&light_wood,2,0,   0);
SetPiece(0x03,Queen ,&light_wood,3,0,   0);
SetPiece(0x04,King  ,&light_wood,4,0,   0);
SetPiece(0x05,Bishop,&light_wood,5,0,   0);
SetPiece(0x06,Knight,&light_wood,6,0,   0);
SetPiece(0x07,Rook  ,&light_wood,7,0,   0);
SetPiece(0x08,Pawn  ,&light_wood,0,1,   0);
SetPiece(0x09,Pawn  ,&light_wood,1,1,   0);
SetPiece(0x0A,Pawn  ,&light_wood,2,1,   0);
SetPiece(0x0B,Pawn  ,&light_wood,3,1,   0);
SetPiece(0x0C,Pawn  ,&light_wood,4,1,   0);
SetPiece(0x0D,Pawn  ,&light_wood,5,1,   0);
SetPiece(0x0E,Pawn  ,&light_wood,6,1,   0);
SetPiece(0x0F,Pawn  ,&light_wood,7,1,   0);
SetPiece(0x10,Rook  , &dark_wood,0,7,   0);
SetPiece(0x11,Knight, &dark_wood,1,7, 180);
SetPiece(0x12,Bishop, &dark_wood,2,7,   0);
SetPiece(0x13,Queen , &dark_wood,3,7,   0);
SetPiece(0x14,King  , &dark_wood,4,7,   0);
SetPiece(0x15,Bishop, &dark_wood,5,7,   0);
SetPiece(0x16,Knight, &dark_wood,6,7, 180);
SetPiece(0x17,Rook  , &dark_wood,7,7,   0);
SetPiece(0x18,Pawn  , &dark_wood,0,6,   0);
SetPiece(0x19,Pawn  , &dark_wood,1,6,   0);
SetPiece(0x1A,Pawn  , &dark_wood,2,6,   0);
SetPiece(0x1B,Pawn  , &dark_wood,3,6,   0);
SetPiece(0x1C,Pawn  , &dark_wood,4,6,   0);
SetPiece(0x1D,Pawn  , &dark_wood,5,6,   0);
SetPiece(0x1E,Pawn  , &dark_wood,6,6,   0);
SetPiece(0x1F,Pawn  , &dark_wood,7,6,   0);
}
```

The stone and wood textures are defined as resources:

```
Agate         BITMAP  "agate.bmp"
BlackGranite  BITMAP  "blackgranite.bmp"
Lapis         BITMAP  "lapis.bmp"
Malachite     BITMAP  "malachite.bmp"
Marble        BITMAP  "marble.bmp"
Oak           BITMAP  "oak.bmp"
```

```
Pedauk          BITMAP  "pedauk.bmp"
Purpleheart     BITMAP  "purpleheart.bmp"
Walnut          BITMAP  "walnut.bmp"
WhiteGranite    BITMAP  "whitegranite.bmp"
Yew             BITMAP  "yew.bmp"
Kewazinga       BITMAP  "kewazinga.bmp"
```

These are loaded by the following code:

```
DWORD LoadTexture(char*rname)
  {
  void*rLock;
  HGLOBAL rLoad;
  HRSRC rFind;
  BITMAPINFOHEADER*bm;
  if((rFind=FindResource(hInst,rname,RT_BITMAP))==NULL)
     Abort(__LINE__,"can't find resource %s\nWindows
     error code %li",rname,GetLastError());
  if((rLoad=LoadResource(hInst,rFind))==NULL)
     Abort(__LINE__,"can't load resource %s\nWindows
     error code %li",rname,GetLastError());
  if((rLock=LockResource(rLoad))==NULL)
     Abort(__LINE__,"can't lock resource %s\nWindows
     error code %li",rname,GetLastError());
  bm=(BITMAPINFOHEADER*)rLock;
  return(InitializeTexture(bm));
  }
void LoadTextures()
  {
  tAgate       =LoadTexture("Agate");
  tBlackGranite=LoadTexture("BlackGranite");
  tKewazinga   =LoadTexture("Kewazinga");
  tLapis       =LoadTexture("Lapis");
  tMalachite   =LoadTexture("Malachite");
  tMarble      =LoadTexture("Marble");
  tOak         =LoadTexture("Oak");
  tPedauk      =LoadTexture("Pedauk");
  tPurpleheart =LoadTexture("Purpleheart");
  tWalnut      =LoadTexture("Walnut");
  tWhiteGranite=LoadTexture("WhiteGranite");
  tYew         =LoadTexture("Yew");
  light_wood  =tYew;
  dark_wood   =tKewazinga;;
  light_stone =tMarble;
  dark_stone  =tBlackGranite;
  }
```

The board and pieces are rendered with the following code:

```
void PrepMesh(MESH*Mesh)
  {
  int i;
  VERTEX n,p,q;
```

```c
    for(i=0;(Mesh[i].color&0x80000000)==0;i++)
      {
      p.x=Mesh[i].v[3]-Mesh[i].v[0];
      p.y=Mesh[i].v[4]-Mesh[i].v[1];
      p.z=Mesh[i].v[5]-Mesh[i].v[2];
      q.x=Mesh[i].v[6]-Mesh[i].v[0];
      q.y=Mesh[i].v[7]-Mesh[i].v[1];
      q.z=Mesh[i].v[8]-Mesh[i].v[2];
      n=CrossProduct(p,q);
      memcpy(Mesh[i].n,(float*)&n,3*sizeof(float));
      }
    }
void glMesh(MESH*Mesh,DWORD color,DWORD texture)
    {
    int i;
    if(fabs(Mesh[0].n[0])+fabs(Mesh[0].n[1])
      +fabs(Mesh[0].n[2])<FLT_EPSILON)
      PrepMesh(Mesh);
    if(texture)
      {
      glColor(WHITE);
      glEnable(GL_TEXTURE_2D);
      BindTexture(GL_TEXTURE_2D,texture);
      }
    else if(color)
      {
      glDisable(GL_TEXTURE_2D);
      glColor(color);
      }
    glBegin(GL_TRIANGLES);
    for(i=0;(Mesh[i].color&0x80000000)==0;i++)
      {
      glNormal3fv(Mesh[i].n);
      if(texture)
        {
        glVertexAndTex3fv(Mesh[i].v  ,texture);
        glVertexAndTex3fv(Mesh[i].v+3,texture);
        glVertexAndTex3fv(Mesh[i].v+6,texture);
        }
      else
        {
        if(color)
          glColor(color);
        else
          glColor(Mesh[i].color);
        glVertex3fv(Mesh[i].v);
        glVertex3fv(Mesh[i].v+3);
        glVertex3fv(Mesh[i].v+6);
        }
      }
```

```
  glEnd();
  if(texture)
    glDisable(GL_TEXTURE_2D);
  }
void SetView(int a,int b,int c,float s,float x,float
   y,float z)
  {
  View.a=a;
  View.b=b;
  View.c=c;
  View.s=s;
  View.x=x;
  View.y=y;
  View.z=z;
  }
void RenderTour()
  {
  int i,n;
  float a,r=0.0125,x1,x2,x3,x4,x5,x6,y=0.0125,
    z1,z2,z3,z4,z5,z6;
  glDisable(GL_TEXTURE_2D);
  glColor(0xFF0000);
  glBegin(GL_QUADS);
  glNormal3f(0.,1.,0.);
  x2=Brd[Tour[0].y];
  z2=Brd[Tour[0].x];
  n=min(64,pending_tour);
  for(i=1;i<n;i++)
    {
    x1=x2;
    z1=z2;
    x2=Brd[Tour[i].y];
    z2=Brd[Tour[i].x];
    a=atan2(z2-z1,x2-x1);
    x3=x1-r*sin(a);
    x4=x2-r*sin(a);
    x5=x1+r*sin(a);
    x6=x2+r*sin(a);
    glVertex3f(x3,y,z3);
    glVertex3f(x4,y,z4);
    glVertex3f(x6,y,z6);
    glVertex3f(x5,y,z5);
    }
  glEnd();
  }
void RenderBoard()
  {
  char board[]="??";
  int i,j,k;
  for(i=0;i<8;i++)
```

```
    {
    board[1]='1'+i;
    for(j=0;j<8;j++)
      {
      board[0]='A'+j;
      k=ObjectIndex(board);
      glStencilFunc(GL_ALWAYS,k,-1);
      if(k==selected)
        glHexahedron(Brd[i],-
3./32.,Brd[j],3./8.,3./16.,3./8.,0xFF0000,0);
      else
        glHexahedron(Brd[i],-
3./32.,Brd[j],3./8.,3./16.,3./8.,0,(i+j)%2?light_ston
  e:dark_stone);
      }
    }
  glStencilFunc(GL_ALWAYS,0,-1);
  }
void RenderPiece(MESH*piece,char*object,DWORD
   texture,float x,float z,float s,float b)
  {
  int k;
  k=ObjectIndex(object);
  glPushMatrix();
  glTranslatef(x,0,z);
  glScalef(s,s,s);
  glStencilFunc(GL_ALWAYS,k,-1);
  glRotatef(b,0,1,0);
  if(k==selected)
    glMesh(piece,0xFF0000,0);
  else
    glMesh(piece,0,texture);
  glStencilFunc(GL_ALWAYS,0,-1);
  glPopMatrix();
  }
void RenderChess()
  {
  int i;
  ScaleTexture(2.);
  RenderBoard();
  if(light_wood==tOak)
    ScaleTexture(1.);
  else if(light_wood==tPedauk)
    ScaleTexture(2.);
  else
    ScaleTexture(25.);
  for(i=0;i<16;i++)
    if(Piece[i].row>=0)
```

```
      RenderPiece(Piece[i].mesh,Piece[i].name,
    *Piece[i].wood,Brd[Piece[i].row],Brd[Piece[i].col],
    0.75,Piece[i].rotation);
  if(dark_wood==tPurpleheart)
    ScaleTexture(5.);
  else
    ScaleTexture(2.);
  for(i=16;i<32;i++)
    if(Piece[i].row>=0)
      RenderPiece(Piece[i].mesh,Piece[i].name,
    *Piece[i].wood,Brd[Piece[i].row],Brd[Piece[i].col],
    0.75,Piece[i].rotation);
  if(pending_tour>0)
    RenderTour();
  }
void RenderScene()
  {
  float lp[4];
  if(!pDC)
    return;
  glClearDepth(1);
  glClearStencil(0);
  glClearColor(0,0,0,0);
  glClear(GL_COLOR_BUFFER_BIT|GL_DEPTH_BUFFER_BIT|
    GL_STENCIL_BUFFER_BIT);
  glEnable(GL_DEPTH_TEST);
  glDepthFunc(GL_LESS);
  glFrontFace(GL_CCW);
  glDisable(GL_CULL_FACE);
  glCullFace(GL_BACK);
  glEnable(GL_STENCIL_TEST);
  glStencilOp(GL_KEEP,GL_KEEP,GL_REPLACE);
  glStencilFunc(GL_ALWAYS,0,-1);
  glShadeModel(GL_FLAT);
  glDisable(GL_AUTO_NORMAL);
  glEnable(GL_NORMALIZE);
  glDisable(GL_BLEND);
  glColorMaterial(GL_FRONT_AND_BACK,
    GL_AMBIENT_AND_DIFFUSE);
  glEnable(GL_COLOR_MATERIAL);
  glMatrixMode(GL_MODELVIEW);
  glLoadIdentity();
  if(fill_polygons)
    glPolygonMode(GL_FRONT_AND_BACK,GL_FILL);
  else
    glPolygonMode(GL_FRONT_AND_BACK,GL_LINE);
  glLightModeli(GL_LIGHT_MODEL_TWO_SIDE,FALSE);
  glLightModeli(GL_LIGHT_MODEL_LOCAL_VIEWER,FALSE);
  glLightModelfv(GL_LIGHT_MODEL_AMBIENT,
    floatColor(0x000000));
```

```
    glLightfv(GL_LIGHT0,GL_AMBIENT ,floatColor(0x555555));
    glLightfv(GL_LIGHT0,GL_DIFFUSE ,floatColor(0xAAAAAA));
    glLightfv(GL_LIGHT0,GL_SPECULAR,floatColor(0x000000));
      lp[0]=sin(Light.a*M_PI/180)*cos(Light.b*M_PI/180);
      lp[2]=cos(Light.a*M_PI/180)*cos(Light.b*M_PI/180);
      lp[1]=sin(Light.b*M_PI/180);
      lp[3]=0;/* infinite distance to light source */
    glLightfv(GL_LIGHT0,GL_POSITION,lp);
    glEnable(GL_LIGHT0);
    if(enable_lighting)
      glEnable(GL_LIGHTING);
    else
      glDisable(GL_LIGHTING);
    glColor(WHITE);
    glRotatef(View.a,1,0,0);
    glRotatef(View.b,0,1,0);
    glRotatef(View.c,0,0,1);
    glScalef(View.s,View.s,View.s);
    glTranslatef(View.x,View.y,View.z);
    RenderChess();
    glFinish();
    SwapBuffers(pDC);
    }
```

The logic to solve the knight's walk is implemented with this very simple code (at least by chess standards):

```
int MoveOK(int x,int y)
    {
    if(x<0)return(0);
    if(x>7)return(0);
    if(y<0)return(0);
    if(y>7)return(0);
    if(board[y][x])return(0);
    return(1);
    }
int Moves(int x,int y)
    {
    int i,n;
    for(n=i=0;i<8;i++)
      n+=MoveOK(x+move[i].x,y+move[i].y);
    return(n);
    }
int EndTour(int x1,int y1)
    {
    int i,m=0,n1,n2,x2,x3,y2,y3;
    memset(board,0,sizeof(board));
    board[y1][x1]=1;
    Tour[0].x=x1;
    Tour[0].y=y1;
    while(1)
```

```c
      {
      n1=9;
      for(i=0;i<8;i++)
         {
         x2=x1+move[i].x;
         y2=y1+move[i].y;
         if(!MoveOK(x2,y2))
            continue;
         if(m==62)
            {
            x3=x2;
            y3=y2;
            break;
            }
         n2=Moves(x2,y2);
         board[y2][x2]=0;
         if(n2<1||n2>=n1)
            continue;
         x3=x2;
         y3=y2;
         n1=n2;
         }
      if(n1==9&&m!=62)
         return(0);
      m++;
      x1=x3;
      y1=y3;
      board[y3][x3]=m+1;
      Tour[m].x=x3;
      Tour[m].y=y3;
      if(m==63)
         break;
      }
   return(m);
   }
void BeginTour(int s)
   {
   int x1,y1;
   x1=(int)(Object[s][0]-'A');
   y1=(int)(Object[s][1]-'1');
   if(EndTour(x1,y1))
      {
      for(pending_tour=1;pending_tour<=64;pending_tour++)
         {
         Piece[1].col=Tour[pending_tour-1].x;
         Piece[1].row=Tour[pending_tour-1].y;
         RePaint();
         }
      }
   else
```

```
    MessageBox(hMain,"knight's tour was not
    successful","algorithm failure",MB_APPLMODAL|MB_OK);
  }
```

Figure 48. Knight's Tour

Chapter 21. Displaying Three-Dimensional Data

The Field3D example is different from any other contained in the archive as it correlates, interpolates, and displays three-dimensional data rather than some particular shape. Typical output is shown in the figure below:

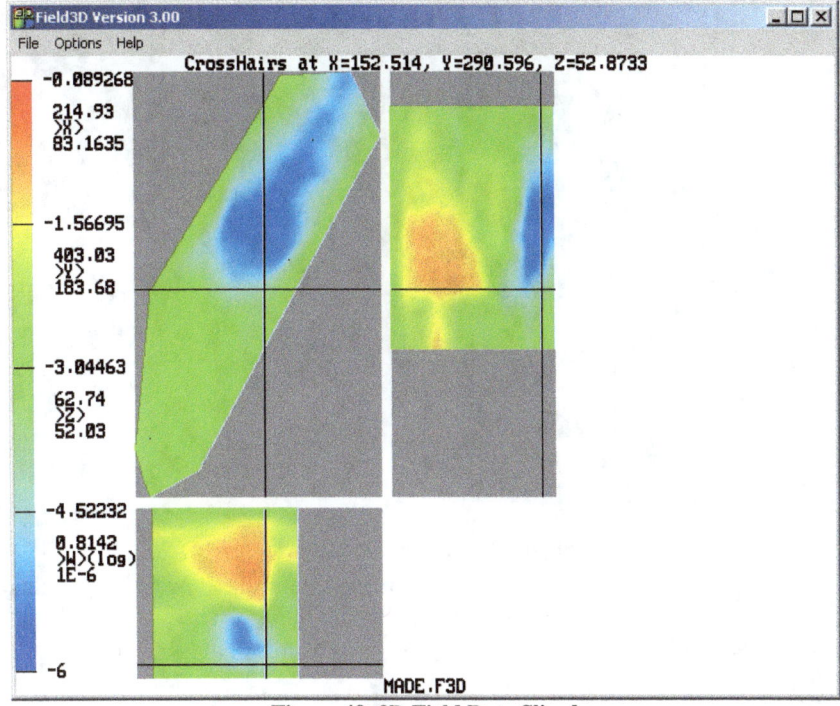

Figure 49. 3D Field Data Sliced

The large rectangle is the X-Y plane, the lower rectangle is the X-Z plane, and the right rectangle is the Y-Z plane. The crosshairs in all three rectangles are at the same location in three-dimensional space. The lower rectangle shows a vertical slice through the data where the horizontal black line passes through it. The right rectangle shows a vertical slice through the data where the vertical black line passes through it. This figure printed and folded along the edges to illustrate the relationship between the three views is shown below:

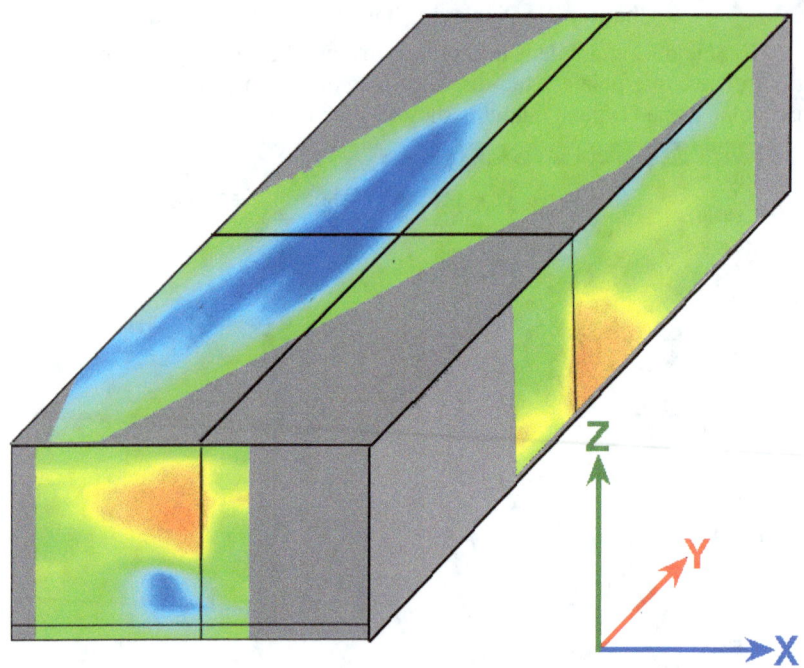

Figure 50. 3D Field Data Block

There are several two- and three-dimensional sets provided with this example (*.DAT) as well as pre-compiled fields (*.F3D). There are also batch files (_make_*.bat) that illustrate the various command line options and re-compile the fields.

This following example shows topography with additional information overlaid. The elevations are color coded from blue (sea level) to red (250 feet).

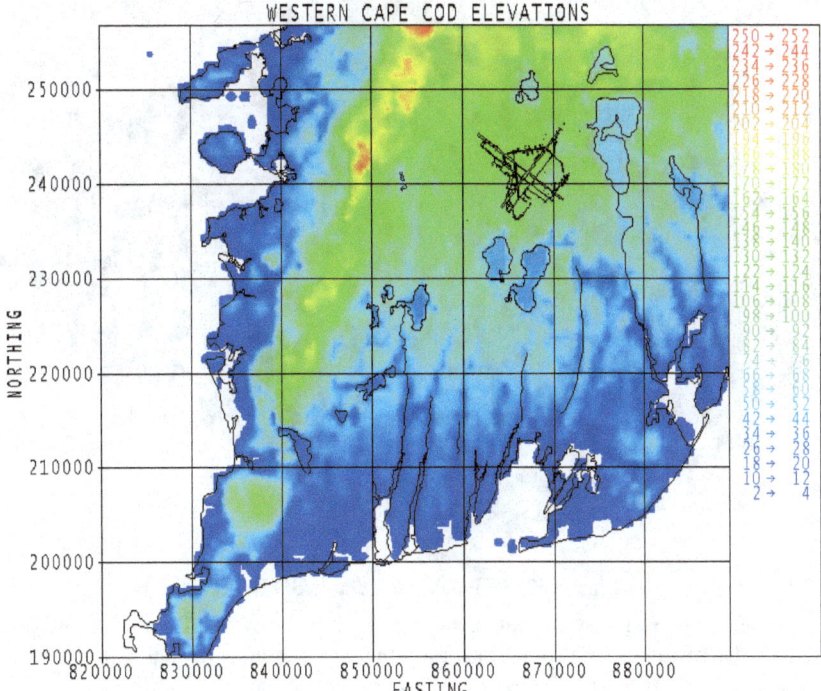

Figure 51. Colored Topographic Data

The same topography in 3D with considerable vertical exaggeration:

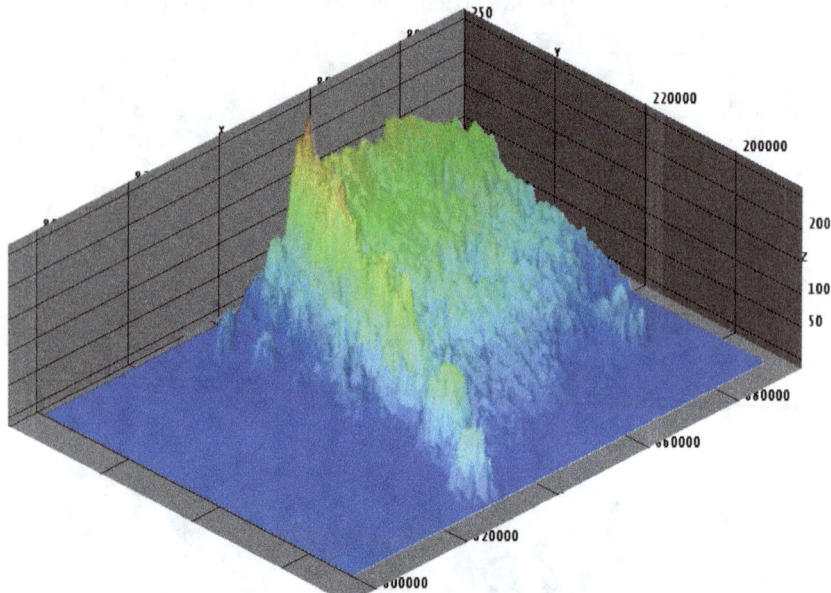

Figure 52. Topographic Data in 3D Relief

Field3D will also write out 2D and 3D table files (*.TB2 and *.TB3) that contain the results of interpolation in a convenient tabular format. Such a table was used to construct the previous two graphics.

Chapter 22. Geometric Shapes

All of the geometric shapes are illustrated in the Demo3D example, which can be found in the online archive in folder examples\Demo3D. We first build a small function to receive a polygon and pass this along to the rendering engine. The polygons should be convex and non-overlapping. Concave and/or overlapping polygons should be first subdivided into triangles and combined to form a *mesh*, which we will discuss in the next chapter. All simple geometric shapes can be built up from polygons. For instance, a cylinder is formed entirely from quadrangles:

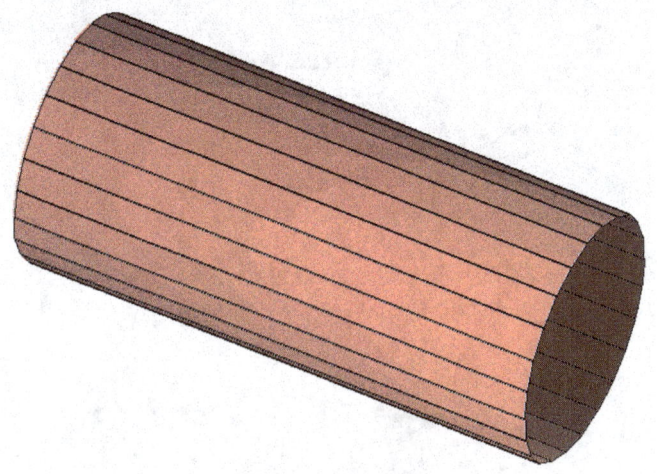

Figure 53. 3D Tube

Spheroids are formed of quadrangles plus triangles at the poles.

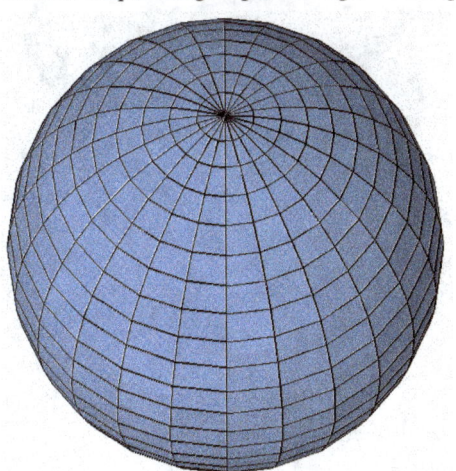

Figure 54. 3D Sphere

A torus is formed entirely of quadrangles.

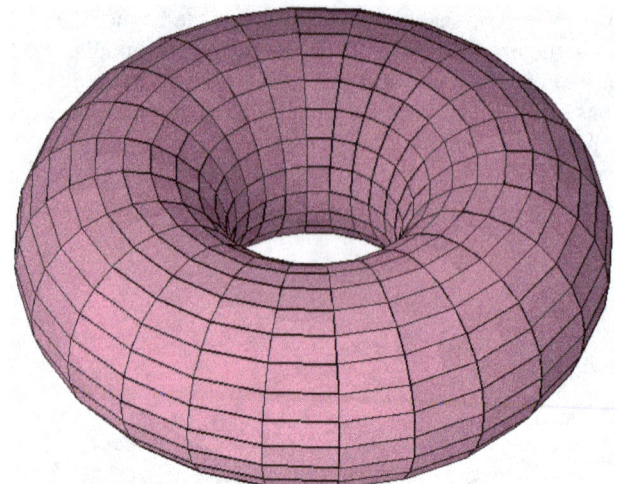

Figure 55. 3D Torus

A cone is formed from triangles and a disc (i.e., a washer) is formed from quadrangles. More elaborate shapes such as a spring are easily formed from these basic polygons.

Figure 56. 3D Coil

Many simple shapes can be created by extruding quadrangles along a curve.

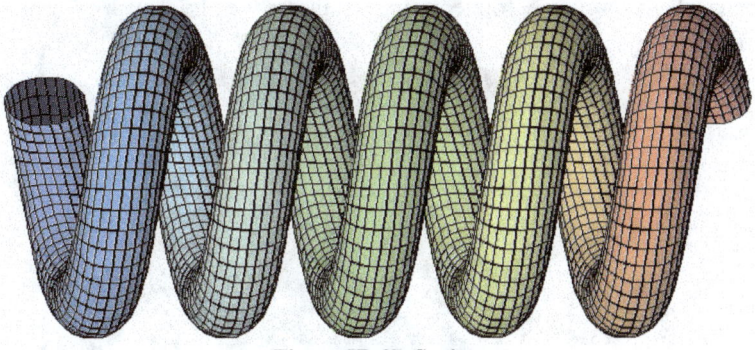

Figure 57. 3D Spring

Simple distortions can also be applied.

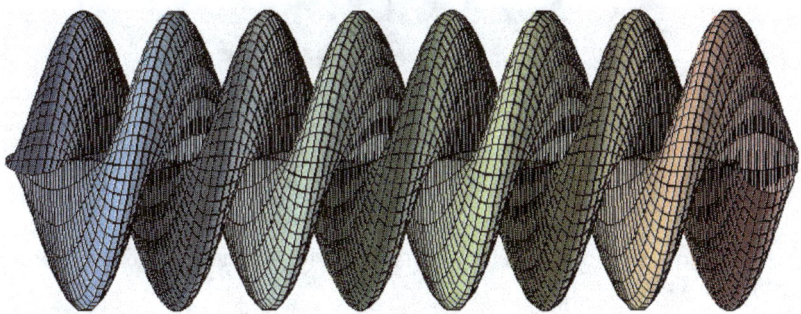

Figure 58. 3D Screw

Distortions, stretching, and twists can be combined.

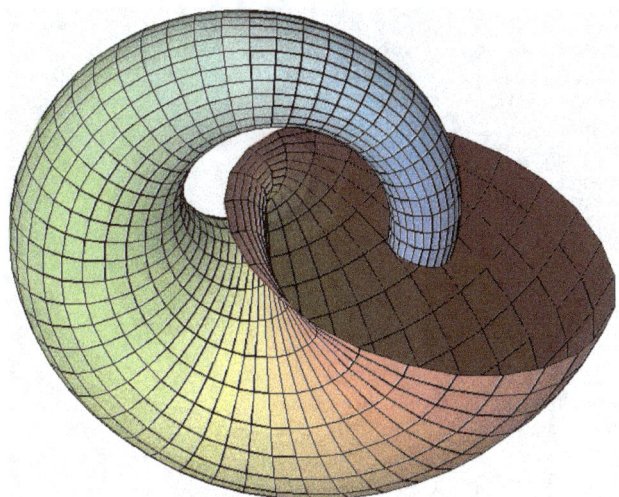

Figure 59. 3D Seashell

The entire range of polyhedra can be quickly assembled from a few polygons. Walls are easily formed using hexahedra (i.e., bricks).

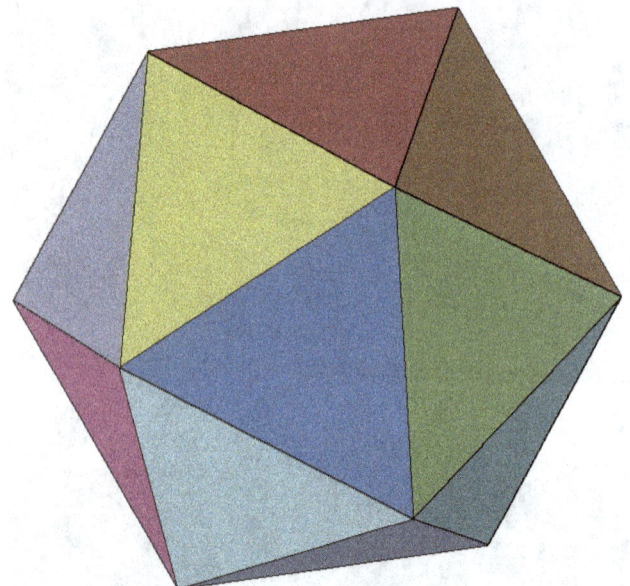

Figure 60. Dodecahedron

The following simple functions can be used to pass each of these shapes and more to the rendering engine.

```
void RenderTriangle(VECTOR V1,VECTOR V2,VECTOR V3,COLOR
   c)
  {
  VECTOR N;
  glBegin(GL_TRIANGLES);
  glMaterialfv(glFace(),GL_AMBIENT_AND_DIFFUSE,c);
  N=vNormal(V1,V2,V3);
  glNormal3d(N.x,N.y,N.z);
  glVertex3d(V1.x,V1.y,V1.z);
  glVertex3d(V2.x,V2.y,V2.z);
  glVertex3d(V3.x,V3.y,V3.z);
  glEnd();
  }
void RenderQuadrangle(VECTOR V1,VECTOR V2,VECTOR
   V3,VECTOR V4,COLOR c)
  {
  VECTOR N;
  glBegin(GL_QUADS);
  glMaterialfv(glFace(),GL_AMBIENT_AND_DIFFUSE,c);
  N=vNormal(V1,V2,V3);
  glNormal3d(N.x,N.y,N.z);
  glVertex3d(V1.x,V1.y,V1.z);
```

```
glVertex3d(V2.x,V2.y,V2.z);
glVertex3d(V3.x,V3.y,V3.z);
glVertex3d(V4.x,V4.y,V4.z);
glEnd();
}
```

Along with defining the coordinates of the vertices and color, we must also define the outward normal so that the rendering engine can properly apply lighting. The outward normal vector is the cross product of the two vectors forming the vertices of the triangle.

```
VECTOR vNormal(VECTOR V1,VECTOR V2,VECTOR V3)
    {
    double a1,a2,a3,b1,b2,b3,r;
    static VECTOR N;
    a1=V2.x-V1.x;
    a2=V2.y-V1.y;
    a3=V2.z-V1.z;
    b1=V3.x-V1.x;
    b2=V3.y-V1.y;
    b3=V3.z-V1.z;
    N.x=a2*b3-a3*b2;
    N.y=a3*b1-a1*b3;
    N.z=a1*b2-a2*b1;
    r=sqrt(N.x*N.x+N.y*N.y+N.z*N.z);
    if(r>DBL_EPSILON)
       {
       N.x/=r;
       N.y/=r;
       N.z/=r;
       }
    else
       {
       N.x=0;
       N.y=0;
       N.z=1;
       }
    return(N);
    }
```

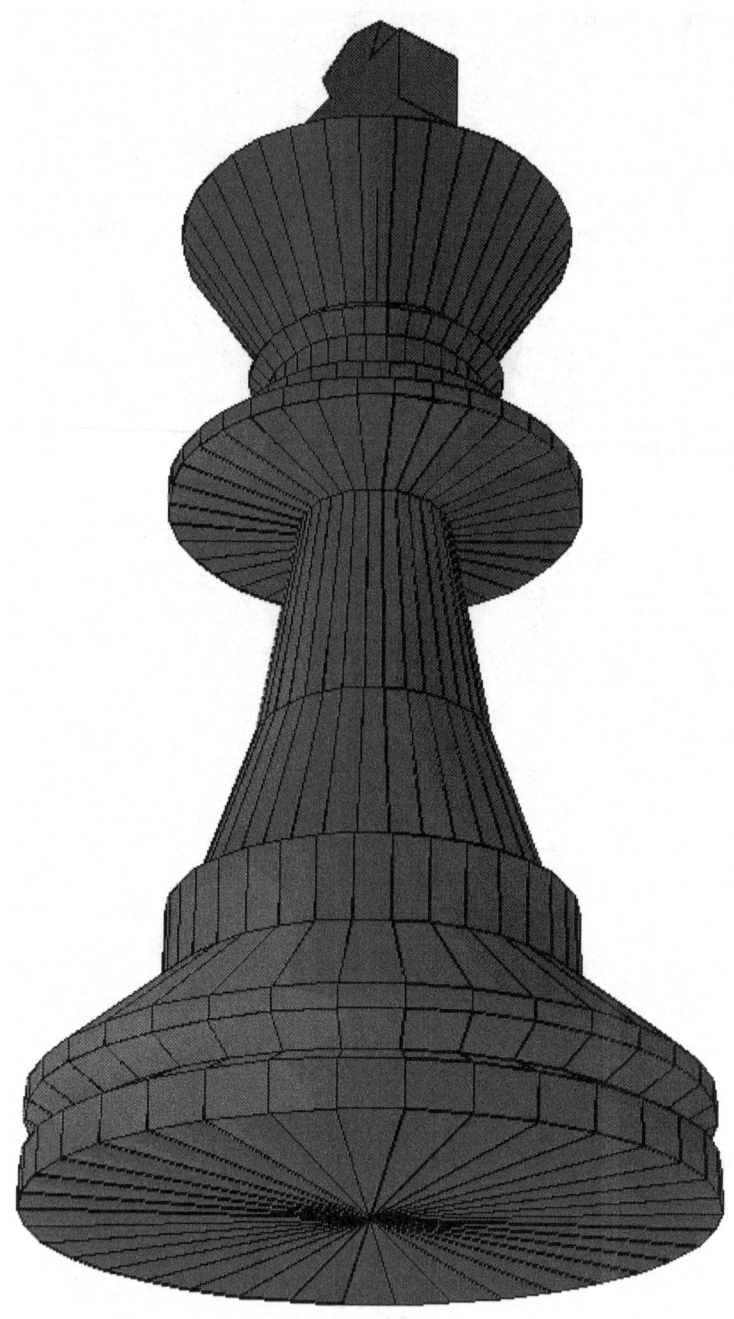

Figure 61. Chess King

Chapter 23. Meshes

A mesh is an unstructured assemblage of polygons, most often triangles or quadrangles. It's basically the same as a finite element grid and programs designed to generate such grids can be used to create and manipulate these 3D objects. This surface was created from triangles.

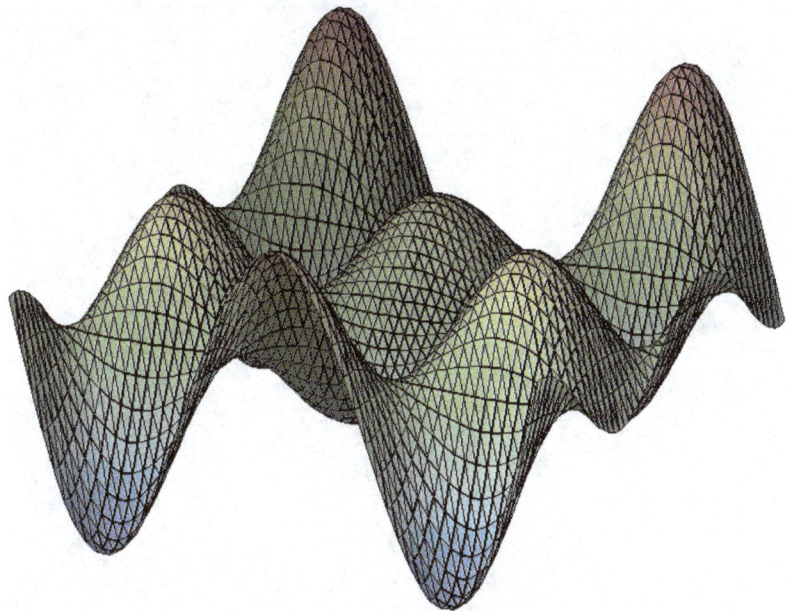

Figure 62. Undulating Surface

This is a more complex mesh, fitted to the topography:

Figure 63. Topographic Mesh

Several mesh-generating tools are available on the web. There is a free tool with source code (elem3.c) on my web site listed in the Forward. You will find it in the archive accompanying the text, *Differential Equations*. It was used to produce the following mesh.

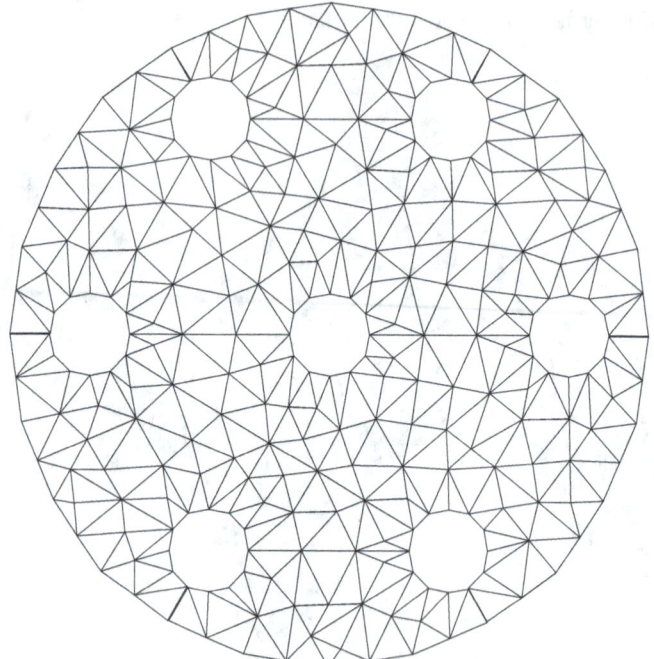

Figure 64. Flange Triangular Mesh

and also this 3D rendering:

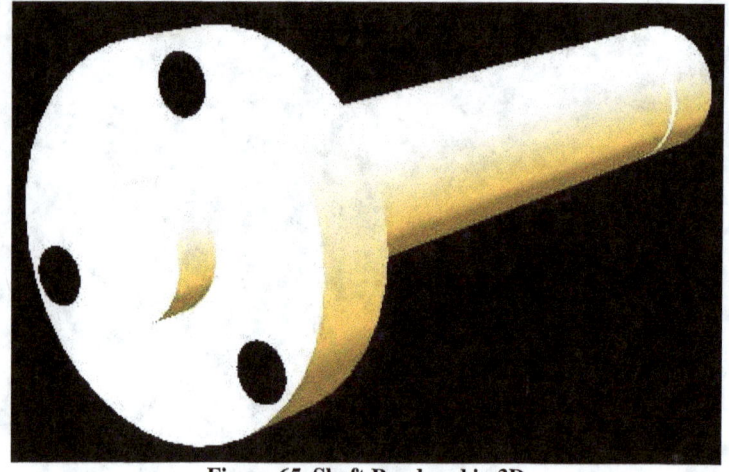

Figure 65. Shaft Rendered in 3D

It is most efficient to define and deliver polygons in a mesh structure, each polygon having an assigned color or texture. As the three components of RGB only occupy the lower 24 of 32 bits in a standard unsigned integer, any value in the high byte (-1, which is 0xFFFFFFFF) can be used to terminate a list.

```
MESH mesh[]={
    {1,2,3,4,5,6,7,8,9,blue},
    {2,3,4,5,6,7,8,9,1,red},
    {3,4,5,6,7,8,9,1,2,green},
    {0,0,0,0,0,0,0,0,0,-1}};
```

The most famous model associated with OpenGL™ is the teapot, as the developers used this object to test their work along the way. This teapot is a distorted ellipsoid plus two warped curving tubes.

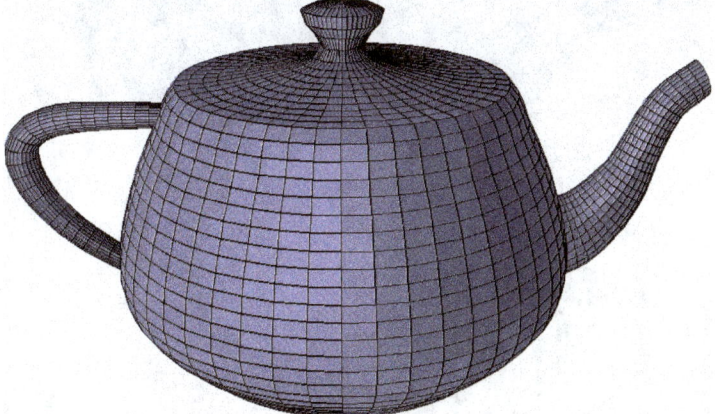

Figure 66. Teapot Mesh from Side

The ellipsoid is composed of quadrangles with triangles at the poles and the tubes are entirely quadrangles.

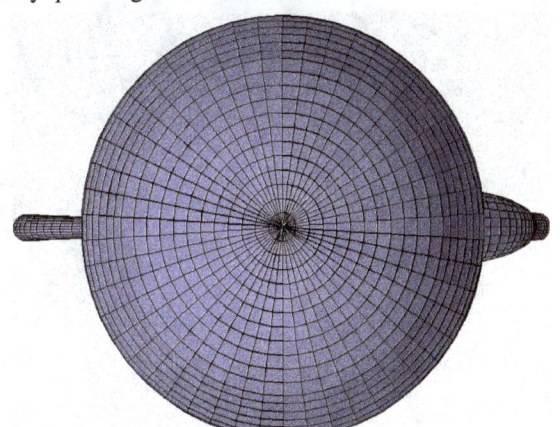

Figure 67. Teapot Mesh from Below

OpenGL™ provides smooth shading.

Figure 68. Teapot Smooth Rendering

A Klein bottle can be formed entirely from quadrangles.

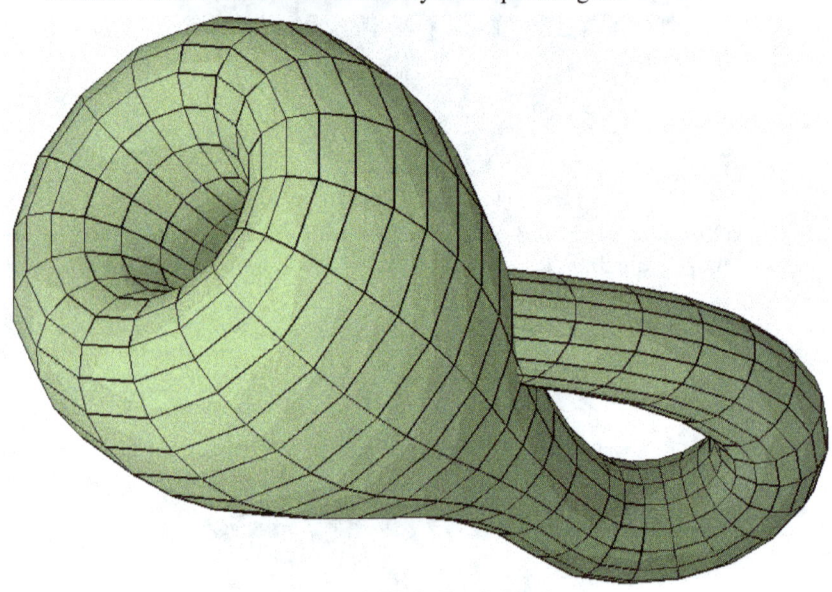

Figure 69. Klein Bottle Mesh

For more on meshes, see Appendix F.

Chapter 24. Complex Objects

Complex objects are most easily constructed as a mesh or collection of meshes. The board and chess pieces are mesh objects.

Figure 70. Chess Set Mesh

The final result after painting is shown below.

Figure 71. Chess Set Textured Rendering

Each piece is a mesh at the origin (x=y=z=0), as shown below:
```
PIECE bishop[]={
{-1652,    -7,    0,-1168,    -7, 1168,-1504,   66,    0},
{-1652,    -7,    0,-1504,    66,    0,-1064,   66,-1064},
{-1652,    -7,    0,-1064,    66,-1064,-1168,   -7,-1168},
{-1652,    -7,    0,-1168,    -7,-1168, -884,    9,    0},
{-1652,    -7,    0, -884,     9,    0, -625,    9,  625},
{-1652,    -7,    0, -625,     9,  625,-1168,   -7, 1168},
{-1644,   413,    0,-1163,   413, 1163,-1409,  717,    0},
{-1644,   413,    0,-1409,   717,    0, -996,  717, -996},
```

{-1644, 413, 0, -996, 717, -996,-1163, 413,-1163},

These are then drawn at the desired location and rotation by a small section of code:

```
void RenderPiece(MESH*piece,char*object,DWORD
    texture,float x,float z,float s,float b)
  {
  int k;
  k=ObjectIndex(object);
  glPushMatrix();
  glTranslatef(x,0,z);
  glScalef(s,s,s);
  glStencilFunc(GL_ALWAYS,k,-1);
  glRotatef(b,0,1,0);
  if(k==selected)
    glMesh(piece,0xFF0000,0);
  else
    glMesh(piece,0,texture);
  glStencilFunc(GL_ALWAYS,0,-1);
  glPopMatrix();
  }
```

The board is a collection of hexahedra (bricks):

```
void RenderBoard()
  {
  char board[]="??";
  int i,j,k;
  for(i=0;i<8;i++)
    {
    board[1]='1'+i;
    for(j=0;j<8;j++)
      {
      board[0]='A'+j;
      k=ObjectIndex(board);
      glStencilFunc(GL_ALWAYS,k,-1);
      if(k==selected)
        glHexahedron(Brd[i],-3./32.,Brd[j],
          3./8.,3./16.,3./8.,0xFF0000,0);
      else
        glHexahedron(Brd[i],-3./32.,Brd[j],
          3./8.,3./16.,3./8.,0,
          (i+j)%2?light_stone:dark_stone);
      }
    }
  glStencilFunc(GL_ALWAYS,0,-1);
  }
```

Three-dimensional models for all sorts of things (e.g., man, fire extinguisher, and forklift palette) are available online and can be readily adapted to the mesh structure best suited to construct your ensemble within the OpenGL™ context, as illustrated by this next figure:

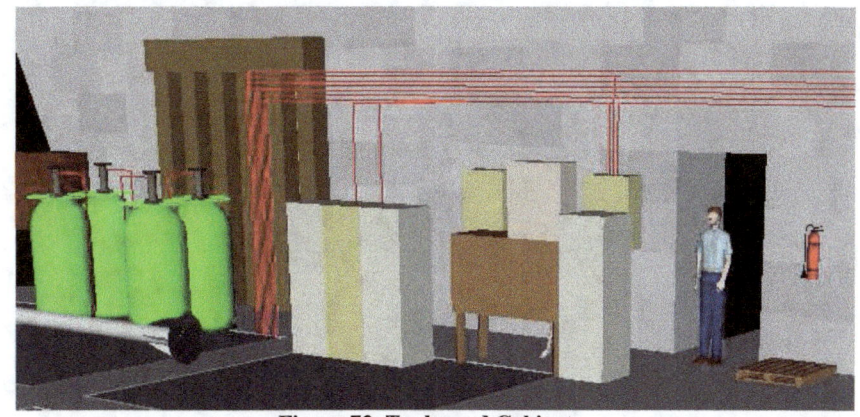

Figure 72. Tanks and Cabinets

Other objects (e.g., tanks, cabinets, and panels) can be created with geometric shapes, such as the iconic (and unusually-shaped) water tower associated with the East Tennessee Technology Park since the Manhattan Project.

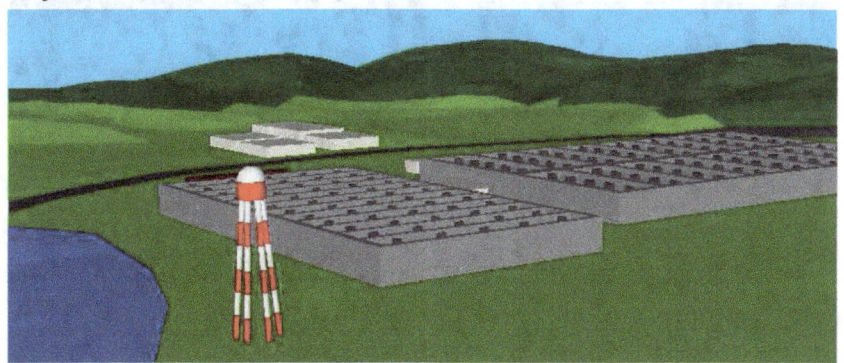

Figure 73. Buildings and Water Tower

As illustrated with the chess pieces, many objects can be quickly rendered bi the OpenGL™ engine so that even complex assemblies, such as the following section, can be created. This assembly consists of six ribbed tanks, twelve centrifugal compressors, twelve electric motors with shaft, housing, and mounting block, twenty pipes, walls, and slab.

```
MESH Motor0[]={
   { 0.762F, 0.000F, 0.429F, 0.660F, 0.381F, 0.429F,
     0.667F, 0.000F, 0.594F,0.F,0.F,0.F,dodger_blue},
   { 0.577F, 0.333F, 0.594F, 0.667F, 0.000F, 0.594F,
     0.660F, 0.381F, 0.429F,0.F,0.F,0.F,dodger_blue},
   { 0.667F, 0.000F, 0.594F, 0.577F, 0.333F, 0.594F,
     0.476F, 0.000F, 0.594F,0.F,0.F,0.F,dodger_blue},
   { 0.412F, 0.238F, 0.594F, 0.476F, 0.000F, 0.594F,
     0.577F, 0.333F, 0.594F,0.F,0.F,0.F,dodger_blue},
```

```
etc...
```

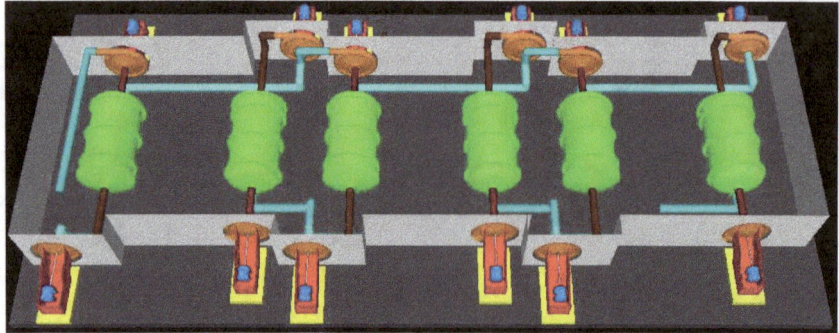

Figure 74. Drums, Motors, Compressors, and Pipes

Any level of complexity can be assembled in this way.

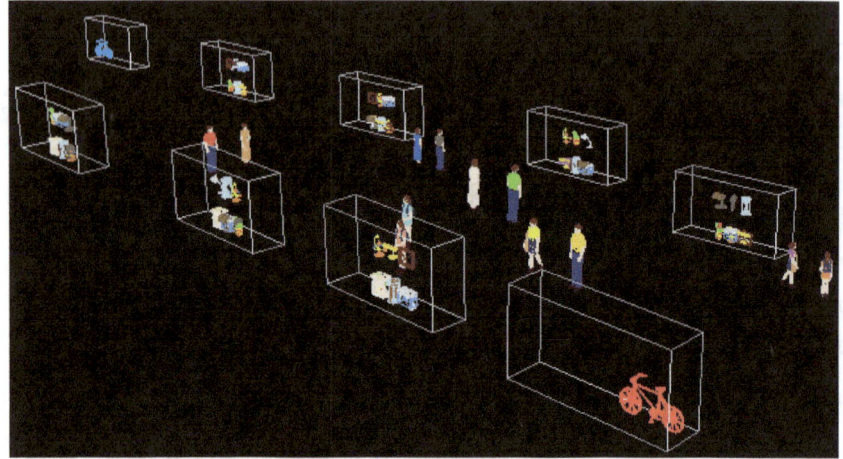

Figure 75. Transparent Display Cases

For more on complex objects, see Appendix F.

Chapter 25. Textured Objects

Except for the chess pieces, all of the objects presented thus far have been simply colored. Textures are an important aspect of OpenGL™ that provides realism. Textures are bitmaps (i.e., flat colored images) that are draped over the polygons. These must be properly prepared before they can be used. Texture preparation involves four steps:

1) Load into memory
2) Convert to correct format
3) Associate with an index
4) Bind to the vertices

The image format expected by OpenGL™ is unlike Windows® or JPEG, as development of OpenGL™ predates the widespread availability of both Windows® and JPEG (see Appendix C for more details). Images can be loaded in several ways, including:

1) Data statement (very large)
2) Resource
3) File

A simple program can be written to convert any binary file (such as a JPEG) to a data statement. Resources are specified in a RC file, processed by the resource compiler, and linked with the program. These must then be loaded into active memory (see Appendix D for more details). Once converted to the proper format (see Appendix C for details), an index must be issued by the rendering engine through a call to glGenTextures(). You will always refer to this texture by the assigned index. After receiving the index, the image is associated with it through a call to glBindTexture().

Textures (i.e., bitmap images) are two-dimensional (i.e., flat). You must define 2D single precision floating point coordinates of the texture (zero to one) with the 3D vertices of your objects as you pass each point to the rendering engine. The simplest sequence is illustrated in the following code snippet that paints a picture onto a rectangle (hence 0,0 to 1,0 to 1,1 to 0,1):

```
loop through polygons
    {
    BindTexture(GL_TEXTURE_2D,texture_index);
    glEnable(GL_TEXTURE_2D);
    glColor(white);
    glBegin(GL_QUADS);
    glNormal3f(0,0,1);
    glTexCoord2d(0,0);glVertex3f(x-w/2,z-h/2,y);
    glTexCoord2d(1,0);glVertex3f(x+w/2,z-h/2,y);
    glTexCoord2d(1,1);glVertex3f(x+w/2,z+h/2,y);
    glTexCoord2d(0,1);glVertex3f(x-w/2,z+h/2,y);
    glEnd();
    glDisable(GL_TEXTURE_2D);
```

}

First bind the texture using the index provided. Enable textures. Use white light. Begin a sequence of (in this case one) quadrangle. Specify the outward normal vector. Specify four texture coordinates and four polygon points sequentially. End the quadrangle sequence. Disable textures before you paint anything else. Draping textures over more complex options requires some creative mathematics, as illustrated in the chess program, which may be found in the online archive in folder examples\chess.

Figure 76. Wood and Marble Textures

Not only are textures rectangular, both dimensions (height and width) must be a power of two. This makes draping textures over some shapes challenging. Several illustrations of texture draping can be found in the codes contained in the online archive in the examples folder.

One such transformation is spherical, as illustrated in this next figure:

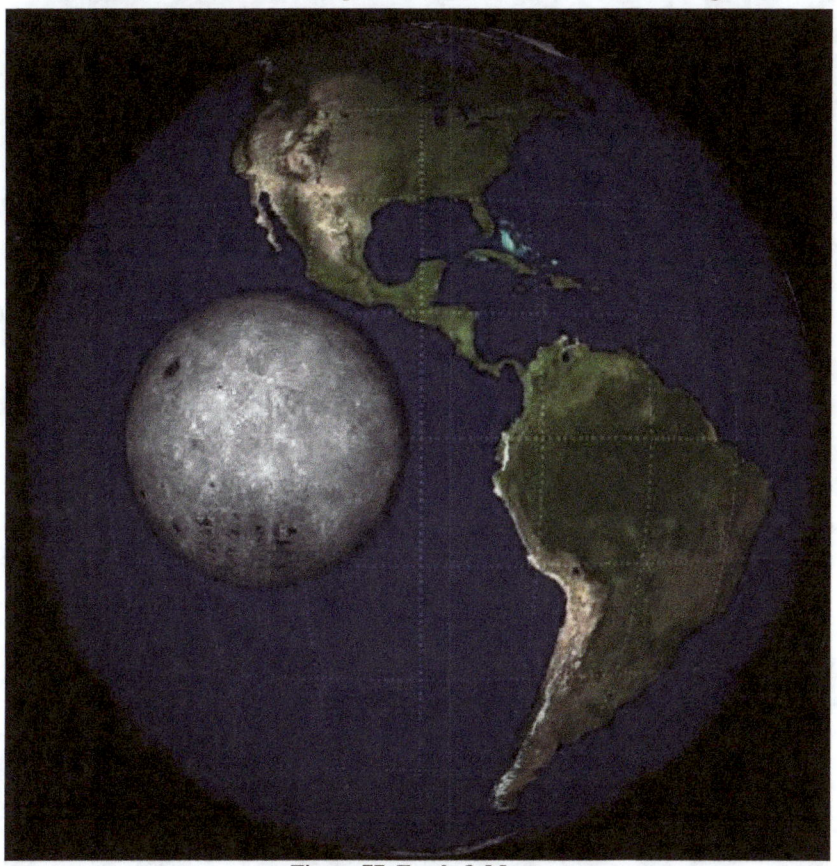

Figure 77. Earth & Moon

The original flat undistorted image used for these textures is rectangular:

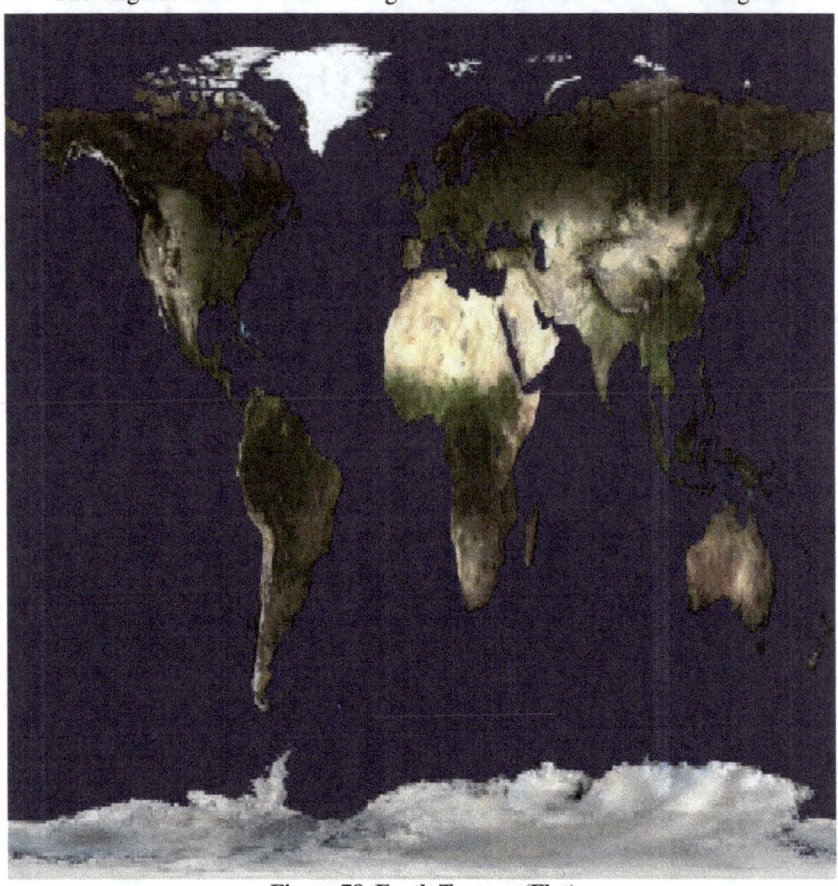

Figure 78. Earth Texture (Flat)

The texture coordinates are (0,0) in the bottom left corner and (1,1) in the upper right. In order to wrap this around a sphere (coordinates r,θ,φ), we apply the relationships:

$$x = \frac{1+\cos(\theta)}{2}$$
$$y = \frac{1+\cos(\varphi)}{2} \quad (25.1)$$

The moon texture is also flat:

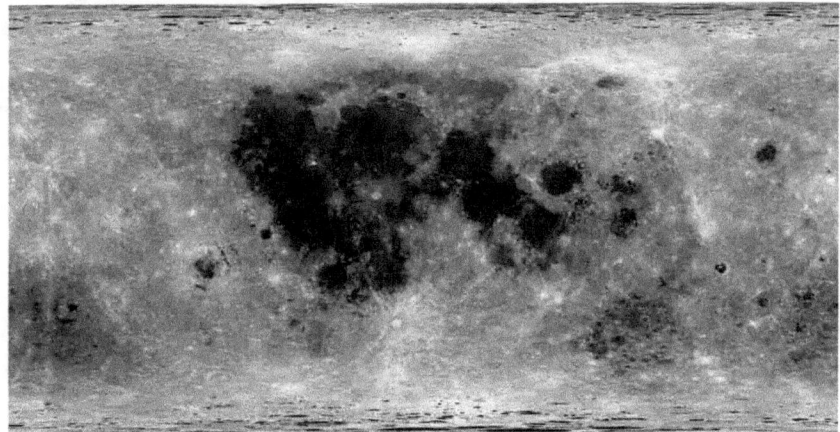

Figure 79. Moon Texture

Chapter 26. Viewpoint

The OpenGL™ rendering engine works with a view port (a frame containing a distorted but flat picture of the objects) and a camera (the eye of the observer).

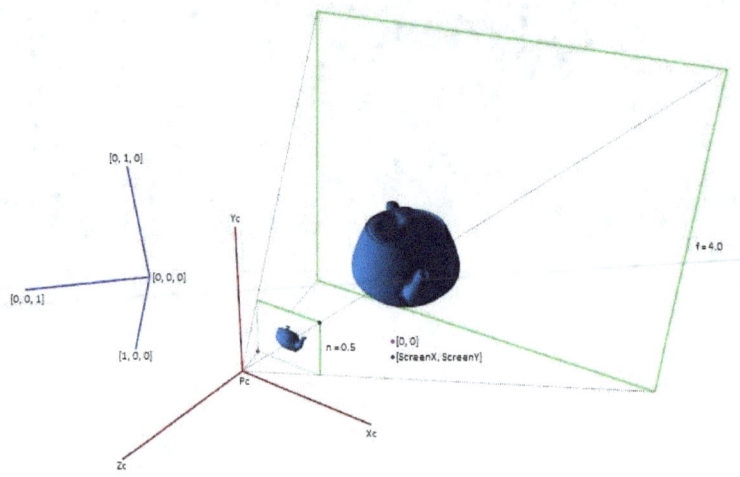

Figure 80. Viewpoint

Setting the view port is simple and must be adjusted whenever the target window is changed inside the GUI with a call to the engine:

```
SetViewport(width,height);
```

The camera is a little more complicated, having three angles (roll, pitch, and yaw) and three translations (heave, sway, and surge), best described by the motions of a ship.

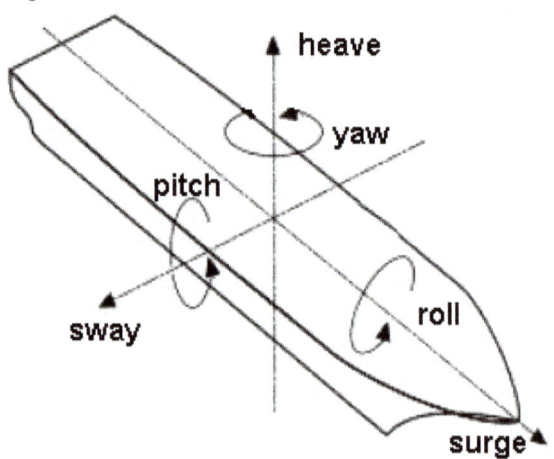

Figure 81. 3D Motions of a Ship

The OpenGL™ axis orientation began from 2D representations, as this came to computers first. The X-axis is from left to right. The Y-axis is from bottom to top (on a flat display). The Z-axis then arises from the cross product of X and Y, which is positive out of the display toward the viewer and negative into the display away from the viewer.

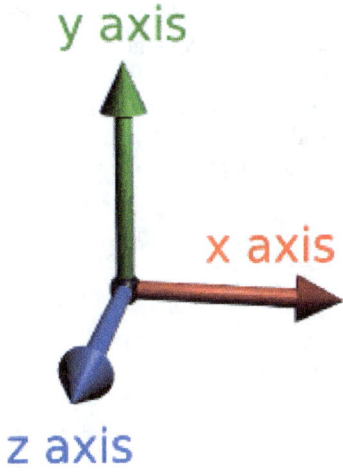

Figure 82. 3D Axis Vectors

Thus, surge is in the positive X direction, heave is in the positive Y direction and sway is in the positive Z direction. The rotations are defined by the right-hand thumb rule from the three axis directions, as indicated on the ship. After setting the view port and before drawing the objects, we set the six camera variables by three rotations (which must be must be performed in three steps in order to work as expected by the typical observer), three translations (which can be performed in a single step), and an optional scaling (stretching or shrinking in all three dimensions). The scaling can be done before or after the translation, though the effect is different. This is illustrated by the following code snippet:

```
glRotatef((float)view.a,1.F,0.F,0.F);
glRotatef((float)view.b,0.F,1.F,0.F);
glRotatef((float)view.c,0.F,0.F,1.F);
glScalef(view.s,view.s,view.s);
glTranslatef(view.x,view.y,view.z);
```

For example, when the user clicks on a button, moves a slider, or depresses a key, the scene is cleared, the updated camera variables are sent to the rendering engine, followed by the objects, and the result is painted back into the space provided by the GUI. In this way the user can rotate, translate, and zoom the scene.

Chapter 27. Lighting

We will not discuss complex lighting in this text. The reader is directed to my previous text, *3D Rendering in Windows®*, and many other articles on the subject. Our focus here is on 3D models that do something in response to user inputs, for example, illustrate procedures for training. The reactor simulator provided as an example throughout this text was used for this very purpose. Maximal realism in rendering might be desirable for some applications. Here we are concerned with function over form—how it works more so than how it looks. While more than one light is available (limited to two on some systems), we will use only one simple white light (index zero), whose position is defined in spherical coordinates and is sufficiently distant from the objects as to be essentially infinite. This is accomplished with a few calls to the OpenGL™ rendering engine:

```
glLightModeli(GL_LIGHT_MODEL_TWO_SIDE,FALSE);
glLightModeli(GL_LIGHT_MODEL_LOCAL_VIEWER,FALSE);
glLightModelfv(GL_LIGHT_MODEL_AMBIENT,
   floatColor(0x000000));
glLightfv(GL_LIGHT0,GL_AMBIENT ,floatColor(0x777777));
glLightfv(GL_LIGHT0,GL_DIFFUSE ,floatColor(0x999999));
glLightfv(GL_LIGHT0,GL_SPECULAR,floatColor(0x000000));
lp[0]=sin(Light.a*M_PI/180)*cos(Light.b*M_PI/180);
lp[2]=cos(Light.a*M_PI/180)*cos(Light.b*M_PI/180);
lp[1]=sin(Light.b*M_PI/180);
lp[3]=0;/* infinite distance to light source */
glLightfv(GL_LIGHT0,GL_POSITION,lp);
glEnable(GL_LIGHT0);
glEnable(GL_LIGHTING);
```

Figure 83. T-Rex 3D Model

Figure 84. Stonehenge 3D Model

Chapter 28. Simple Motion

An example of simple motion would be rotating the view through 360° in steps of 15° about the Y-axis (red vector). The following code (which can be found in the SWSA5 example in the online archive) accomplishes this. The steps (clear, rebuild, paint) are all performed in user-defined function RePaint().

```
if(msg.message==WM_COMMAND&&msg.wParam==PUSH_ROTATE)
  {
  int b;
  for(b=0;b<360;b+=15)
    {
    view.b=b;
    RePaint();
    }
  SetFocus(hMain);
  return(TRUE);
  }
```

After pushing a button or clicking on some object, it is necessary to return focus to the main program using SetFocus(hMain); otherwise, the 3D keystrokes will not be directed to the correct message stream. This is an important detail of Windows® GUI programming. The end result is something like the following:

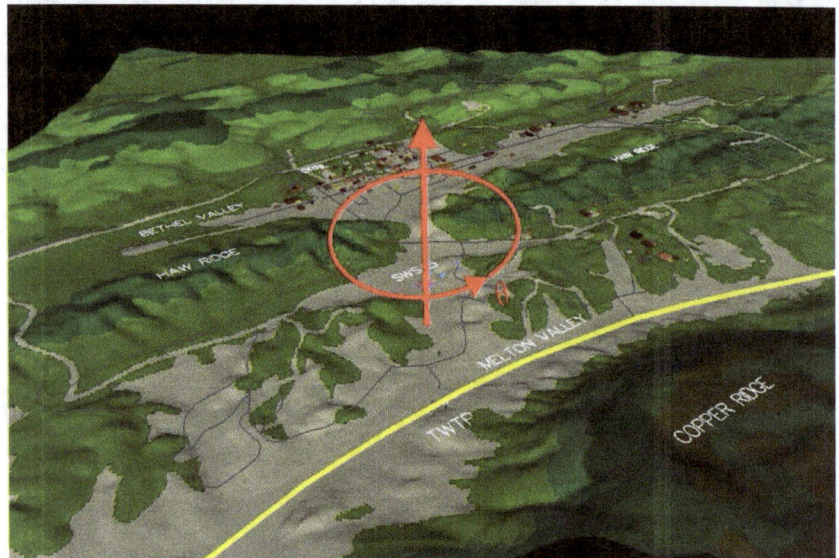

Figure 85. Rotation about Axis

Rotation about the X-axis is accomplished using view.a and about the Z-axis using view.c then repainting. This moves the object via changing the view structure:

```
struct{int a,b,c,h,w;float s,x,y,z;}view;
```

116

If, instead, we wanted to follow along Melton Valley, as indicated by the orange curve in the preceding figure, we would move the camera, not the object, by changing the camera structure:

```
struct{float a,b,c;}camera;
```

We step the camera along the X-axis (camera.a) and the Z-axis (camera.c), repainting at each step, following the arc indicated by the thick yellow curve. The scene has been conveniently scaled to fit into a zero to one frame. The applicable code is:

```
if(msg.message==WM_COMMAND&&msg.wParam==PUSH_PATH)
  {
  float path[]={
    {0.24F,0.00F},
    {0.28F,0.05F},
    {0.32F,0.09F},
    {0.35F,0.13F},
    {0.39F,0.17F},
    {0.43F,0.20F},
    {0.47F,0.24F},
    {0.51F,0.27F},
    {0.54F,0.30F},
    {0.58F,0.33F},
    {0.62F,0.36F},
    {0.66F,0.38F},
    {0.70F,0.40F},
    {0.73F,0.42F},
    {0.77F,0.44F},
    {0.81F,0.46F},
    {0.85F,0.48F},
    {0.89F,0.49F},
    {0.92F,0.50F},
    {0.96F,0.51F},
    {1.00F,0.52F},
    {FLT_MAX}};
  for(i=0;path[i]!=FLT_MAX;i++)
    {
    camera.a-=path[i++];
    camera.c+=path[i];
    RePaint();
    }
  SetFocus(hMain);
  return(TRUE);
  }
```

Note that floating point numbers are double precision by default; whereas, OpenGL™ expects single precision floats. The compiler will issue a warning if the data statements do not include the designation F. Several of the examples include a "tour" button that implements just such a stepping process. While the camera and view structures could be combined, I prefer to keep them separate so that it is clear in the code which one is being modified.

Moving Objects within a Scene

These examples have considered fixed objects within a scene, moving the entire scene or moving the camera with respect to the scene. We might want to move some objects within a scene. Perhaps the simplest of these is the Earth and Moon demo, where the Earth rotates and the Moon orbits. This implementation is not astronomically correct, as this would be quite boring and slow indeed. It takes 29 days, 12 hours, 44 minutes, and 3 seconds for the Moon to orbit the Earth. In this demo it's only 8 days (see turn/8 below). The moon also rotates so that the same side is always facing the Earth. This would require an additional step, not included in the following simple code. The loosely implemented orbiting requires two steps, the first being:

```
if(msg.message=WM_COMMAND&&msg.wParam==PUSH_ROTATE)
    {
    int t;
    for(t=120;t>0;t--)
        {
        turn=t;
        RePaint();
        }
    SetFocus(hMain);
    return(TRUE);
    }
```

and the second being:

```
void RePaint(void)
    {
/* set lighting */
    glClear(GL_COLOR_BUFFER_BIT|GL_DEPTH_BUFFER_BIT);
    glLightfv(GL_LIGHT0,GL_POSITION,LightPos);
    glEnable(GL_TEXTURE_2D);
    glLightfv(GL_LIGHT0,GL_DIFFUSE,White);
    glLightfv(GL_LIGHT0,GL_SPECULAR,Black);
/* rotate view */
    glPushMatrix();
    glRotatef(90.,1.,0.,0.);
/* draw Earth */
    glPushMatrix();
    glRotatef(turn,0.,0.,1.);
    glTexImage2D(GL_TEXTURE_2D,0,3,nEarth,nEarth,
        0,GL_RGB,GL_UNSIGNED_BYTE,tEarth);
    glCallList(gEarth);
    glPopMatrix();
/* draw Moon */
    glTexImage2D(GL_TEXTURE_2D,0,3,nMoon,nMoon,
        0,GL_RGB,GL_UNSIGNED_BYTE,tMoon);
    glRotatef(turn/8.,0.,0.,1.);
```

```
glTranslatef(0.,3.,0.);
glCallList(gMoon);
glPopMatrix();
glutSwapBuffers();
}
```

We note several things here. First, the steps: clear, lighting, rotate, render Earth, render Moon, swap buffers. The last step paints the rendered result into the window provided by the GUI. Function glRotatef() is called performed before rendering the Earth and Moon plus glTranslatef() is called before rendering the Moon. This puts the two objects in the correct place. Each texture is selected just before rendering the sphere by calling glTexImage2D().

While we could draw the two spheres (Earth and Moon) by feeding triangles around each pole and quadrangles over the rest of the surface. We use a convenient feature of OpenGL: lists. Using lists may not make rendering any faster, but it does simplify parts of the code making the overall flow more clear. A sphere is a special type of set recognized by OpenGL™ and so defining a list that happens to be a sphere is a simple process (see Appendix E for more on working with lists).

```
Quadric=gluNewQuadric();
gluQuadricTexture(Quadric,GL_TRUE);
gEarth=glGenLists(1);
glNewList(gEarth,GL_COMPILE);
gluSphere(Quadric,2.,24,24);
glEndList();
```

This type of object is called a *quadric*, we want it to include a texture (bitmap), we must be assigned an integer by calling glGenLists(), we add one sphere, and then close out the list. We can now refer to the list by the index: gEarth. The same is done to create gMoon.

Chapter 29. Linkage Motion

We have already seen this simple type of motion in several examples, including: bluepony, gears, geartrain, origami, and rollercoaster. This is the technique used in the MSRE demo. We will begin with bluepony. The outer loop moves the whole pony around the OpenGL™ sign, much like the Moon orbiting the Earth. This is accomplished by the following code snippet:

```
xPos=WalkRadius*cos(WalkAngle*M_PI/180);
zPos=WalkRadius*sin(WalkAngle*M_PI/180);
glEnable(GL_LIGHTING);
glPushMatrix();
glTranslatef(xPos,0,zPos);
glRotatef(90-WalkAngle,0,1,0);
DrawPony(LegAngle);
glPopMatrix();
```

The sin() and cos() provide the orbiting location in the XZ plane. The pony is rotated along the orbit (variable WalkAngle) with a call to glRotatef(), which comes *after* the call to glTranslatef(). The pony is perpendicular to the radius (variable WalkRadius) by setting the rotation angle to 90-WalkAangle. Notice the call to glPushMatrix() and later glPopMatrix(). These save the transformation, which is changed during the pony drawing. The variable LegAngle is passed to the function rendering the pony, which we examine next...

```
void DrawPony(float legAngle)
  {
  glCallList(Body);
  glCallList(Mane);
  glPushMatrix();
  glTranslatef(FrontLegPos[0],FrontLegPos[1],
    FrontLegPos[2]);
  glRotatef(legAngle,0.0,0.0,1.0);
  glCallList(FrontLeg);
  glPopMatrix();
  glPushMatrix();
  glTranslatef(FrontLegPos[0],FrontLegPos[1],-
    FrontLegPos[2]);
  glRotatef(-legAngle,0.0,0.0,1.0);
  glCallList(FrontLeg);
  glPopMatrix();
  glPushMatrix();
  glTranslatef(BackLegPos[0],BackLegPos[1],
    BackLegPos[2]);
  glRotatef(-legAngle,0.0,0.0,1.0);
  glCallList(BackLeg);
  glPopMatrix();
  glPushMatrix();
  glTranslatef(BackLegPos[0],BackLegPos[1],-
    BackLegPos[2]);
```

```
glRotatef(legAngle,0.0,0.0,1.0);
glCallList(BackLeg);
glPopMatrix();
}
```

Note the convenient use of lists to draw the parts of the pony. Notice also the section of code surrounding each part that is altered to produce the leg motion. This particular procedure has five steps:

1) Push the transformation matrix onto the stack
2) Apply the translation (x, y, z sliding)
3) Apply the rotation (α, θ, φ turning)
4) Render list
5) Pop the transformation off the stack

The two gear examples (gears.c and geartrain.c) are even simpler. Both were written by Brian Paul (author of bluepony) and adapted by Mark J. Kilgard, author of the GLUT® OpenGL™ Utility Library. Here we see geartrain:

Figure 86. Geartrain by Shobhan Kumar Dutta

Gears (or similar objects) of the same shape, even of different sizes, can be defined by a single section of code, as the diameter, depth, tooth pitch, and number of teeth can be specified in an argument. These can be built beforehand and kept in lists or generated each time. There are three distinct gear shapes in this example. We don't need to worry about meshing of the teeth, provided they are properly shaped, translated to the correct location, and set to the appropriate rotation before rendering. There is only one type of shaft, drawn four times. There is also only one belt. Rendering the scene can be facilitated with a few arrays so as to use three outer loops:

```
for(k=0;k<number_of_axles;k++)
  {
  for(i=0;i<number_of_gears-1;i++)
    {
    for(j=0;j<number_of_gears;j++)
```

The primary gear position is set and the others are calculated from it. One section of code illustrates how the gears are properly synchronized:

```
for(i=0;i<number_of_gears;i++)
  {
  x=y=z=0.;
  axle_index=axle_find(g[i].axle_name);
  g[i].axis=a[axle_index].axis;
  g[i].motored=a[axle_index].motored;
  if(a[axle_index].motored)
    {
    g[i].direction=a[axle_index].direction;

  g[i].angular_velocity=a[axle_index].angular_velocity;
    }
  if(g[i].axis==0)
    x=1.0;
  else if(g[i].axis==1)
    y=1.0;
  else
    z=1.0;
  g[i].position[0]=a[axle_index].position[0]
    +x*g[i].relative_position;
  g[i].position[1]=a[axle_index].position[1]
    +y*g[i].relative_position;
  g[i].position[2]=a[axle_index].position[2]
    +z*g[i].relative_position;
  }
```

Combined rotation and translation of the shaft in the MSRE demo is accomplished with only a few lines of code:

```
for(a=90;a>=0;a-=15)
  {
  PosiObject(crane,Vector(60.1-r*sin(a*M_PI/180),
    2.+r*cos(a*M_PI/180),27.4F),FALSE);
  PosiObject(probe_angle,Vector(0.F,0.F,a),TRUE);
  }
```

Dynamic repositioning of single and multiple (combined) objects is accomplished with only a few lines of code:

```
struct{int cols,rows,step;float*data,*high,*lift;
  }Animate;
void PosiObject(int object,VECTOR v,int next_step)
  {
  int j=Animate.cols*Animate.step+3*object;
  Animate.data[j+1]=v.x;
  Animate.data[j+2]=v.y+Animate.lift[object];
  Animate.data[j+3]=v.z;
  if(next_step)
    NextStep();
  }
void PosiObjects(float x,float z,int object,...)
  {
  int j;
  va_list arg_marker;
  va_start(arg_marker,object);
  while(object>=0)
    {
    j=Animate.cols*Animate.step+3*object;
    Animate.data[j+1]=x;
    Animate.data[j+3]=z;
    object=(int)va_arg(arg_marker,int);
    }
  NextStep();
  }
```

Steps along the process are stacked in a growing pile, which is reallocated as needed:

```
void NextStep()
  {
  int j;
  if(++Animate.step>=Animate.rows)
    {
    Animate.rows+=100;
    Animate.data=reallocate(__LINE__,Animate.data,
      Animate.cols*Animate.step,Animate.cols*
      Animate.rows,sizeof(float));
    }
  for(j=1;j<Animate.cols;j++)
    Animate.data[Animate.cols* Animate.step   +j]=
    Animate.data[Animate.cols*(Animate.step-1)+j];
  }
```

Note that there are two allocation functions in Windows®: malloc() and calloc(). The first does not clear the memory, while the second does. There was a reallocate function in DOS, but this was not carried over to Windows®. You must provide your own. Reallocation (expansion or contraction of an existing block of memory) involves three steps:

```
1) Allocate a new block
2) Copy the old block into the new
```

3) Free the old block

This is accomplished by the following code:

```
void*reallocate(int line,void*old_ptr,unsigned
    old_count,unsigned new_count,unsigned size)
 {
 void*new_ptr;
 if((new_ptr=calloc(new_count,size))==NULL)
    Abort(line,"can't reallocate memory %ux%u=%u "
      "-> %ux%u=%u bytes",old_count,size,old_count*
      size,new_count,size,new_count*size);
 if(old_ptr&&old_count)
    {
    memcpy(new_ptr,old_ptr,min(old_count,new_count)
      *size);
    free(old_ptr);
    }
 return(new_ptr);
 }
```

It is important to check for failure to allocate memory blocks, as such will result in a fatal exception and a program crash. While there may be plenty of available memory, allocation is not always successful and it is good practice to check. Checking also aids in troubleshooting.

The next linkage motion we will consider is the miniature steam engine example created by Troy Robinette using Mark Kilgard's OpenGL™ Utility Toolkit, GLUT®. This model includes a crankshaft, flywheel, connecting rod, piston, cylinder, and pivot pin. The wire frame is shown on the next page. The motions are familiar. The piston slides up and down in the cylinder. In this case, rather than accentuating a wristpin, the rod and piston are rigid and the cylinder rocks back-and-forth to maintain alignment.

The position of each object is related by trigonometric relationships. The crankshaft and flywheel simply rotate. The rod boss follows the crank pin. The angle of the cylinder, piston, and rod are given by the Pythagorean theorem. The position of each part is determined from the crank angle, which is advanced to produce the animated effect.

The rendering sequence is as before: clear, set view and camera, render objects, and finally paint. This last step is accomplished by a call to the GLUT function glutPostRedisplay(). The lighting is unremarkable. An optional checkerboard texture is included for illustration and variety. Lists are used for each of the objects, which makes the code (steam.c) more readable. Use of the GLUT® library eliminates the need for a specific GUI.

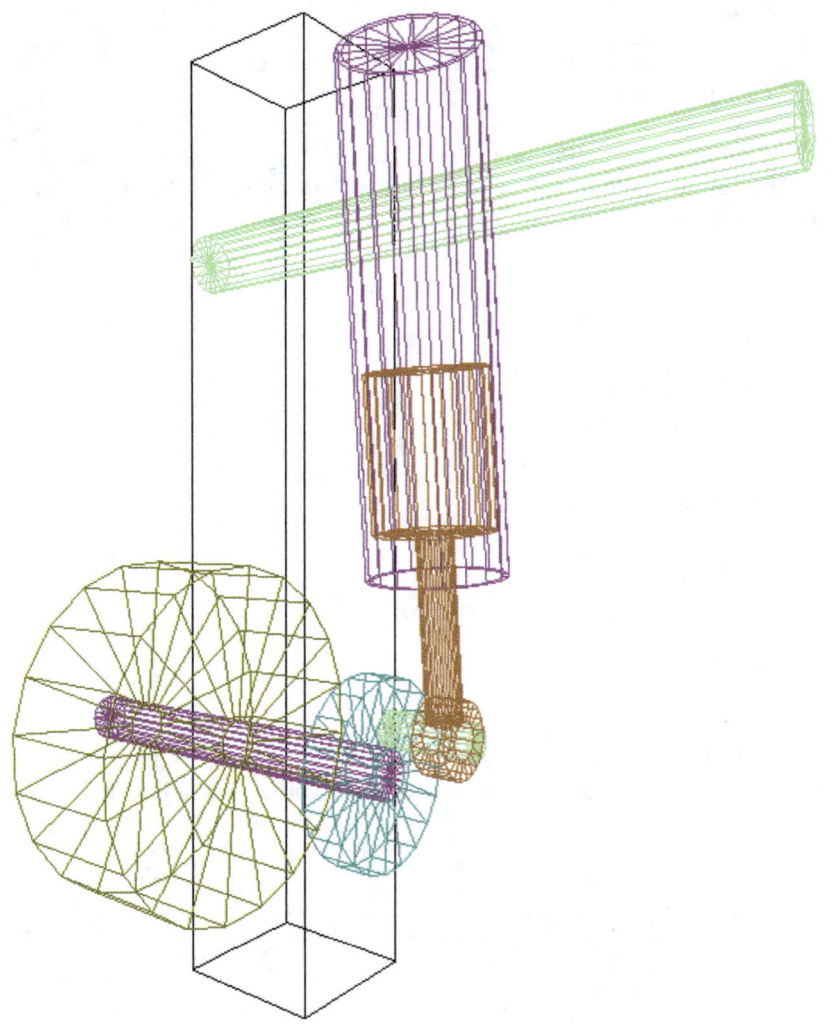

Figure 87. Miniature Steam Engine by Troy Robinette

In order to reinforce the step-by-step approach of such models, we will consider just a few drawing procedures, beginning with the cylinder:

```
void draw_cylinder(GLUquadricObj*object,GLdouble
    outerRadius,GLdouble innerRadius,GLdouble lenght)
{
glPushMatrix();
gluCylinder(object,outerRadius,outerRadius,
   lenght,20,1);
glPushMatrix();
glRotatef(180,0.0,1.0,0.0);
gluDisk(object,innerRadius,outerRadius,20,1);
```

```
glPopMatrix();
glTranslatef(0.0,0.0,lenght);
gluDisk(object,innerRadius,outerRadius,20,1);
glPopMatrix();
}
```

Notice the call to glPushMatrix() at the beginning and glPopMatrix() at the end. This preserves orientation of the scene and other objects. Only this object is impacted by the call to glRotatef() and glTranslatef(). The piston is quite similar:

```
void draw_piston(void)
{
glPushMatrix();
glColor4f(0.3,0.6,0.9,1.0);
glPushMatrix();
glRotatef(90,0.0,1.0,0.0);
glTranslatef(0.0,0.0,-0.07);
myCylinder(obj,0.125,0.06,0.12);
glPopMatrix();
glRotatef(-90,1.0,0.0,0.0);
glTranslatef(0.0,0.0,0.05);
myCylinder(obj,0.06,0.0,0.6);
glTranslatef(0.0,0.0,0.6);
myCylinder(obj,0.2,0.0,0.5);
glPopMatrix();
}
```

There is an outer loop to rotate the assembly and the option for clockwise or counterclockwise. Because this example doesn't need much in the way of user interface code, it is a clear and concise example of programmed linkage motion.

```
do
  {
  draw_engine_pole();
  glPushMatrix();
  glTranslatef(0.5,1.4,0.0);
  draw_cylinder_head();
  glPopMatrix();
  glPushMatrix();
  glTranslatef(0.0,-0.8,0.0);
  draw_crank();
  glPopMatrix();
  }
  while(pass>0);
```

Figure 88. Miniature Steam Engine by Troy Robinette

Linkage motion us used throughout the MSRE example, which may be found in the online archive. The MSRE scene is depicted on the cover. The cask is run through its paces using linkage motion, as shown in these next figures:

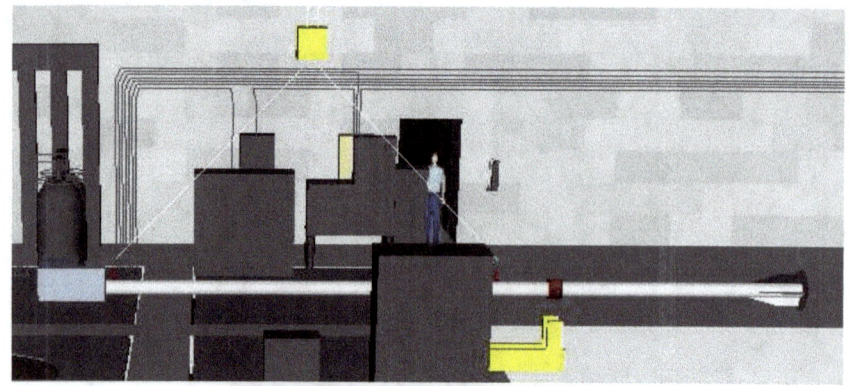

Figure 89. Molten Salt Reactor Model

Each of the three dimensional components of the motion is interpolated (as a table) from the initial time to the final time, as shown in the following code:

```
VECTOR InterpolatePosition(int object,float t)
  {
  return(Vector(
    InterpolateTable(Animate.data,Animate.cols,
      Animate.step,3*object+1,t),
    InterpolateTable(Animate.data,Animate.cols,
      Animate.step,3*object+2,t),
    InterpolateTable(Animate.data,Animate.cols,
      Animate.step,3*object+3,t))
    );
  }
```

Throughout a sequence, each of the moving objects is advanced in the same way, as listed in the code below:

```
void UpdateObjectPositions(float t)
  {
  VECTOR v;
  Container.bot=InterpolatePosition(cage_bottom,t);
  Container.can=InterpolatePosition(canister   ,t);
  Container.cas=InterpolatePosition(casing     ,t);
  Container.hat=InterpolatePosition(cell_hatch ,t);
  Container.lid=InterpolatePosition(casing_lid ,t);
  Container.plg=InterpolatePosition(casing_plug,t);
  Container.top=InterpolatePosition(cage_top   ,t);
  Container.trk=InterpolatePosition(truck      ,t);
  Crane6       =InterpolatePosition(crane_6ton ,t);
  Crane30      =InterpolatePosition(crane_30ton,t);
  GloveBox     =InterpolatePosition(glove_box  ,t);
  Cask.position=InterpolatePosition(probe_cask ,t);
  Shield[0]    =InterpolatePosition(shield1    ,t);
  Shield[1]    =InterpolatePosition(shield2    ,t);
  Shield[2]    =InterpolatePosition(shield3    ,t);
  v=InterpolatePosition(crane_6ext ,t);crane6_ext =v.x;
```

```
v=InterpolatePosition(crane_6rig ,t);
crane6_rig =v.x>0.5;
v=InterpolatePosition(crane_30rig,t);
crane30_rig=v.x>0.5;
v=InterpolatePosition(probe_sling,t);
Cask.sling =v.x>0.5;
v=InterpolatePosition(probe_angle,t);
Cask.angle =v.z;
}
```

The initial positions of the objects are set in the following code:

```
void InitializeObjects()
  {
  Animate.step=0;
  memset(Animate.data,0,Animate.cols*Animate.rows
    *sizeof(float));
  PosiObject(cage_bottom,Vector( 12.0F,   0.0F,
    18.0F),FALSE);
  PosiObject(canister    ,Vector( 31.8F,-18.6F,
    30.1F),FALSE);
  PosiObject(casing      ,Vector(  6.0F,   0.0F,
    18.0F),FALSE);
  PosiObject(casing_lid ,Vector(  6.0F,   7.8F,
    18.0F),FALSE);
  PosiObject(casing_plug,Vector(  6.0F,   0.0F,
    18.0F),FALSE);
  PosiObject(cage_top    ,Vector(  6.0F,   0.0F,
    38.0F),FALSE);
  PosiObject(cell_hatch ,Vector( 31.8F,  -0.4F,
    30.1F),FALSE);
  PosiObject(crane_6ton ,Vector(125.0F,  32.0F,
    2.0F),FALSE);
  PosiObject(crane_30ton,Vector(  3.0F,  29.0F,
    9.0F),FALSE);
  PosiObject(probe_angle,Vector(  0.0F,   0.0F,
    90.0F),FALSE);
  PosiObject(probe_cask ,Vector( 29.1F,   1.0F,
    13.5F),FALSE);
  PosiObject(truck       ,Vector(-20.0F,   0.0F,
    28.0F),FALSE);
  PosiObject(glove_box  ,Vector(GloveBoxPositions[
    active_tank],-12.0F,31.5F),FALSE);
  PosiObject(shield1     ,Vector(GloveBoxPositions[
    shield_position[
    active_tank][0]],-14.0F,31.5F),FALSE);
  PosiObject(shield2     ,Vector(GloveBoxPositions[
    shield_position[active_tank][1]],
    -14.0F,31.5F),FALSE);
  PosiObject(shield3     ,Vector(GloveBoxPositions[
    shield_position[active_tank][2]],-14.0F,
```

```
    31.5F),FALSE);
  NextStep();
  }
```

The animations are also initialized in an allocated list, as shown below:

```
void InitializeAnimation()
  {
  Animate.cols=1+3*things;
  Animate.rows=100;
  Animate.data=allocate(__LINE__,Animate.rows
    *Animate.cols,sizeof(float));
  Animate.high=allocate(__LINE__,Animate.cols,
    sizeof(float));
  Animate.lift=allocate(__LINE__,Animate.cols,
    sizeof(float));
  Animate.high[cage_bottom]= 5.3F;
  Animate.high[canister   ]= 8.5F;
  Animate.high[casing     ]= 9.2F;
  Animate.high[casing_lid ]= 1.1F;
  Animate.high[casing_plug]= 0.4F;
  Animate.high[cage_top   ]= 4.8F;
  Animate.high[cell_hatch ]= 0.4F;
  Animate.high[crane_6ton ]= 2.0F;
  Animate.high[crane_30ton]= 4.5F;
  Animate.high[glove_box  ]= 6.0F;
  Animate.high[shield1    ]= 2.0F;
  Animate.high[shield2    ]= 2.0F;
  Animate.high[shield3    ]= 2.0F;
  Animate.high[truck      ]=11.4F;
  Animate.lift[cage_bottom]= 0.0F;
  Animate.lift[canister   ]= 0.0F;
  Animate.lift[casing     ]=-0.8F;
  Animate.lift[casing_lid ]= 0.0F;
  Animate.lift[casing_plug]= 0.0F;
  Animate.lift[cage_top   ]=-5.5F;
  Animate.lift[cell_hatch ]= 0.0F;
  Animate.lift[crane_6ton ]= 0.7F;
  Animate.lift[crane_30ton]= 2.5F;
  Animate.lift[glove_box  ]= 0.0F;
  Animate.lift[shield1    ]= 1.0F;
  Animate.lift[shield2    ]= 1.0F;
  Animate.lift[shield3    ]= 1.0F;
  Animate.lift[truck      ]= 0.0F;
  InitializeObjects();
  UpdateObjectPositions(0);
  }
```

The two cranes slide along the tracks in both X and Z while transporting, lifting, and lowering, the cask.

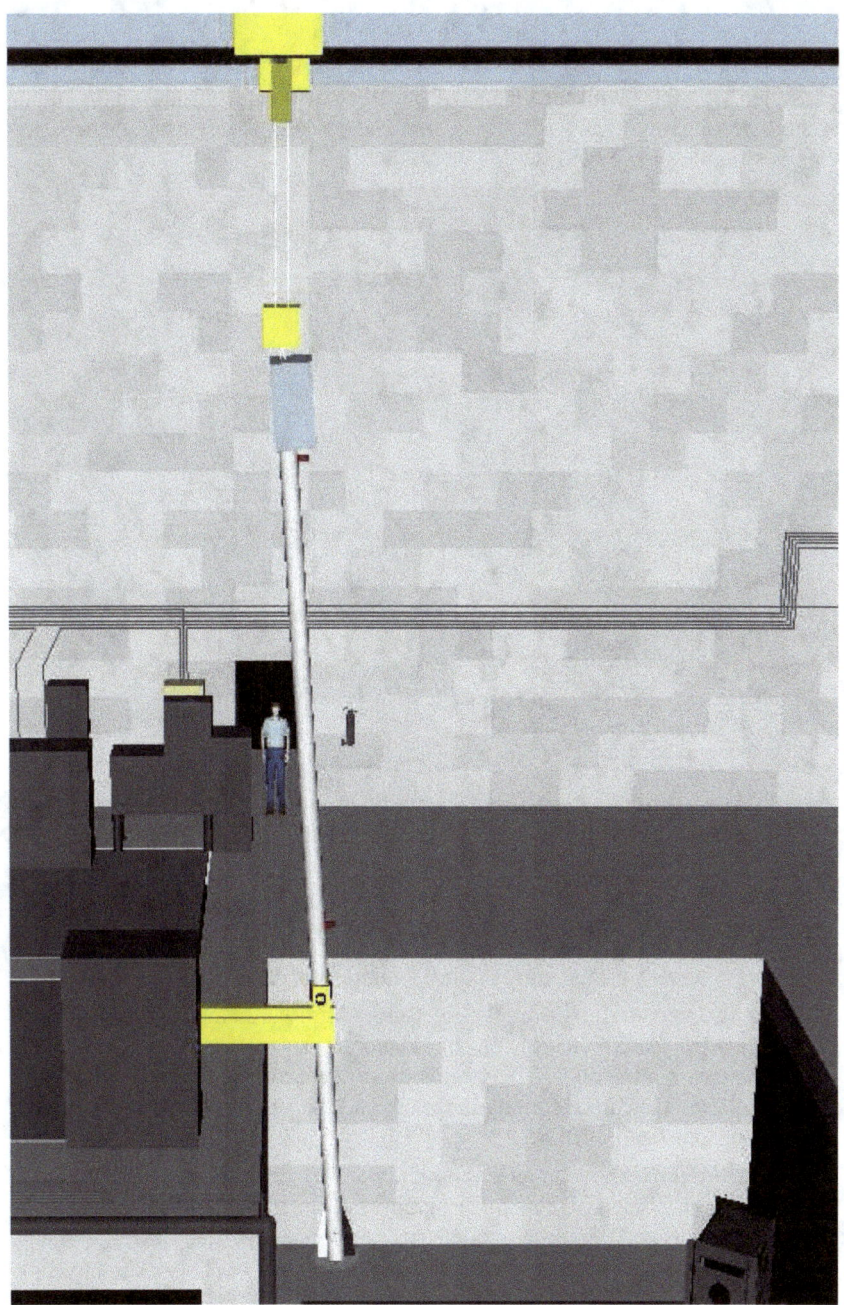

Figure 90. Traveling Crane

Chapter 30. Track Motion

The clearest and most concise example of track motion is the rollercoaster example that comes with the OpenGL™ SDK. You can also find it in the online archive accompanying *3D Rendering in Windows®* in folder examples\coaster. One position is shown below:

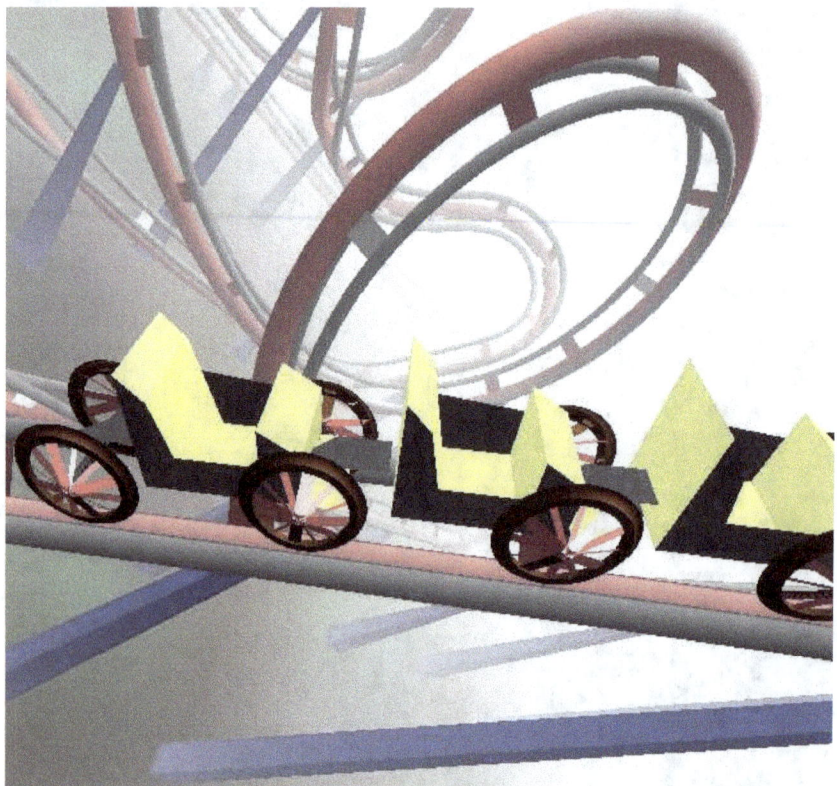

Figure 91. Coaster Example with Fog

This is a wonderfully complex, yet straightforward implementation of an articulating wheeled carriage on an elaborate track reminiscent of many amusement park attractions. The wheels even rotate to add further realism. The camera follows the carriage along the track and the sky moves with the camera to give a perception of distance.

There are three code modules (coaster.c, defrc.c, and matrix.c) that make up this model. The first is the main program and the last facilitates the needed vector calculations. The second code (defrc.c) defines the track using a unique script, which is so very remarkable and creative[7]—a real treat compared to some

---

[7] If you ever find out who wrote this, please send me an Email so that I can properly credit the creative genius!

lengthy numeric data statements, such as this author has employed in so many models. The track description is so delightful that we will begin there. Definition takes the form of sequential text statements. Those beginning with an asterisk are comments. Below is an excerpt:

```
char*coaster[]={
  "*first (all gentle) slope",
  "pitch 16 10",
  "wait 10",
  "*weather rectify",
  "pitch 0 10",
  "wait 100",
  "pitch -16 10",
  "wait 10",
  "pitch 0 10",
  "wait 10",
  "*",
  "*first bend (right)",
  "*begin turning",
  "alignment 40 30",
  "wait 20",
  "*initial curve",
  "heading -45 10",
  "wait 10",
  "*end screw",
  "alignment 0 30",
  "wait 79",
  "*turn out early",
  "alignment -10 30",
  "wait 10",
  "*end bend",
  "heading 0 10",
  "wait 20",
  "*end printouts",
  "alignment 0 10",
  "wait 160",
  "*",
  "*second turn (right)",
  "*start turning",
  "alignment 10 10",
  "wait 20",
  "*initial curve",
  "heading -45 10",
  "wait 10",
  "*end screw",
  "alignment 0 30",
  "wait 79",
  "*turn out early",
  "alignment -40 30",
  and so forth...,NULL};
```

Let us next examine the very compact code that interprets these statements. It is surrounded by a for() statement that advances through the list until reaching a NULL text pointer. The keywords (pitch, alignment, heading, roll, and wait) are contained in the scanf() statement, which illustrates the most excellent compactness of the C programming language compared to all others.

```c
for(in=0;coaster[in];in++)
  {
  if(coaster[in][0]=='*')
    continue;
  else if(sscanf(coaster[in],"pitch %lf %d",&a,&i))
    {
    pitch.speed=(a-pitch.value)/i;
    pitch.steps=i;
    }
  else if(sscanf(coaster[in],"alignment %lf %d",
    &a,&i))
    {
    alignment.speed=(a-alignment.value)/i;
    alignment.steps=i;
    }
  else if(sscanf(coaster[in],"heading %lf %d",&a,&i))
    {
    heading.speed=(a-heading.value)/i;
    heading.steps=i;
    }
  else if(sscanf(coaster[in],"roll %lf %d",&a,&i))
    {
    roll.speed=(a-roll.value)/i;
    roll.steps=i;
    }
  else if(sscanf(coaster[in],"wait %d",&i))
    etc...
  }
```

Lists are used in the same pattern of function calls to render each wheel.

```c
void display_wheel(float w)
  {
  int ww=w;
  glPopMatrix();
  glPushMatrix();
  glTranslatef(x[ww],y[ww],z[ww]);
  glRotatef(r3[ww]*180/M_PI,0.0,0.0,1.0);
  glRotatef(-r2[ww]*180/M_PI,0.0,1.0,0.0);
  glRotatef(r1[ww]*180/M_PI,1.0,0.0,0.0);
  glTranslatef(-0.15*(w-ww),0.8,0.0);
  glRotatef(-w,0.0,0.0,1.0);
  glCallList(2);
  glEnd();
  }
```

Here is a different view of the elaborate track:

Figure 92. Coaster Example without Fog

Track motion is also used in the MSRE example with the two cranes and also the truck that removes the contaminated waste in it's special container. The two cranes travel along two different XZ tracks, which must avoid each other plus only one can be used at a time.

```
VECTOR Crane6;
float crane6_ext;
int crane6_rig;
void ParkCrane6()
  {
  Crane6.x=125.F;
  Crane6.y= 32.F;
  Crane6.z=  2.F;
  }
```

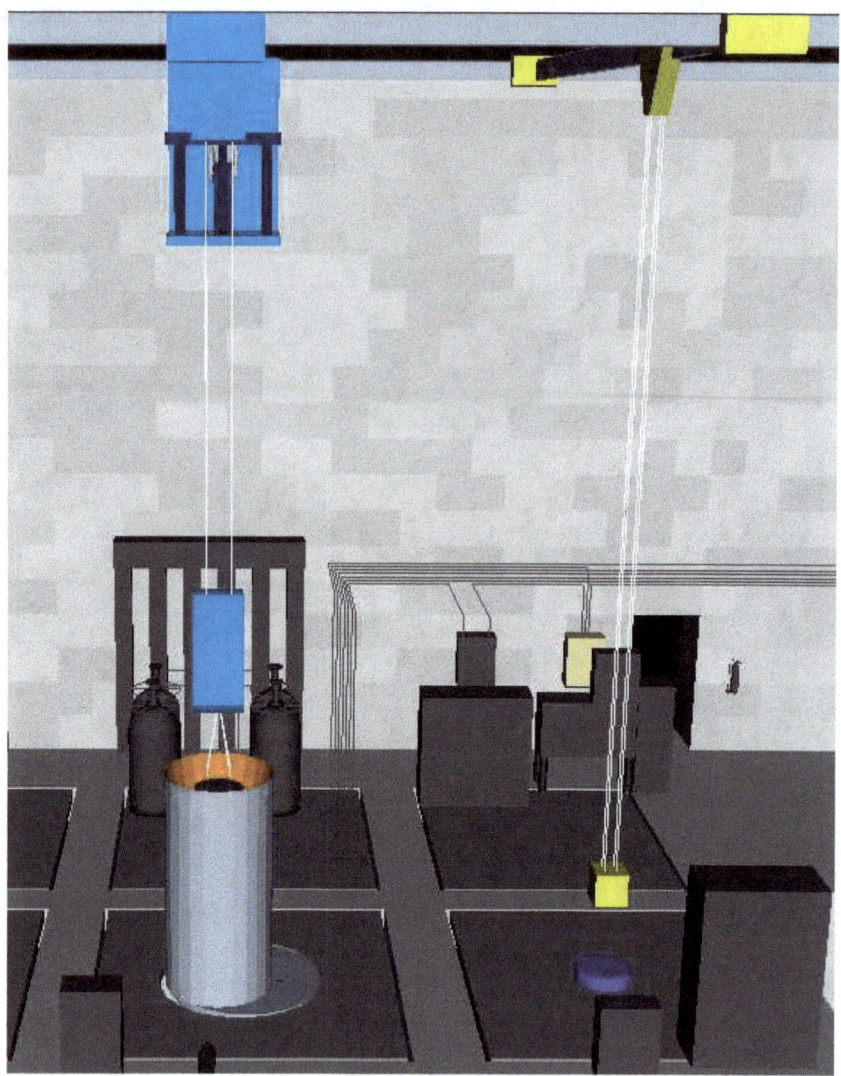

Figure 93. Hoist and Cylinder

```
VECTOR Crane30={120.0,29.0,3.0};
int crane30_rig;
void ParkCrane30()
  {
  Crane30.x=120.0;
  Crane30.y= 29.0;
  Crane30.z=  3.0;
  }
```

Figure 94. Container and Flatbed Truck

Chapter 31. Reflecting Motion

For reflecting motion we consider Brian Paul's bounce demo, which is included with the Mesa SDK (and can also be found in the online archive). The scene contains a ball, a floor, and a wall—simple enough objects (sphere and two flat planes). The basic scene is shown below:

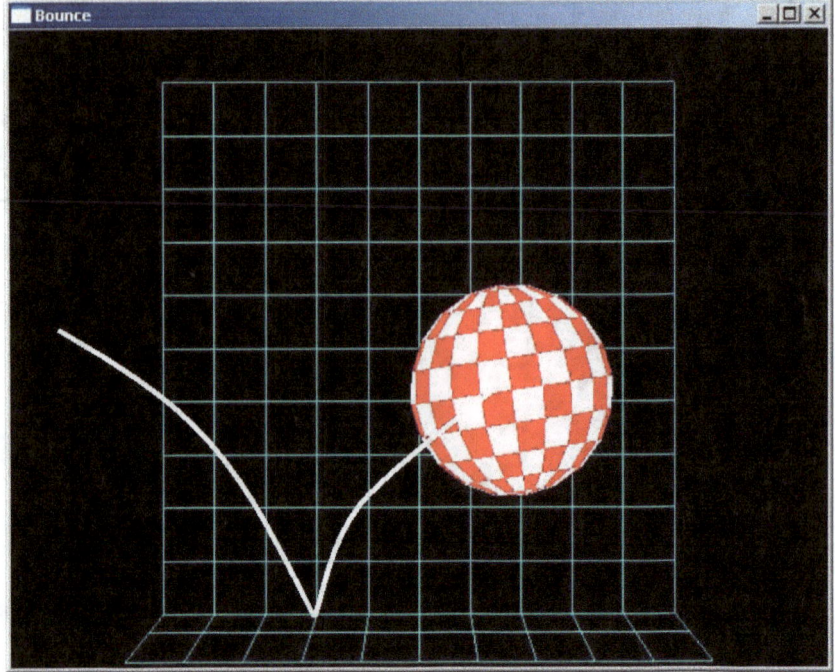

Figure 95. Bouncing Ball

The checkerboard pattern adds some complexity but the wall and ball are easily drawn without resorting to lists. Only the position and orientation as a function of time are needed. While it is straightforward enough to describe simple harmonic motion with a few trig functions, this implementation is even less complicated. Brian Paul's bounce demo uses an initial velocity vector followed by simple reflection. When the ball reaches a boundary of the invisible box (Xmin,Ymin) to (Xmax,Ymax), the velocity components are reversed, sending it back in the other direction. The code is quite simple:

```
void idle(void)
  {
  static float vel0=-100.0;
  Zrot+=Zstep;
  Xpos+=Xvel;
  if(Xpos>=Xmax)
     {
     Xpos=Xmax;
     Xvel=-Xvel;
```

```
      Zstep=-Zstep;
      }
    if(Xpos<=Xmin)
      {
      Xpos=Xmin;
      Xvel=-Xvel;
      Zstep=-Zstep;
      }
    Ypos+=Yvel;
    Yvel+=G;
    if(Ypos<Ymin)
      {
      Ypos=Ymin;
      if(vel0==-100.0)
         vel0=fabs(Yvel);
      Yvel=vel0;
      }
    glutPostRedisplay();
    }
```

A similar reflection calculation is used in molecular modeling, as illustrated below:

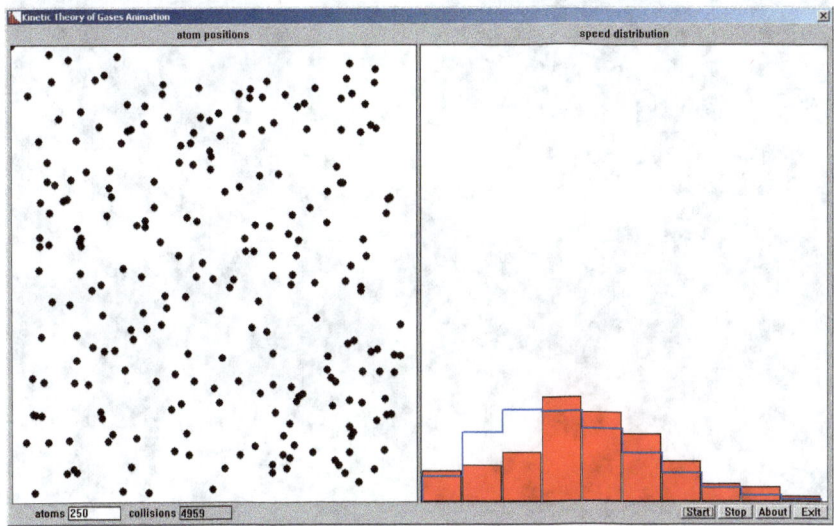

Figure 96. Molecules Collide

Chapter 32. Bouncing Motion

For bouncing motion we consider Mark Kilgard's reflect example included in the OpenGL™ SDK (and can also be found in the online archive). While the primary purpose of this example is to demonstrate how to generate a reflected image, the dinosaur also bounces and so we examine it here rather than reinventing the wheel and proliferating unnecessary examples. The typical scene is depicted below:

Figure 97. Dino Bounce

The vertical position (i.e., bounce) is a simple sine wave:
```
void idle(void)
  {
  static float time;
  time=glutGet(GLUT_ELAPSED_TIME)/500.;
  jump=3.*fabs(sin(time));
  glutPostRedisplay();
  }
```

Constructing the dinosaur by extruding polygons (i.e., making a third dimension from a two-dimensional form). The extrusion setup is straightforward:

```
void makeDinosaur(void)
{
  extrudeSolidFromPolygon(body,sizeof(body),
    bodyWidth,BODY_SIDE,BODY_EDGE,BODY_WHOLE);
  extrudeSolidFromPolygon(arm,sizeof(arm),
    bodyWidth/4,ARM_SIDE,ARM_EDGE,ARM_WHOLE);
  extrudeSolidFromPolygon(leg,sizeof(leg),
    bodyWidth/2,LEG_SIDE,LEG_EDGE,LEG_WHOLE);
  extrudeSolidFromPolygon(eye,sizeof(eye),
    bodyWidth+0.2,EYE_SIDE,EYE_EDGE,EYE_WHOLE);
}
```

The function extrudeSolidFromPolygon() function can be used in other models. It transforms each part into a list glNewList(), fills it with calls to glBegin(GL_QUAD_STRIP) and glVertex3f(), and then closes it off with a call to glEnd() and glEndList(). The first glEnd() closes off the glBegin(GL_QUAD_STRIP) and the second closes off the list. The dinosaur is drawn by rendering the lists sequentially:

```
void drawDinosaur(void)
{
  glPushMatrix();
  glTranslatef(0.,jump,0.);
  glMaterialfv(GL_FRONT,GL_DIFFUSE,skinColor);
  glCallList(BODY_WHOLE);
  glPushMatrix();
  glTranslatef(0.,0.,bodyWidth);
  glCallList(ARM_WHOLE);
  glCallList(LEG_WHOLE);
  glTranslatef(0.,0.,-bodyWidth-bodyWidth/4);
  glCallList(ARM_WHOLE);
  glTranslatef(0.,0.,-bodyWidth/4);
  glCallList(LEG_WHOLE);
  glTranslatef(0.,0.,bodyWidth/2-0.1);
  glMaterialfv(GL_FRONT,GL_DIFFUSE,eyeColor);
  glCallList(EYE_WHOLE);
  glPopMatrix();
  glPopMatrix();
}
```

While reflections are not the main focus of this text, it is worth noting here with this example that the reflection is actually a second dinosaur, drawn upside down and backwards with altered lighting. There are many helpful comments in the source code (reflect.c), describing the details required, including back face culling and how the orientation flips and must be reversed.

Chapter 33. Sliding Motion

The first example of sliding motion we will consider is the chess demo written by Henk Kok that comes with the GLUT® distribution package. The files can also be found in the online archive in the folder examples\OpenGL\chess. Not only do the pieces slide around, when one is captured, it sinks into the board. There are seven files that accomplish the task of rendering this model.

- main.c sets up the application and launches the GLUT® context
- animate.c moves the pieces
- chess.c defines the board and pieces
- chess.h declares the functions and variables
- pathplan.c defines the available path for a piece
- texture.c defines textures (e.g., marble)
- chess.inp contains the moves in succinct notation

The notation in chess.inp is interesting. This is an excerpt: d2d4, g8f6, c2c4, g7g6, b1c3, f8g7, e2e4, d7d6... The texture is not visible:

Figure 98. Chess Pieces with Shading

As we have seen before, lists are used to facilitate the process. The following is an example of building a list for the king (konig) and queen (dame):

```
glNewList(KONING+8*i,GL_COMPILE);
do_koning();
width[KONING+8*i]=bwidth;
height[KONING+8*i]=bheight;
glEndList();
glNewList(DAME+8*i,GL_COMPILE);
do_dame();
width[DAME+8*i]=bwidth;
height[DAME+8*i]=bheight;
```

```
glEndList();
```

The pieces are drawn at the proper location by first translating, then rotating. The position and view are preserved by pushing and then popping the transformation matrix.

```
glPushMatrix();
glTranslatef(x-1.,((x==CX2&&y==CY2)?CZ2:0.),8.-y);
glScalef(1.2,1.2,1.2);
glCallList(pc+list[0]);
glPopMatrix();
```

The following section of code is illustrative:

```
#define MOVE_FRAC 8
switch(path[X][Y])
   {
   case NORTH:     NY--;break;
   case SOUTH:     NY++;break;
   case WEST:      NX--;break;
   case EAST:      NX++;break;
   case NORTHWEST:NX--;NY--;break;
   case NORTHEAST:NX++;NY--;break;
   case SOUTHWEST:NX--;NY++;break;
   case SOUTHEAST:NX++;NY++;break;
   }
CX1=(X*(MOVE_FRAC-frac)+NX*frac)/MOVE_FRAC;
CY1=(Y*(MOVE_FRAC-frac)+NY*frac)/MOVE_FRAC;
```

Here we see the eight possible directions (four sides plus four corners) a piece can move linked to the change in XY position. Movement is broken up into eight steps (see MOVE_FRAC definition above). These are performed sequentially. The end result appears to be a smooth sliding motion. The rate arises from a combination of the default idle timer and the processing duration. There is also a wait or skip variable (extern int speed) that can be adjusted with the UP and DOWN keys. Even this simplistic process produces a satisfactory result, indicating that complicated stepping schemes may not always be necessary when constructing such models.

The next sliding motion we will consider is that present in Kevin Smith's glpuzzle demp, which is included in the OpenGL™ SDK (may also be found in the online archive). This application slides pieces in response to mouse movement using the trackball utility files (trackball.c and trackball.h). The scene is quite simple to encode and render:

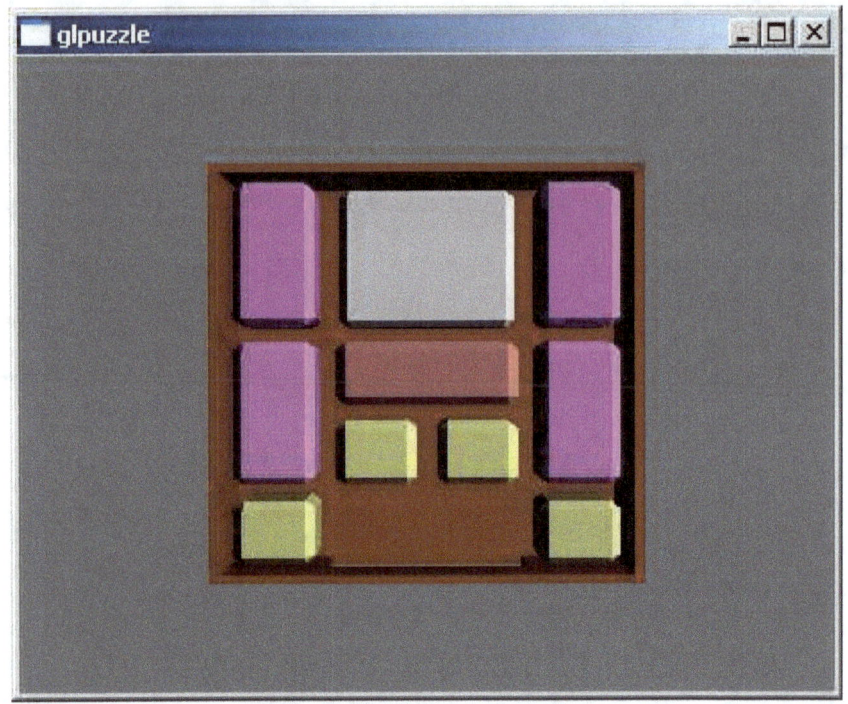

Figure 99. GL Puzzle Example

Perhaps the most complex part of this code is keeping track of where the pieces are and what moves are legitimate. This is done in the main source code. Not surprisingly, this is handled in function canmove() with assistance from canmove0(). There is also a function to determine which piece has been selected: selectpiece() as well as one to remove a piece: nukepiece(). Piece repositioning begins with function: grabpiece(). You will find this code quite readable and easy to follow with the functions named so naturally. The shapes and lighting are uncomplicated, which keeps focus on the selection and movement.

Knight's Tour

The knight's tour demo also slides the pieces across the board. The *tour* describes 64 sequential moves, landing on each square only once. The algorithm is quite simple and surprisingly effective. It uses a stack to keep previous partially successful sequences. When a path ends in failure, the stack is popped and the last partially successful one is continued. At each juncture, the move having the largest number of potential next moves beyond that space is selected. The following section of code implements this logic:

```
int MoveOK(int x,int y)
   {
   if(x<0)
```

```c
    return(0);
  if(x>7)
    return(0);
  if(y<0)
    return(0);
  if(y>7)
    return(0);
  if(board[y][x])
    return(0);
  return(1);
  }
int Moves(int x,int y)
  {
  int i,n;
  for(n=i=0;i<8;i++)
    n+=MoveOK(x+move[i].x,y+move[i].y);
  return(n);
  }
int EndTour(int x1,int y1)
  {
  int i,m=0,n1,n2,x2,x3,y2,y3;
  memset(board,0,sizeof(board));
  board[y1][x1]=1;
  Tour[0].x=x1;
  Tour[0].y=y1;
  while(1)
    {
    n1=9;
    for(i=0;i<8;i++)
      {
      x2=x1+move[i].x;
      y2=y1+move[i].y;
      if(!MoveOK(x2,y2))
        continue;
      if(m==62)
        {
        x3=x2;
        y3=y2;
        break;
        }
      n2=Moves(x2,y2);
      board[y2][x2]=0;
      if(n2<1||n2>=n1)
        continue;
      x3=x2;
      y3=y2;
      n1=n2;
      }
    if(n1==9&&m!=62)
      return(0);
```

```
      m++;
      x1=x3;
      y1=y3;
      board[y3][x3]=m+1;
      Tour[m].x=x3;
      Tour[m].y=y3;
      if(m==63)
        break;
      }
   return(m);
   }
void BeginTour(int s)
   {
   int x1,y1;
   x1=(int)(Object[s][0]-'A');
   y1=(int)(Object[s][1]-'1');
   if(EndTour(x1,y1))
      {
      for(pending_tour=1;pending_tour<=64;pending_tour++)
         {
         Piece[1].col=Tour[pending_tour-1].x;
         Piece[1].row=Tour[pending_tour-1].y;
         RePaint();
         }
      }
   else
      MessageBox(hMain,"knight's tour was not
      successful","algorithm failure",MB_APPLMODAL|MB_OK);
   }
```

Function MoveOK() returns 0 or 1 (yes or no). Function Moves() counts the number of potential next moves. BeginTour() initiates the process. EndTour() finds the path. Function RePaint() moves the knight after the path has been loaded into an array. The tour is rendered by the following instructions:

```
void RenderTour()
   {
   int i,n;
   float a,r=0.0125,x1,x2,x3,x4,x5,x6,y=0.0125,
      z1,z2,z3,z4,z5,z6;
   glDisable(GL_TEXTURE_2D);
   glColor(0xFF0000);
   glBegin(GL_QUADS);
   glNormal3f(0.,1.,0.);
   x2=Brd[Tour[0].y];
   z2=Brd[Tour[0].x];
   n=min(64,pending_tour);
   for(i=1;i<n;i++)
      {
      x1=x2;
      z1=z2;
```

```
        x2=Brd[Tour[i].y];
        z2=Brd[Tour[i].x];
        a=atan2(z2-z1,x2-x1);
        x3=x1-r*sin(a);
        x4=x2-r*sin(a);
        x5=x1+r*sin(a);
        x6=x2+r*sin(a);
        z3=z1+r*cos(a);
        z4=z2+r*cos(a);
        z5=z1-r*cos(a);
        z6=z2-r*cos(a);
        glVertex3f(x3,y,z3);
        glVertex3f(x4,y,z4);
        glVertex3f(x6,y,z6);
        glVertex3f(x5,y,z5);
        }
    glEnd();
}
```

Different paths result depending on the initial square. The end result is shown below:

Figure 100. One of Many Possible Successful Tours

Chapter 34. Combining Simple Motions

The Olympic ring demo included in the OpenGL™ SDK is simple and easy to follow. The rings are a torus and are rendered each in turn with quadrangles by the following function:

```
void FillTorus(float rc,int numc,float rt,int numt)
{
int i,j,k;
double s,t,x,y,z;
for(i=0;i<numc;i++)
   {
   glBegin(GL_QUAD_STRIP);
   for(j=0;j<=numt;j++)
      {
      for(k=1;k>=0;k--)
         {
         s=(i+k)%numc+0.5;
         t=j%numt;
         x=cos(t*2*M_PI/numt)*cos(s*2*M_PI/numc);
         y=sin(t*2*M_PI/numt)*cos(s*2*M_PI/numc);
         z=sin(s*2*M_PI/numc);
         glNormal3f(x,y,z);
         x=(rt+rc*cos(s*2*M_PI/numc))*cos(t*2*M_PI/numt);
         y=(rt+rc*cos(s*2*M_PI/numc))*sin(t*2*M_PI/numt);
         z=rc*sin(s*2*M_PI/numc);
         glVertex3f(x,y,z);
         }
      }
   glEnd();
   }
}
```

The initial ring positions and rotations are defined during setup within function InitializeRings().

```
for(i=0;i<RINGS;i++)
   {
   offsets[i][0]=Rand();
   offsets[i][1]=Rand();
   offsets[i][2]=Rand();
   angs[i]=260.*Rand();
   rotAxis[i][0]=Rand();
   rotAxis[i][1]=Rand();
   rotAxis[i][2]=Rand();
   iters[i]=(deviation*Rand()+60.);
   }
```

That these are random isn't material, only that they are removed from their final positions, which are also defined in this same function:

```
dests[BLUERING][0]=-spacing;
dests[BLUERING][1]=top_y;
```

```
dests[BLUERING][2]=top_z;
dests[BLACKRING][0]=0.;
dests[BLACKRING][1]=top_y;
dests[BLACKRING][2]=top_z;
dests[REDRING][0]=spacing;
dests[REDRING][1]=top_y;
dests[REDRING][2]=top_z;
dests[YELLOWRING][0]=-spacing/2.;
dests[YELLOWRING][1]=bottom_y;
dests[YELLOWRING][2]=bottom_z;
dests[GREENRING][0]=spacing/2.;
dests[GREENRING][1]=bottom_y;
dests[GREENRING][2]=bottom_z;
```

The initial position of the rings is shown in this first figure:

Figure 101. Olympic Rings in Motion

The transition is then from the initial to the final destinations in steps. The number of steps for each transition is nominally random and stored in array iters[]. This randomness is also immaterial to the end result, although it does provide some variety. As the random numbers are not seeded, these will always be the same. The iterative transition is performed in such a way as to appear rapid at first, slowing as each ring's destination is approached. The following code accomplishes this effect:

```
float Clamp(int iters_left,float t)
  {
  if(iters_left<3)
    return(0.);
  return(iters_left-2)*t/iters_left;
  }
```

```
for(i=0;i<RINGS;i++)
  {
  if(iters[i])
    {
    for(j=0;j<3;j++)
      offsets[i][j]=Clamp(iters[i],offsets[i][j]);
    angs[i]=Clamp(iters[i],angs[i]);
    iters[i]--;
    }
  }
```

The final result is shown in this second figure:

Figure 102. Olympic Rings Final Position

<u>Lorenz Attractor</u>

The next combined simple motion we will consider is that of the Lorenz attractor demo written by Aaron Ferrucci and included in the OpenGL™ SDK (may also be found in the online archive). The following description accompanies this demo:

> This program shows some particles stuck in a Lorenz attractor (the parameters used are r=28,b=8/3,sigma=10). The eye is attracted to the red particle, with a force directly proportionate to distance. A command line puts the whole mess inside a box made of hexagons. I think this helps to maintain the illusion of 3 dimensions, but it can slow things down. Other options allow you to play with the redraw rate and the number of new lines per redraw. So you can customize it to the speed of your machine.

The biggest difference between this example and the previous ones is that the motion follows a specific pattern described by the physics controlling the motion of the particles. The position of the particles is calculated at each time step in the following function:

```
void move_eye(void)
  {
  /* first move the eye */
  eyev[0]+=gravity*(rv[rp][0]-eyex[0]);
  eyev[1]+=gravity*(rv[rp][1]-eyex[1]);
```

```
eyev[2]+=gravity*(rv[rp][2]-eyex[2]);
/* adjust position using new velocity */
eyex[0]+=eyev[0]*dt;
eyex[1]+=eyev[1]*dt;
eyex[2]+=eyev[2]*dt;
/* move the lookat point */
/* it catches up to the red point if it's moving
 slowly enough */
eyel[0]+=LG*(rv[rp][0]-eyel[0]);
eyel[1]+=LG*(rv[rp][1]-eyel[1]);
eyel[2]+=LG*(rv[rp][2]-eyel[2]);
/* change view */
gluLookAt(eyex[0],eyex[1],eyex[2],eyel[0],
  eyel[1],eyel[2],0,1,0);
}
```

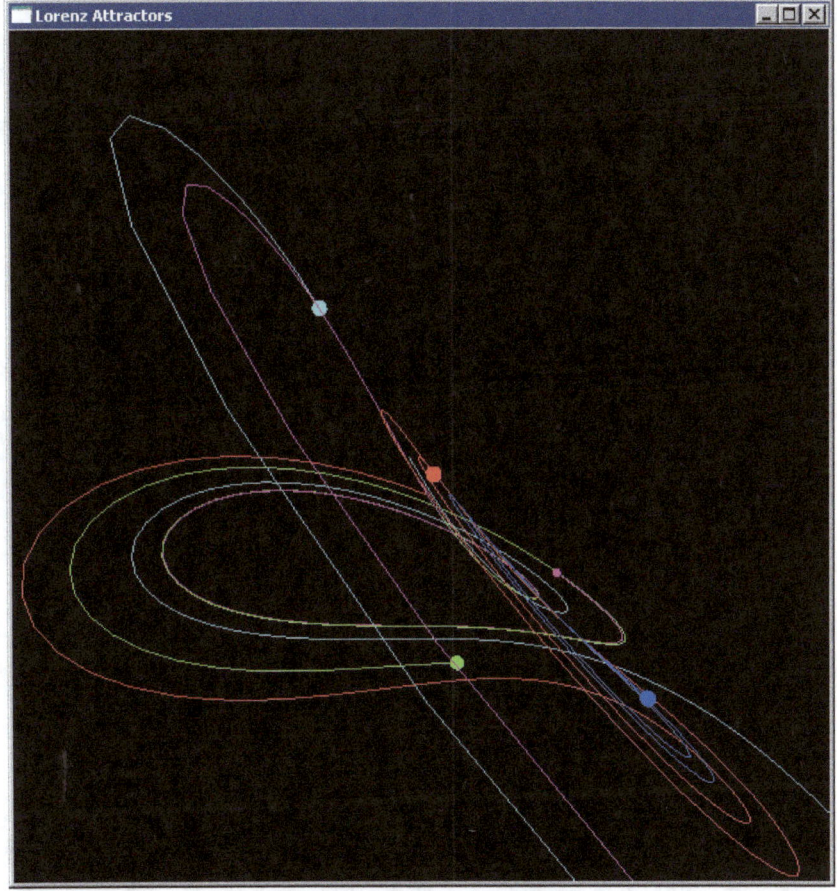

Figure 103. Lorenz Attractors

The GLUT® function call gluLookAt() facilitates the necessary adjustments to give a desirable overall effect of motion and viewpoint. The preceding figure is typical of the resulting animation. Notice that the main rendering function (listed below) draws the particles and also the trails as curves of the same color.

```
void redraw(void)
  {
  glClear(GL_COLOR_BUFFER_BIT|GL_DEPTH_BUFFER_BIT);
  if(hexflag)
     draw_hexcube();
  glColor3f(1.0,0.0,0.0);
  drawLines(rp,rv);
  sphdraw(rv[rp]);
  glColor3f(0.0,0.0,1.0);
  drawLines(bp,bv);
  sphdraw(bv[bp]);
  glColor3f(0.0,1.0,0.0);
  drawLines(gp,gv);
  sphdraw(gv[gp]);
  glColor3f(1.0,0.0,1.0);
  drawLines(yp,yv);
  sphdraw(yv[yp]);
  glColor3f(0.0,1.0,1.0);
  drawLines(mp,mv);
  sphdraw(mv[mp]);
  glutSwapBuffers();
  }
```

The particles are drawn using a list for compactness:

```
void sphdraw(float args[3])
  {
  glPushMatrix();
  glTranslatef(args[0],args[1],args[2]);
  glCallList(asphere);
  glPopMatrix();
  }
```

The view is saved and restored by pushing it onto the stack before rendering and then popping it off before continuing. The track lines are added by this function:

```
void next_line(float v[][3],int *p)
  {
  dx=sigma*(v[*p][1]-v[*p][0])*dt;
  dy=(r*v[*p][0]-v[*p][1]+v[*p][0]*v[*p][2])*dt;
  dz=(v[*p][0]*v[*p][1]+b*v[*p][2])*dt;
  v[(*p+1)&POINTMASK][0]=v[*p][0]+dx;
  v[(*p+1)&POINTMASK][1]=v[*p][1]+dy;
  v[(*p+1)&POINTMASK][2]=v[*p][2]-dz;
  *p=(*p+1)&POINTMASK;
  }
```

The track lines are drawn in four steps by the following function:

```c
#define LINE_STEP 4
void drawLines(int index,float array[POINTMASK][3])
  {
  int p;
  int i;
  p=(index+1)&POINTMASK;
  i=LINE_STEP-(p%LINE_STEP);
  if(i==LINE_STEP)
     i=0;
  glBegin(GL_LINE_STRIP);
  /* draw points in order from oldest to newest */
  while(p!=index)
     {
     if(i==0)
        {
        glVertex3fv(array[p]);
        i=LINE_STEP;
        }
     i--;
     p=(p+1)&POINTMASK;
     }
  glVertex3fv(array[index]);
  glEnd();
  }
```

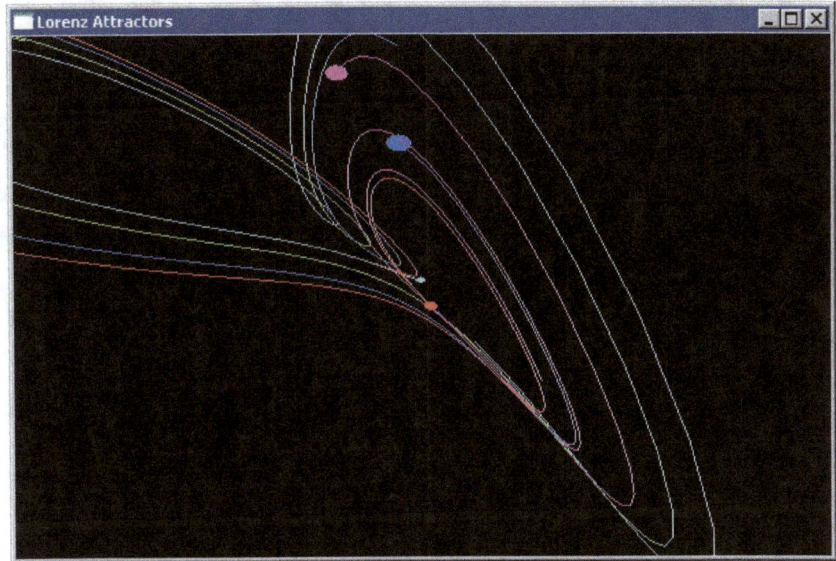

Figure 104. Lorenz Attractor Zoom In

The ETTP demo includes a six-foot man to give scale and proportion:

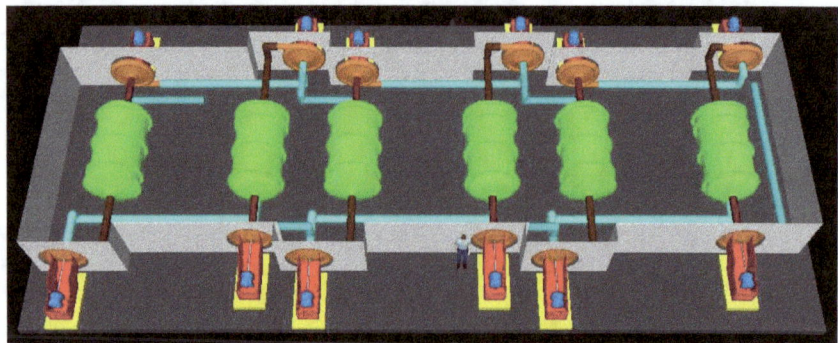

Figure 105. Equipment Default Colors

It also uses colors to indicate stages of preparation for decommissioning:

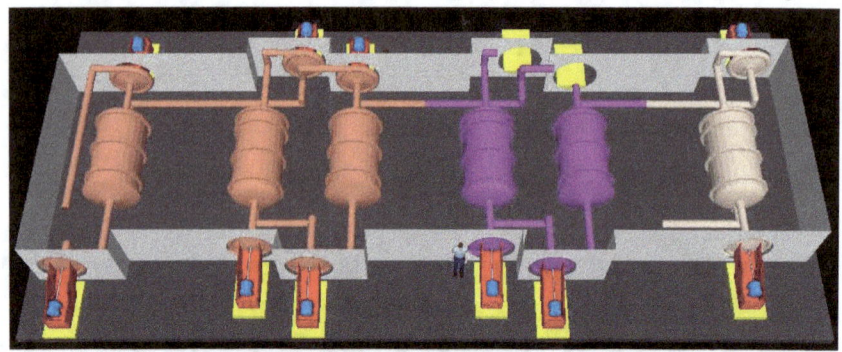

Figure 106. Colors Show Stage of Processing

The parts are disassembled in order using a combination of sliding and rotating motions. This animated model was used for training in preparation for disassembly.

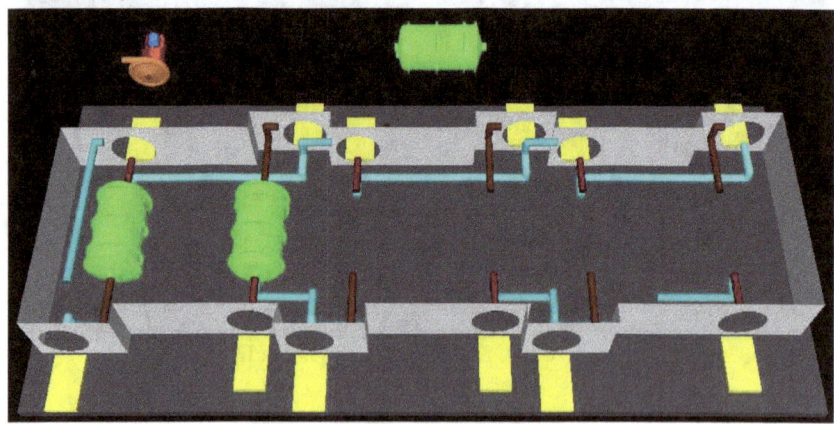

Figure 107. Disassembly Animation

The steps to remove one of the electric motors is shown in the following code segment:

```
int RemoveMotor()
  {
  float s;
  static float motor[]={
     0.04F, 0.04F,
    -0.89F, 0.40F,
    -0.43F, 0.35F,
    -0.28F, 0.40F,
     0.18F, 0.35F,
     0.33F, 0.40F,
     0.80F, 0.35F,
     0.89F,-0.40F,
     0.43F,-0.35F,
     0.28F,-0.40F,
    -0.18F,-0.35F,
    -0.33F,-0.40F,
    -0.80F,-0.35F,
     FLT_MAX};
  while(dismantle.motor.i<12)
     {
     if(!(_show[dismantle.motor.i]&_motor))
       {
       dismantle.motor.i++;
       continue;
       }
     if(dismantle.motor.j>=dismantle.motor.n)
       {
       dismantle.motor.j=0;
       dismantle.motor.k++;
       if(dismantle.motor.k==1)
         {
         _move[dismantle.motor.i]|=_motor|_mount
           |_shaft|_compr;
         memset(&_Move,0,sizeof(_Move));
         dismantle.motor.dz=(float)(fabs(motor[
           2*(dismantle.motor.i+1)+1])-0.6);
         dismantle.motor.n=(int)max(1,
           fabs(dismantle.motor.dz)/0.05)+1;
         s=max(motor[0],motor[1])/2;
         dismantle.motor.dz/=dismantle.motor.n*s;
         }
       else if(dismantle.motor.k==2)
         {
         dismantle.motor.dx=-sneg((float)(1.2+motor[
         2*(dismantle.motor.i+1)]),dismantle.motor.i<6);
         dismantle.motor.n=(int)max(1,
           fabs(dismantle.motor.dx)/0.05)+1;
         s=max(motor[0],motor[1])/2;
```

```
            dismantle.motor.dx/=dismantle.motor.n*s;
            }
        else
            {
            _move[dismantle.motor.i]^=_motor|_mount|
              _shaft|_compr;
            _show[dismantle.motor.i]|=_motor|_mount|
              _shaft|_compr;
            _show[dismantle.motor.i]^=_motor|_mount|
              _shaft|_compr;
            dismantle.motor.i++;
            dismantle.motor.j=0;
            dismantle.motor.k=0;
            dismantle.motor.n=0;
            continue;
            }
        }
    if(dismantle.motor.k==1)
      _Move.z+=dismantle.motor.dz;
    else if(dismantle.motor.k==2)
      _Move.x+=dismantle.motor.dx;
    SetWindowText(hStat,"REMOVING MOTORS AND
    COMPRESSORS");
    RePaint();
    dismantle.motor.j++;
    return(0);
    }
  return(1);
  }
```

The procedure to remove one of the pipes is much simpler:

```
int RemovePipe()
  {
  while(dismantle.pipe.i<24)
      {
      if(dismantle.pipe.i<12)
          {
          if(!(_show[dismantle.pipe.i]&_pipe1))
              {
              dismantle.pipe.i++;
              continue;
              }
          }
      else
          {
          if(!(_show[dismantle.pipe.i-12]&_pipe2))
              {
              dismantle.pipe.i++;
              continue;
              }
```

```
      }
    if(dismantle.pipe.i<12)
      _show[dismantle.pipe.i]^=_pipe1;
    else
      _show[dismantle.pipe.i-12]^=_pipe2;
    SetWindowText(hStat,"REMOVING PIPES");
    RePaint();
    dismantle.pipe.i++;
    return(0);
    }
  return(1);
  }
```

Each of these utilizes a stepping motion along a predetermined path from the current position to the final one, which is out of view. The camera position and point of view of the observer can be changed during this process in order to give any number of perspectives on the same motion. This was particularly helpful during the dismantling. The program originally kept an inventory of components and the state of each, including the name of the user, the computer used, and the time of any changes. All of the changes could be reversed or advanced in order to produce a view representing the state of the entire system at any time during the decommissioning process.

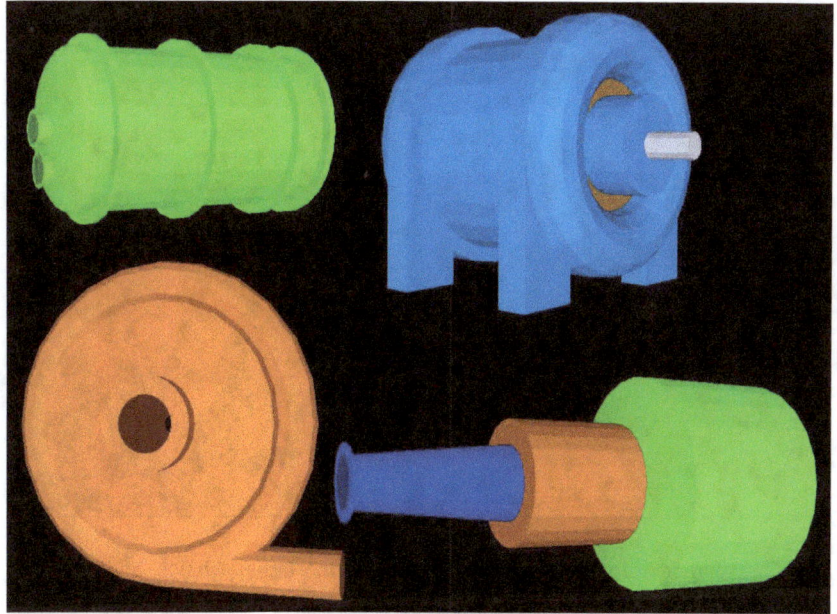

Figure 108. Components

Chapter 35. Swimming Motion

Our example of swimming motion is Mark Kilgard's Atlantis demo, which comes with the GLUT® distribution package. The code is conveniently broken down into sections:

- atlantis.c: the main program
- dolphin.c: defines the dolphin object
- shark.c: defines the shark object
- whale.c: defines the whale object
- swim.c: defines the swimming motions

The swim code module also includes a function SharkMiss() that avoids collisions and also provides the appearance of fleeing the denizens. As is the case with all of Kilgard's codes, Atlantis is clearly written with meaningful function and variable names like fish->attack and SHARKSPEED. There are even two object names (momwhale and babywhale) of type fishrec. The angles are named psi and theta. The position calculations are also easily identified:

```
x=fish->xt-fish->x;
y=fish->yt-fish->y;
z=fish->zt-fish->z;
```

The final result is quite satisfactory:

Figure 109. Atlantis Example

The smaller dolphins even flap faster than the larger whales, adding to the realism. Another detail adding to the realism is articulation and segmentation, controlled by the natural variables:

```
fish->vtail+=(fish->dtheta-fish->vtail)/10;
if(fish->vtail>0.5)
   fish->vtail=0.5;
else if(fish->vtail<-0.5)
```

```
fish->vtail=-0.5;
segup=thrash*fish->vtail;
```
Here we see a closer view of mama and baby whale. Notice the articulating segments indicated by the red lines.

Figure 110. Whale Articulation Lines

All of the fish move about the center in a circular motion, much like the Moon orbiting the Earth. They move at different speeds and also articulate (see variables involving "thrash"). The whale orientation and position is updated by the following code:

```
void WhalePilot(fishRec*fish)
  {
  fish->phi=-20.;
  fish->theta=0.;
  fish->psi-=0.5;
  fish->x+=WHALESPEED*fish->v*
     cos(fish->psi/RAD)*cos(fish->theta/RAD);
  fish->y+=WHALESPEED*fish->v*
     sin(fish->psi/RAD)*cos(fish->theta/RAD);
  fish->z+=WHALESPEED*fish->v*sin(fish->theta/RAD);
  }
```

Some variation is added though a random number comparison:

```
if(rand()%100>98)
   sign=1-sign;
fish->psi+=sign;
if(fish->psi>180.)
   fish->psi-=360.;
if(fish->psi<-180.)
   fish->psi+=360.;
```

The other fish lurch forward (i.e., "spurt") when too close to a shark:

```
if(fish->attack)
   {
   if(fish->v<1.1)
```

```
      fish->spurt=1;
    if(fish->spurt)
      fish->v+=0.2;
    if(fish->v>5.)
      fish->spurt=0;
    if((fish->v>1.)&&(!fish->spurt))
      fish->v-=0.2;
    }
```
There is even a large-scale variation to assure escape from a shark encounter:
```
void SharkMiss(int i)
  {
  int j;
  float avoid,thetal;
  float X,Y,Z,R;
  for(j=0; j<NUM_SHARKS; j++)
    {
    if(j!=i)
      {
      X=sharks[j].x-sharks[i].x;
      Y=sharks[j].y-sharks[i].y;
      Z=sharks[j].z-sharks[i].z;
      R=sqrt(X*X+Y*Y+Z*Z);
      avoid=1.;
      thetal=sharks[i].theta;
      if(R<SHARKSIZE)
        {
        if(Z>0.)
          sharks[i].theta-=avoid;
        else
          sharks[i].theta+=avoid;
        }
      sharks[i].dtheta+=(sharks[i].theta-thetal);
      }
    }
  }
```
Not only are Kilgard's programs well written and efficient, they clear, rather than obfuscated, as seems so often to be the case with much sample code. The function driving the animation, indicated by a call to the GLUT® utility function glutIdleFunc(Animate), couldn't be any more concise:
```
void Animate(void)
  {
  int i;
  static now,then=-1;
  if(then==-1)
    then=GetTickCount();
  else
    {
```

```
      now=GetTickCount();
      if(now<=then)
         return;
      then=now;
      }
   for(i=0;i<NUM_SHARKS;i++)
     {
     SharkPilot(&sharks[i]);
     SharkMiss(i);
     }
WhalePilot(&dolph);
dolph.phi++;
glutPostRedisplay();
WhalePilot(&momWhale);
momWhale.phi++;
WhalePilot(&babyWhale);
babyWhale.phi++;
}
```

Figure 111. Close-Up of Sharks

Chapter 36. Stretching Motion

Our example of stretching motion, morph3d.c, was developed by Brian Paul and Marcelo Vianna and comes with the Mesa SDK (also included in the online archive accompanying *3D Rendering in Windows®*). This demo consists of five geometric shapes (tetrahedron, cube (hexahedron), octahedron, dodecahedron, and icosahedron), which are drawn on top of each other. The conglomerate swirls about on the screen inside a box so that it is sometimes closer and sometimes farther from the observer.

The shapes are also distorted as time progresses. The distortions are cyclical, so that the appearance is stretched and squished over and over again. As one of the five shapes is stretched and the others squished, that one becomes dominant, appearing to engulf the others. Gross movement is simple and has been covered in previous chapters. The surfaces (polygons) are simply colored, making the primary focus of this demo the cyclical distortions.

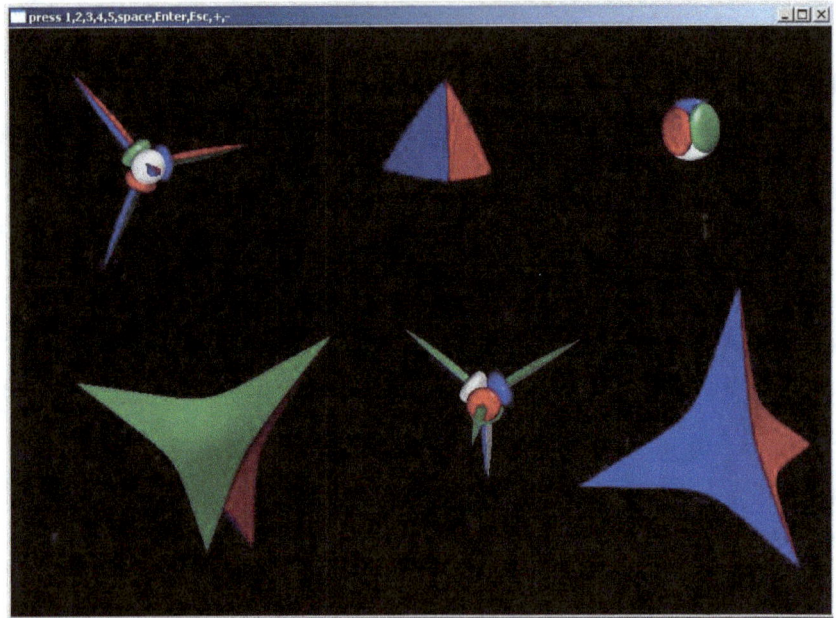

Figure 112. Morph3D by Brian Paul & Marcelo Vianna

All of the polyhedral objects are drawn one face at a time, rotating and translating the polygons as needed to obtain the desired undistorted shape. The tetrahedron is the simplest, so it will be listed here. The others are similar with more calls.

```
void draw_cube(void)
  {
  GLuint list;
  list=glGenLists(1);
  glNewList(list,GL_COMPILE);
```

```
    SQUARE(2,seno,edgedivisions,0.5);
    glEndList();
    glMaterialfv(GL_FRONT_AND_BACK,GL_DIFFUSE,
       MaterialColor[0]);
    glCallList(list);
    glRotatef(cubeangle,1,0,0);
    glMaterialfv(GL_FRONT_AND_BACK,GL_DIFFUSE,
       MaterialColor[1]);
    glCallList(list);
    glRotatef(cubeangle,1,0,0);
    glMaterialfv(GL_FRONT_AND_BACK,GL_DIFFUSE,
       MaterialColor[2]);
    glCallList(list);
    glRotatef(cubeangle,1,0,0);
    glMaterialfv(GL_FRONT_AND_BACK,GL_DIFFUSE,
       MaterialColor[3]);
    glCallList(list);
    glRotatef(cubeangle,0,1,0);
    glMaterialfv(GL_FRONT_AND_BACK,GL_DIFFUSE,
       MaterialColor[4]);
    glCallList(list);
    glRotatef(2*cubeangle,0,1,0);
    glMaterialfv(GL_FRONT_AND_BACK,GL_DIFFUSE,
       MaterialColor[5]);
    glCallList(list);
    glDeleteLists(list,1);
}
```

Each of the faces is a list glCallList() consisting of a single distorted polygon. The same list is used glGenLists(1) and the colors are changed before each face glMaterialfV() with MaterialColor[face_index]. Each distorted triangle is generated in the following function:

```
void TRIANGLE(GLfloat Edge,GLfloat Amp,
     int Divisions,GLfloat Z)
{
GLfloat Xf,Yf,Xa,Yb,Xf2,Yf2;
GLfloat Factor,Factor1,Factor2;
GLfloat VertX,VertY,VertZ,NeiAX,NeiAY,NeiAZ,
   NeiBX,NeiBY,NeiBZ;
GLfloat Ax,Ay,Bx;
int Ri,Ti;
GLfloat Vr=(Edge)*SQRT3/3;
GLfloat AmpVr2=(Amp)/sqr(Vr);
GLfloat Zf=(Edge)*(Z);
Ax=(Edge)*(+0.5/(Divisions));
   Ay=(Edge)*(-SQRT3/(2*Divisions));
Bx=(Edge)*(-0.5/(Divisions));
for(Ri=1;Ri<=(Divisions);Ri++)
   {
   glBegin(GL_TRIANGLE_STRIP);
```

```
for(Ti=0;Ti<Ri;Ti++)
  {
  Xf=(float)(Ri-Ti)*Ax+(float)Ti*Bx;
  Yf=Vr+(float)(Ri-Ti)*Ay+(float)Ti*Ay;
  Xa=Xf+0.001;
  Yb=Yf+0.001;
  Factor=1-(((Xf2=sqr(Xf))+(Yf2=sqr(Yf)))*AmpVr2);
  Factor1=1-((sqr(Xa)+Yf2)*AmpVr2);
  Factor2=1-((Xf2+sqr(Yb))*AmpVr2);
  VertX=Factor*Xf;
  VertY=Factor*Yf;
  VertZ=Factor*Zf;
  NeiAX=Factor1*Xa-VertX;
  NeiAY=Factor1*Yf-VertY;
  NeiAZ=Factor1*Zf-VertZ;
  NeiBX=Factor2*Xf-VertX;
  NeiBY=Factor2*Yb-VertY;
  NeiBZ=Factor2*Zf-VertZ;
  glNormal3f(VectMul(NeiAX,NeiAY,NeiAZ,
    NeiBX,NeiBY,NeiBZ));
  glVertex3f(VertX,VertY,VertZ);
  Xf=(float)(Ri-Ti-1)*Ax+(float)Ti*Bx;
  Yf=Vr+(float)(Ri-Ti-1)*Ay+(float)Ti*Ay;
  Xa=Xf+0.001;
  Yb=Yf+0.001;
  Factor=1-(((Xf2=sqr(Xf))+(Yf2=sqr(Yf)))*AmpVr2);
  Factor1=1-((sqr(Xa)+Yf2)*AmpVr2);
  Factor2=1-((Xf2+sqr(Yb))*AmpVr2);
  VertX=Factor*Xf;
  VertY=Factor*Yf;
  VertZ=Factor*Zf;
  NeiAX=Factor1*Xa-VertX;
  NeiAY=Factor1*Yf-VertY;
  NeiAZ=Factor1*Zf-VertZ;
  NeiBX=Factor2*Xf-VertX;
  NeiBY=Factor2*Yb-VertY;
  NeiBZ=Factor2*Zf-VertZ;
  glNormal3f(VectMul(NeiAX,NeiAY,NeiAZ,
    NeiBX,NeiBY,NeiBZ));
  glVertex3f(VertX,VertY,VertZ);
  }
Xf=(float)Ri*Bx;
Yf=Vr+(float)Ri*Ay;
Xa=Xf+0.001;
Yb=Yf+0.001;
Factor=1-(((Xf2=sqr(Xf))+(Yf2=sqr(Yf)))*AmpVr2);
Factor1=1-((sqr(Xa)+Yf2)*AmpVr2);
Factor2=1-((Xf2+sqr(Yb))*AmpVr2);
VertX=Factor*Xf;
VertY=Factor*Yf;
```

```
        VertZ=Factor*Zf;
        NeiAX=Factor1*Xa-VertX;
        NeiAY=Factor1*Yf-VertY;
        NeiAZ=Factor1*Zf-VertZ;
        NeiBX=Factor2*Xf-VertX;
        NeiBY=Factor2*Yb-VertY;
        NeiBZ=Factor2*Zf-VertZ;
        glNormal3f(VectMul(NeiAX,NeiAY,NeiAZ,
            NeiBX,NeiBY,NeiBZ));
        glVertex3f(VertX,VertY,VertZ);
        glEnd();
        }
    }
```

Notice the user-defined number of increments passed as an integer argument, Divisions, and defined at the top of the code in a data statement. The distortion factors (Factor, Factor1, and Factor2) are related by the Pythagorean Theorem in 3D so as to maintain the proper overall shape. The motion is advanced by incrementing variable "step" by 0.05 in the idle function, listed below.

```
void draw(void)
    {
    glClear(GL_COLOR_BUFFER_BIT|GL_DEPTH_BUFFER_BIT);
    glPushMatrix();
    glTranslatef(0.,0.,-10.);
    glScalef(Scale*WindH/WindW,Scale,Scale);
    glTranslatef(2.5*WindW/WindH*sin(step*1.11),
        2.5*cos(step*1.25*1.11),0);
    glRotatef(step*100,1,0,0);
    glRotatef(step*95,0,1,0);
    glRotatef(step*90,0,0,1);
    seno=(sin(step)+1./3.)*(4./5.)*Magnitude;
    draw_object();
    glPopMatrix();
    glFlush();
    glutSwapBuffers();
    step+=0.05;
    }
```

Chapter 37. Exploding Motion

For exploding motion we turn to Mark Kilgard's pointburst demo, which is included in the GLUT® distribution package (and also in the online archive). As with all of Kilgard's work, this is concise and well written. The code is readable and easily understood. In this demo droplets come bursting across the horizon and bounce along the surface.

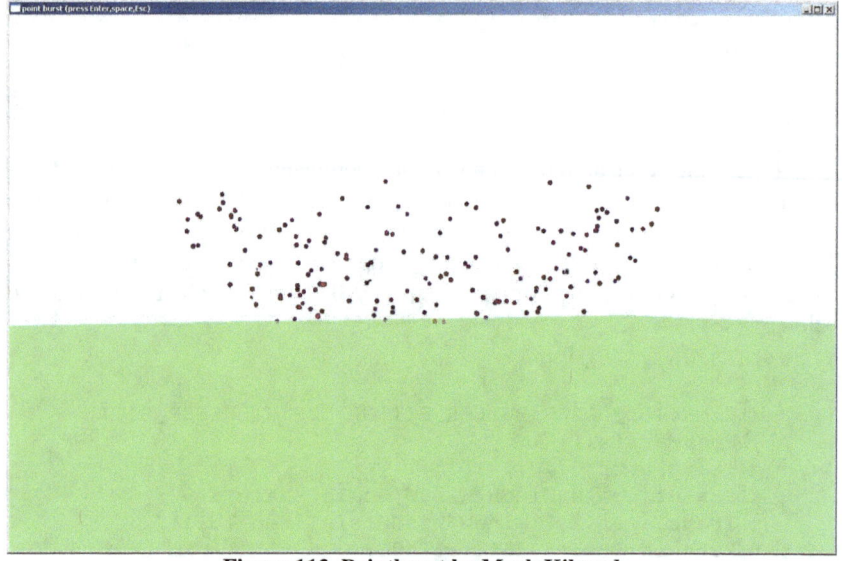

Figure 113. Pointburst by Mark Kilgard

The droplet shape is defined in a data statement like a bitmap character:

```
char*circles[]={
    "....xxxx........",
    "..xxxxxxxx......",
    ".xxxxxxxxxx.....",
    ".xxx....xxx.....",
    "xxx......xxx....",
    "xxx......xxx....",
    "xxx......xxx....",
    "xxx......xxx....",
    ".xxx....xxx.....",
    ".xxxxxxxxxx.....",
    "..xxxxxxxx......",
    "....xxxx........",
    "................",
    "................",
    "................",
    "................",};
```

This could easily be changed to some other simple shape. The same could be defined be much fewer hexadecimal integers, as the character strings are transformed into the latter before use by the following code.

```
for(t=0;t<16;t++)
  {
  for(s=0;s<16;s++)
    {
    if(circles[t][s]=='x')
      {
      loc[0]=0x1F;
      loc[1]=0x1F;
      loc[2]=0x8F;
      }
    else
      loc[0]=loc[1]=loc[2]=0xCA;
    loc+=3;
```

A closer view against a black background is shown below:

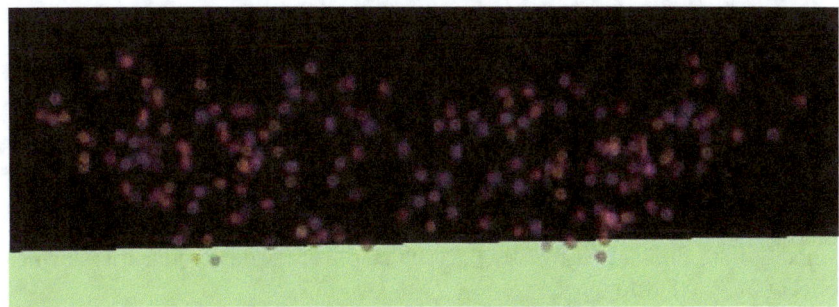

Figure 114. Pointburst Spheres

An even closer view shows how the shape is drawn:

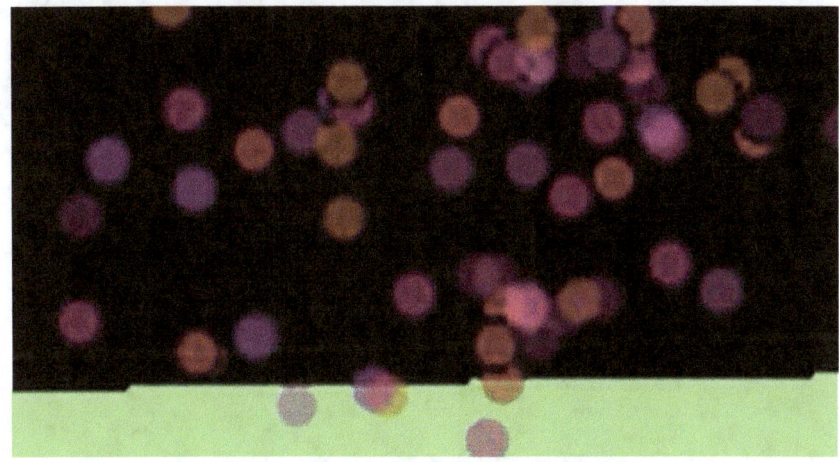

Figure 115. Pointburst Spheres Enlarged

The droplet positions are kept in a list, which is initialized and then updated with each time step (see TIME_DELTA below). The initial positions and velocities are randomized:

```
void makePointList(void)
   {
   float angle,velocity,direction;
   int i;
   motion=1;
   for(i=0;i<numPoints;i++)
      {
      pointList[i][0]=0.0;
      pointList[i][1]=0.0;
      pointList[i][2]=0.0;
      pointTime[i]=0.0;
      angle=(RANDOM_RANGE(60.0,70.0))*M_PI/180.0;
      direction=RANDOM_RANGE(0.0,360.0)*M_PI/180.0;
      pointDirection[i][0]=cos(direction);
      pointDirection[i][1]=sin(direction);
      velocity=MEAN_VELOCITY+RANDOM_RANGE(-0.8,1.);
      pointVelocity[i][0]=velocity*cos(angle);
      pointVelocity[i][1]=velocity*sin(angle);
      colorList[i]=rand()%NUM_COLORS;
      }
   theTime=0.0;
   }
```

The positions are updated based on the velocities and time step and the velocities are diminished by 80% at each step to provide a geometric slowing effect (see *=0.8 below).

```
void updatePointList(void)
   {
   float distance;
   int i;
   motion=0;
   for(i=0;i<numPoints;i++)
      {
      distance=pointVelocity[i][0]*theTime;
      pointList[i][0]=pointDirection[i][0]*distance;
      pointList[i][2]=pointDirection[i][1]*distance;
      pointList[i][1]=(pointVelocity[i][1]
         -0.5*GRAVITY*pointTime[i])*pointTime[i];
      if(pointList[i][1]<=0.0)
         {
         if(distance>EDGE)
            {
            colorList[i]=NUM_COLORS; /* Not moving. */
            continue;
            }
         pointVelocity[i][1]*=0.8;
         pointTime[i]=0.;
```

```
      }
    motion=1;
    pointTime[i]+=TIME_DELTA;
    }
  theTime+=TIME_DELTA;
  if(!motion&&!spin)
    {
    if(repeat)
      makePointList();
    else
      glutIdleFunc(NULL);
    }
  }
```

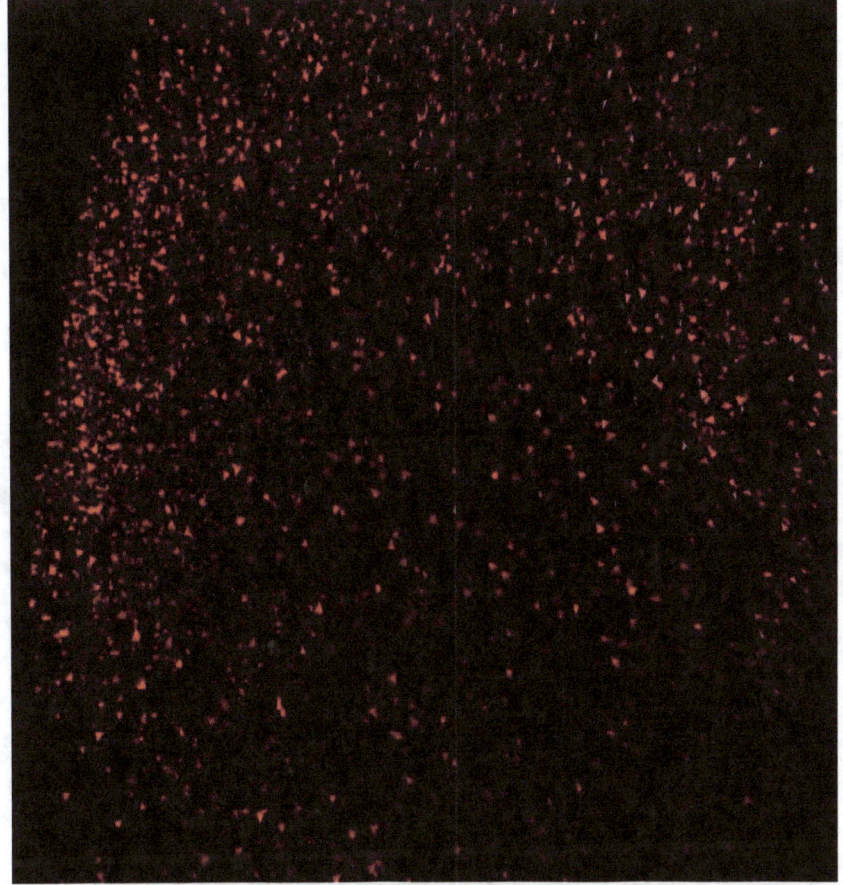

Figure 116. Simulated Explosion

Chapter 38. Soaring Motion

The skyfly demo included in the OpenGL™ SDK is truly amazing for its coding simplicity and seeming visual complexity. The scenery (clouds and terrain) are cleverly created and quite compact, based on two bitmaps (clouds.bw and terrain.bw) that are ready for OpenGL.

Figure 117. SkyFly Terrain

The spatial variability is more than adequate. This next figure shows an object called a *sprite*:

Figure 118. Paper Airplane Sprite

The programming of this demo is a little different from the previous examples in that the camera moves rather than the objects. There are also *sprites*, which look like paper airplanes and continue to move even after the main scene stops. If you are interested in sprites this is a good example to consider. The paper airplanes are defined as follows:

```
float paper_plane_vertexes[]={
/*Nx    Ny    Nz    Vx     Vy     Vz  */
  0.2,  0.0,  0.98,-0.10,  0.00,  0.02,
  0.0,  0.0,  1.00,-0.36,  0.20,-0.04,
  0.0,  0.0,  1.00, 0.36,  0.01,  0.00,
  0.0,  0.0,-1.00,-0.32,  0.02,  0.00,
  0.0,  1.0,  0.00, 0.48,  0.00,-0.06,
  0.0,  1.0,  0.00,-0.30,  0.00,-0.12,
  0.0,-1.0,  0.00, 0.36,-0.01,  0.00,
  0.0,-1.0,  0.00,-0.32,-0.02,  0.00,
  0.0,  0.0,-1.00, 0.36,-0.01,  0.00,
  0.0,  0.0,-1.00,-0.36,-0.20,-0.04,
 -0.2,  0.0,  0.98,-0.10,  0.00,  0.02,
 -0.2,  0.0,-0.98,-0.10,  0.00,  0.02,
  0.0,  0.0,-1.00,-0.36,  0.20,-0.04,
  0.0,  0.0,-1.00, 0.36,  0.01,  0.00,
  0.0,  0.0,  1.00,-0.32,  0.02,  0.00,
  0.0,-1.0,  0.00, 0.48,  0.00,-0.06,
  0.0,-1.0,  0.00,-0.30,  0.00,-0.12,
  0.0,  1.0,  0.00, 0.36,-0.01,  0.00,
  0.0,  1.0,  0.00,-0.32,-0.02,  0.00,
  0.0,  0.0,  1.00, 0.36,-0.01,  0.00,
  0.0,  0.0,  1.00,-0.36,-0.20,-0.04,
  0.2,  0.0,-0.98,-0.10,  0.00,  0.02};
```

The sprites are drawn with the following code:

```
void put_paper_plane(float*source,perfobj_t*pobj)
  {
  int j;
  perfobj_vert_t*pdataptr=(perfobj_vert_t*)pobj->vdata;
  unsigned int*flagsptr=pobj->flags;
  float*sp=source;
  *flagsptr++=PD_DRAW_PAPER_PLANE;
  for(j=0;j<22;j++)
    {
    putn3fdata(sp+0,pdataptr);
    putv3fdata(sp+3,pdataptr);
    sp+=6;
    pdataptr++;
    }
  *flagsptr++=PD_END;
  }

void init_paper_planes(void)
  {
```

```
    perfobj_t*pobj;
    /* create various perf-objs for planes */
    pobj=&(SharedData->paper_plane_obj);
    pobj->flags=SharedData->paper_plane_flags;
    pobj->vdata=(float*)SharedData->paper_plane_verts;
    put_paper_plane(paper_plane_vertexes,pobj);
    pobj=&(SharedData->paper_plane_start_obj);
    pobj->flags=SharedData->paper_plane_start_flags;
    *(pobj->flags)=PD_PAPER_PLANE_MODE;
    *(pobj->flags+1)=PLANES_START;
    *(pobj->flags+2)=PD_END;
    pobj=&(SharedData->paper_plane_2ndpass_obj);
    pobj->flags=SharedData->paper_plane_2ndpass_flags;
    *(pobj->flags)=PD_PAPER_PLANE_MODE;
    *(pobj->flags+1)=PLANES_SECOND_PASS;
    *(pobj->flags+2)=PD_END;
    pobj=&(SharedData->paper_plane_end_obj);
    pobj->flags=SharedData->paper_plane_end_flags;
    *(pobj->flags)=PD_PAPER_PLANE_MODE;
    *(pobj->flags+1)=PLANES_END;
    *(pobj->flags+2)=PD_END;
    }
```

The soaring sensation is produced by the following section of code:

```
void fly(perfobj_t*viewer_pos)
    {
    float terrain_z,xpos,ypos,xcntr,ycntr;
    float delta_speed=.003;
    xcntr=Wxsize/2;
    ycntr=Wysize/2;
    if(Xgetbutton(RKEY))
       init_positions();
    if(Xgetbutton(SPACEKEY))
       Keyboard_mode=!Keyboard_mode;
    if(Keyboard_mode)
        {
        /* step-at-a-time debugging mode */
        if(Keyboard_mode && Xgetbutton(LEFTARROWKEY))
          Azimuth-=0.025;
        if(Keyboard_mode && Xgetbutton(RIGHTARROWKEY))
          Azimuth+=0.025;
        if(Keyboard_mode && Xgetbutton(UPARROWKEY))
          {
          X+=cosf(-Azimuth+M_PI/2.)*0.025;
          Y+=sinf(-Azimuth+M_PI/2.)*0.025;
          }
        if(Keyboard_mode && Xgetbutton(DOWNARROWKEY))
          {
          X-=cosf(-Azimuth+M_PI/2.)*0.025;
          Y-=sinf(-Azimuth+M_PI/2.)*0.025;
```

```
      }
    if(Keyboard_mode && Xgetbutton(PAGEUPKEY))
      Z+=0.025;
    if(Keyboard_mode && Xgetbutton(PAGEDOWNKEY))
      Z-=0.025;
    }
  else
    {
    /* simple,mouse-driven flight model */
    if(Xgetbutton(LEFTMOUSE) && Speed<.3)
      Speed+=delta_speed;
    if(Xgetbutton(RIGHTMOUSE) && Speed>-.3)
      Speed-=delta_speed;
    if(Xgetbutton(MIDDLEMOUSE))
      Speed=Speed*.8;
    xpos=(Xgetvaluator(MOUSEX)-xcntr)/
      ((float) Wxsize*14.);
    ypos=(Xgetvaluator(MOUSEY)-ycntr)/
      ((float) Wysize*.5);
    /* move in direction of view */
    Azimuth+=xpos;
    X+=cosf(-Azimuth+M_PI/2.)*Speed;
    Y+=sinf(-Azimuth+M_PI/2.)*Speed;
    Z-=ypos*Speed;
    }
  /* keep from getting too close to terrain */
  terrain_z=terrain_height(X,Y);
  if(Z<terrain_z+.4)
    Z=terrain_z+.4;
  X=max(X,1.);
  X=min(X,GRID_RANGE);
  Y=max(Y,1.);
  Y=min(Y,GRID_RANGE);
  Z=min(Z,20.);
  *((float*) viewer_pos->vdata+0)=X;
  *((float*)viewer_pos->vdata+1)=Y;
  *((float*)viewer_pos->vdata+2)=Z;
  *((float*)viewer_pos->vdata+3)=Azimuth;
  }
```

A deficit method is used to adjust the rate of change of the viewpoint in response to mouse motion. Much of the code is devoted to generating the terrain. While fascinating, this is not the primary concern here, rather motion is our focus. The speed of rendering is a critical aspect of the perceived performance of this demo. Knowing which functions to call and in what order to result in the fastest rendering is critical to achieving this end. With this in mind, consider the following section of code, including comments, which sends a significant portion of the scenery to the rendering engine:

```
/*Notice how the following routines unwind loops and
   pre-compute indexes
```

```
*at compile time. This is crucial in obtaining the
  maximum data transfer
*from cpu to the graphics pipe.
*/

void drawlitmesh_11(float*op)
  {
  glBegin(GL_TRIANGLE_STRIP);
  /* one */
  glNormal3fv((op+PD_V_NORMAL));
  glVertex3fv((op+PD_V_POINT));
  /* two */
  glNormal3fv((op+(PD_V_SIZE+PD_V_NORMAL)));
  glVertex3fv((op+(PD_V_SIZE+PD_V_POINT)));
  /* three */
  glNormal3fv((op+(2*PD_V_SIZE+PD_V_NORMAL)));
  glVertex3fv((op+(2*PD_V_SIZE+PD_V_POINT)));
  /* four */
  glNormal3fv((op+(3*PD_V_SIZE+PD_V_NORMAL)));
  glVertex3fv((op+(3*PD_V_SIZE+PD_V_POINT)));
  /* five */
  glNormal3fv((op+(4*PD_V_SIZE+PD_V_NORMAL)));
  glVertex3fv((op+(4*PD_V_SIZE+PD_V_POINT)));
  /* six */
  glNormal3fv((op+(5*PD_V_SIZE+PD_V_NORMAL)));
  glVertex3fv((op+(5*PD_V_SIZE+PD_V_POINT)));
  /* seven */
  glNormal3fv((op+(6*PD_V_SIZE+PD_V_NORMAL)));
  glVertex3fv((op+(6*PD_V_SIZE+PD_V_POINT)));
  /* eight */
  glNormal3fv((op+(7*PD_V_SIZE+PD_V_NORMAL)));
  glVertex3fv((op+(7*PD_V_SIZE+PD_V_POINT)));
  /* nine */
  glNormal3fv((op+(8*PD_V_SIZE+PD_V_NORMAL)));
  glVertex3fv((op+(8*PD_V_SIZE+PD_V_POINT)));
  /* ten */
  glNormal3fv((op+(9*PD_V_SIZE+PD_V_NORMAL)));
  glVertex3fv((op+(9*PD_V_SIZE+PD_V_POINT)));
  /* eleven */
  glNormal3fv((op+(10*PD_V_SIZE+PD_V_NORMAL)));
  glVertex3fv((op+(10*PD_V_SIZE+PD_V_POINT)));
  glEnd();
  }
```

Fog adds considerably to the realism. A keystroke (f) is included to toggle the fog on and off. This next view is without fog.

Figure 119. SkyFly Horizon

Chapter 39. Reciprocating Motion

We will discuss some general aspects of general 3D rendering, but our primary focus in this text will be implementation within the context of OpenGL™ on the Windows® operating system. For additional details and more specifics, refer to my text, *3D Rendering in Windows®*, available from Amazon. The organization of this book is as follows: Specific material of increasing complexity is presented in the chapters, while foundational material (such as rendering contexts) is covered in the appendices.

Miniature Steam Engine Example

In this chapter we will consider one of the most basic forms of articulation: reciprocating motion (i.e., that of a cylinder fitted with a piston connected to a crankshaft). For this we will use a modified version of Troy Robinette's Miniature Steam Engine model, which uses Mark J. Kilgard's GLUT® library. We covered this model in book one of this series.

There we were primarily interested in simplicity and, thus, relied heavily on the GLUT® library for rendering and program control. Here we will be more interested in the specifics of rendering and also interactivity through the Windows® message loop. To that end, we have made several modifications to the original code, including: removing all references to the GLUT® library and relying solely on the OpenGL™ API; eliminating the superfluous texture; eliminating the lists (these are all simple geometric shapes and do not warrant building special rendering lists); use of standard variable types (BOOL, int, float, double, etc.) and minimization of special variable types (GLshort, GLint, GLfloat, GLdouble, etc.).

To improve readability and consistency with the OpenGL™ API and also the Windows® API, function names are like: DrawPiston(), while variable names are like crank_angle. The original version can be found in archive accompanying my previous book. The modified version in examples\steam.

Windows® Interface

Before we dive into the rendering, we will consider the Windows® interface, which might be thought of as a shell to facilitate the rendering. All Windows® programs have the same basic structure. The entry point (code address where the O/S jumps to after having loaded the program into memory) is WinMain(). For a console application (often mistakenly called a DOS box), the entry point is simply main(). These are not optional and are hard-wired into the linker.

WinMain is passed the current and any previous instance (handle to the process assigned by the O/S) and also the command line (launch arguments, such as if you were to *drop* a file onto the executable). The command line has already been parsed into individual strings and stored in the following external variables along with the environment strings:

```
extern int __argc;
extern char**__argv;
extern char**_environ;
```

We do not use these externals in this particular example but they are always available and often useful. WinMain performs those tasks necessary for a Windows® program to operate. This includes defining objects and procedures followed by a message loop, which will be executed until the program stops. Windows® is a message-based O/S, which sends and receives messages for everything that happens. WinMain must also set up the OpenGL™ rendering context and link this to one or more windows, where the drawing will occur.

```
int WINAPI WinMain(HINSTANCE hCurrent,HINSTANCE
   hPrevious,char*lCommand,int nShow)
   {
   HACCEL acc;
   MSG msg;
   hInst=hCurrent;
   InitCommonControls();
   acc=LoadAccelerators(hInst,"FAST");
   LoadResources();
   RegisterClasses();
   CreateWindows();
   PositionWindows();
   OpenGL();
   SetTimer(hMain,1,10,(TIMERPROC)Animate);
   while(GetMessage(&msg,NULL,0,0))
      if(!TranslateAccelerator(msg.hwnd,acc,&msg))
         if(!TranslateMessage(&msg))
            DispatchMessage(&msg);
   return(0);
   }
```

InitCommonControls() must be called in order to use any of these stock items, which include: status bar, tabs, progress bar, tree view, tool bar, track bar, etc. Here we use the status bar at the bottom of the main windows to display the camera and lighting variables. Accelerators (a list of enhanced keystrokes and corresponding commands) facilitate the use of directional keys and more. One or more resources are also loaded at this point. In this case, the OpenGL™ logo as a bitmap.

After registering classes, creating and positioning windows (including buttons), initializing the rendering context, we create a timer to facilitate animation, and finally enter the message loop. Messages are received from the O/S through GetMessage(). If it is one of the special accelerator keystrokes, that is translated and dispatched. If not, all other messages are translated and dispatched if relevant. The message loop is ended by a null message, upon which WinMain returns a zero to the O/S, which terminates the program.

Windows® classes have nothing to do with classes in C++. Windows® classes are user-defined procedures that can be called by the O/S upon certain events. There must always be a main procedure, MainProc(), not to be confused with WinMain(). For this example, we also create a procedure to paint the OpenGL™ logo into the frame, LogoProc(), and one to receive the OpenGL™ rendering, PlotProc(). The classes are registered by:

```
void RegisterClasses()
  {
  Register("MAIN",MainProc,StockBrush(COLOR_BTNFACE),
    IDC_ARROW,0,0);
  Register("LOGO",LogoProc,StockBrush(COLOR_BTNFACE),
    IDC_ARROW,0,0);
  Register("PLOT",PlotProc,GetStockObject(NULL_BRUSH),
    IDC_CROSS,0,CS_OWNDC);
  }
```

The PLOT window is assigned its own device context to speed drawing by specifying class style CS_OWNDC. Each class is registered by:

```
void Register(char*cName,void*wProc,HBRUSH
    hBrush,char*dCursor,int iExtra,DWORD style)
  {
  WNDCLASS wc;
  memset(&wc,0,sizeof(WNDCLASS));
  wc.hInstance     =hInst;
  wc.hIcon         =LoadIcon(hInst,"ICON");
  wc.style         =CS_HREDRAW|CS_VREDRAW|style;
  wc.lpszClassName=cName;
  wc.lpfnWndProc   =(WNDPROC)wProc;
  wc.hbrBackground=hBrush;
  wc.hCursor       =LoadCursor(NULL,dCursor);
  wc.cbWndExtra    =iExtra;
  if(!RegisterClass(&wc))
    Abort(__LINE__,"can't register '%s' class\nWindows
    error code %i",cName,GetLastError());
  }
```

Windows® and associated objects (push buttons, radio buttons, etc.) are created as with any other Windows® program. The OpenGL™ context is initialized by the following code:

```
void OpenGL()
  {
  HGLRC rDC;
  if((pDC=GetBestPixelFormat(hPlot))==0)
    Abort(__LINE__,"can't find best pixel
    context\nWindows error code %i",GetLastError());
  if((rDC=wglCreateContext(pDC))==0)
    Abort(__LINE__,"can't create OpenGL context\nWindows
    error code %i",GetLastError());
  if(!wglMakeCurrent(pDC,rDC))
    Abort(__LINE__,"can't make OpenGL context
    current\nWindows error code %i",GetLastError());
  glRepaint();
```

}

This begins with selecting a pixel context (see Appendix B), creating the context, making and the context current. Optionally, the scene may now be painted for the first time. Painting the scene before this will not be successful.

Animation

In a Windows® program, animation consists of two parts: creating a timer (which will be called at regular intervals) and providing a procedure. This can be handled in one of two ways. If a separate function is provided, the name of the function is passed as an argument in the timer creation call. If no function is provided (a NULL address is passed in the timer creation call), the WM_TIMER message is sent to the procedure associated with the specified handle (in this hMain), which will then imply MainProc(). The timer is set up by the call:

```
SetTimer(hMain,1,10,(TIMERPROC)Animate);
```

The animation timer for this example is listed below:

```
void WINAPI Animate(HWND hWnd,WPARAM wParam,DWORD
    idEvent,int uTime)
{
if(!animate)
   return;
if(waits)
   {
   waits--;
   return;
   }
crank_angle+=crank_step;
if(crank_angle>360)
   crank_angle=0;
waits=ticks;
glRepaint();
}
```

In order to vary the speed, the procedure counts down (i.e., *waits*) a variable number of *ticks* before changing and redrawing. The only change for this example is the crank angle, which is stepped through 360° by increments of 5°.

Redraw Everything

The default way of creating an animation using OpenGL™ is to redraw everything. While it is possible to erase part of the *screen* that is in memory (tied to the device context within rendering engine) and repaint only a part of the whole scene, there is no convenient way of doing this or deciding which objects might obscure others. Fortunately, the rendering engine is fast enough to provide acceptable results for even somewhat complex scenes. The *flicker* effect is rarely a problem because OpenGL™ renders the scene first in memory and then BitBlt's it into the *plot* window.

The rendering process begins with clearing with glClear(), setting up the lighting, shading, camera, and viewing context. The objects are then rendered in any order. The rendering process ends with glFinish(). The BitBlt is accomplished with a call to SwapBuffers().

```
void glRepaint()
{
if(!pDC)
  return;
glClearColor(0,0,0,0);
glClear(GL_COLOR_BUFFER_BIT|GL_DEPTH_BUFFER_BIT);
glEnable(GL_DEPTH_TEST);
glDepthFunc(GL_LESS);
glShadeModel(GL_SMOOTH);
glLightModeli(GL_LIGHT_MODEL_TWO_SIDE,TRUE);
glDisable(GL_AUTO_NORMAL);
glMatrixMode(GL_MODELVIEW);
glLoadIdentity();
glEnable(GL_LIGHTING);
glLightfv(GL_LIGHT0,GL_AMBIENT ,ambientLight0);
glLightfv(GL_LIGHT0,GL_DIFFUSE ,diffuseLight0);
   positionLight0[0]=(float)(sin(PI*Light.a/180)
      *cos(PI*Light.b/180));
   positionLight0[1]=(float)(sin(PI*Light.b/180));
   positionLight0[2]=(float)(cos(PI*Light.a/180)
      *cos(PI*Light.b/180));
   positionLight0[3]=0;
glLightfv(GL_LIGHT0,GL_POSITION,positionLight0);
glEnable(GL_LIGHT0);
glDisable(GL_TEXTURE_2D);
glTranslated(Objective.x,Objective.y,Objective.z);
glRotated(Objective.a,1,0,0);
glRotated(Objective.b,0,1,0);
glRotated(Objective.c,0,0,1);
glPolygonMode(back?GL_FRONT_AND_BACK:GL_FRONT,
   fill?GL_FILL:GL_LINE);
glScaled(zoom/2.,zoom/2.,zoom/2.);
RenderEngine();
glFinish();
SwapBuffers(pDC);
}
```

Everything up to RenderEngine() is preparation. The two calls after RenderEngine() complete the process. In this case, all of the objects are drawn inside procedure RenderEngine(). This too is broken up into smaller tasks as listed below:

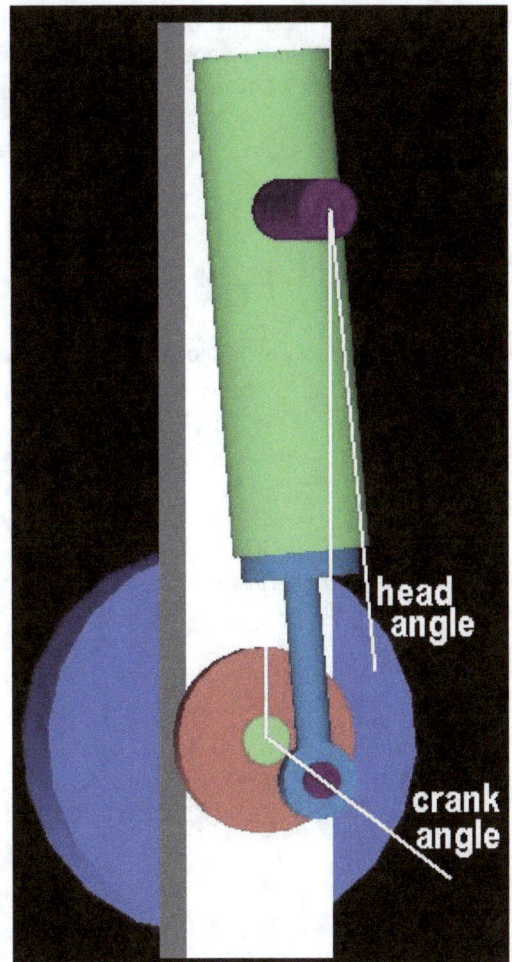

Figure 120. Crank Angle and Head Angle

```
void RenderEngine()
  {
  head_angle=HeadAngle(crank_angle);
  DrawEnginePole();
  glPushMatrix();
  glTranslated(0.5,1.4,0.0);
  DrawCylinderHead();
  glPopMatrix();
  glPushMatrix();
  glTranslated(0.0,-0.8,0.0);
  DrawCrank();
  glPopMatrix();
  }
```

The crank angle is updated in the animation procedure and the head angle is calculated once here to complete the arrangement. This formula can be found on the Web along with a description of reciprocating systems. The formula is provided as a function:

```
double HeadAngle(double deg)
  {
  double theta;
  theta=270.112-deg/58.;
  return(120.*atan((0.15*sin(theta))/
            ((2.7-0.15*cos(theta))))); 
  }
```

The individual parts are broken down into simple geometric shapes (block, cylinder, and disk):

```
void DrawPiston()
  {
  glPushMatrix();
  glColor(0.3F,0.6F,0.9F);
  glPushMatrix();
  glRotated(90.,0.0,1.0,0.0);
  glTranslated(0.0,0.0,-0.07);
  glShaft(0.125,0.06,0.12);
  glPopMatrix();
  glRotated(-90.,1.0,0.0,0.0);
  glTranslated(0.0,0.0,0.05);
  glShaft(0.06,0.0,0.6);
  glTranslated(0.0,0.0,0.6);
  glShaft(0.2,0.0,0.5);
  glPopMatrix();
  }
void DrawEnginePole()
  {
  glPushMatrix();
  glColor(0.9F,0.9F,0.9F);
  glBox(0.5,3.0,0.5);
  glColor(0.5F,0.1F,0.5F);
  glRotated(90.,0.0,1.0,0.0);
  glTranslated(0.0,0.9,-0.4);
  glShaft(0.1,0.0,2);
  glPopMatrix();
  }
void DrawCylinderHead()
  {
  glPushMatrix();
  glColor(0.5F,1.0F,0.5F);
  glRotated(90.,1.0,0.0,0.0);
  glTranslated(0,0.0,0.4);
  glRotated(head_angle,1,0,0);
  glTranslated(0,0.0,-0.4);
  glShaft(0.23,0.21,1.6);
```

```
        glRotated(180.,1.0,0.0,0.0);
        glRing(0.,0.23,20);
        glPopMatrix();
        }
void DrawFlywheel()
        {
        glPushMatrix();
        glColor(0.5F,0.5F,1.0F);
        glRotated(90.,0.0,1.0,0.0);
        glShaft(0.625,0.08,0.5);
        glPopMatrix();
        }
void DrawCrankbell()
        {
        glPushMatrix();
        glColor(1.0F,0.5F,0.5F);
        glRotated(90.,0.0,1.0,0.0);
        glShaft(0.3,0.08,0.12);
        glColor(0.5F,0.1F,0.5F);
        glTranslated(0.0,0.2,0.0);
        glShaft(0.06,0.0,0.34);
        glTranslated(0.0,0.0,0.22);
        glRotated(90.,0.0,1.0,0.0);
        glRotated(crank_angle-head_angle,1.0,0.0,0.0);
        DrawPiston();
        glPopMatrix();
        }
void DrawCrank()
        {
        glPushMatrix();
        glRotated(crank_angle,1.0,0.0,0.0);
        glPushMatrix();
        glRotated(90.,0.0,1.0,0.0);
        glTranslated(0.0,0.0,-1.0);
        glShaft(0.08,0.0,1.4);
        glPopMatrix();
        glPushMatrix();
        glTranslated(0.28,0.0,0.0);
        DrawCrankbell();
        glPopMatrix();
        glPushMatrix();
        glTranslated(-0.77,0.0,0.0);
        DrawFlywheel();
        glPopMatrix();
        glPopMatrix();
        }
```

These individual procedures further break down the drawing process to generic geometric objects. Rather than drawing an arbitrary hexahedron at some particular location and orientation, it is simpler to modify the transformation matrix through which all objects pass and draw a generic object. In order to preserve the transformation within the rendering context, we first save it with glPushMatrix(), perform the desired actions, and then restore it with glPopMatrix().

Not only does this simplify the basic drawing functions, it also facilitates debugging. We know that the generic objects will be drawn correctly. If the final objects are not rendered as desired, the problem must be in the preparation (rotate, translate, scale, etc.) or preservation (push, draw, pop). This sequence and program structure, including separating those procedures unique to Windows® from those pertaining to OpenGL™ makes the code more understandable.

Degrees of Freedom

This example essentially has only one degree of freedom: crank angle. The head angle is uniquely defined by the linkage from the crank angle and so it is not independent. There are also only a few objects impacted by changing the crank angle. Rotation, scaling, lighting, etc. are merely viewing aspects and not articulations. This is perhaps the simplest system of the type covered in this text.

Animation Rate

Live animation rate is limited by the time to render and paint and also process messages. These are not optional steps and would be present in most any O/S and certainly any multi-user or multi-processing system. If the rate is insufficient, the only practical remedy is screen capture and building an animated file, such as a GIF.

Chapter 40. Simple Leg Motion

For this next example we will begin Brian Paul's Blue Pony example, which also utilizes the GLUT® library. In order to focus on the leg motion alone, we will eliminate the billboard logo, replacing it with a red panel. This eliminates the texture reading, conversion, and drawing code, as this does not contribute to our discussion of articulation. The original code uses 2D polygons to define the parts of the pony (body, mane, and legs). These were first tessellated (converted to triangles) and then extruded (to provide thickness). As these operations rely on the GLUT® library and are not directly related to articulation, the pony will be transformed into 3D triangles, which are easily drawn. This operation was performed externally and the results stored in a static data statement (see file pony.3dv in folder examples\pony). For more details on working with finite elements, refer to the previous two texts.

Figure 121. Pony Example (solid)

We will also replace the dependence on the GLUT® library with foundational calls to the OpenGL™ API alone. Finally, we will replace the original GUI functions (also from the GLUT® library) with Windows® API calls, as with the steam engine in Chapter 39. In fact, the user interface, program control, and message loop will be identical to the previous one. Even the animation procedure will be the same so that the only difference between the two will be replacing RenderEngine() with RenderPony(). The triangles can be seen in the wire frame view.

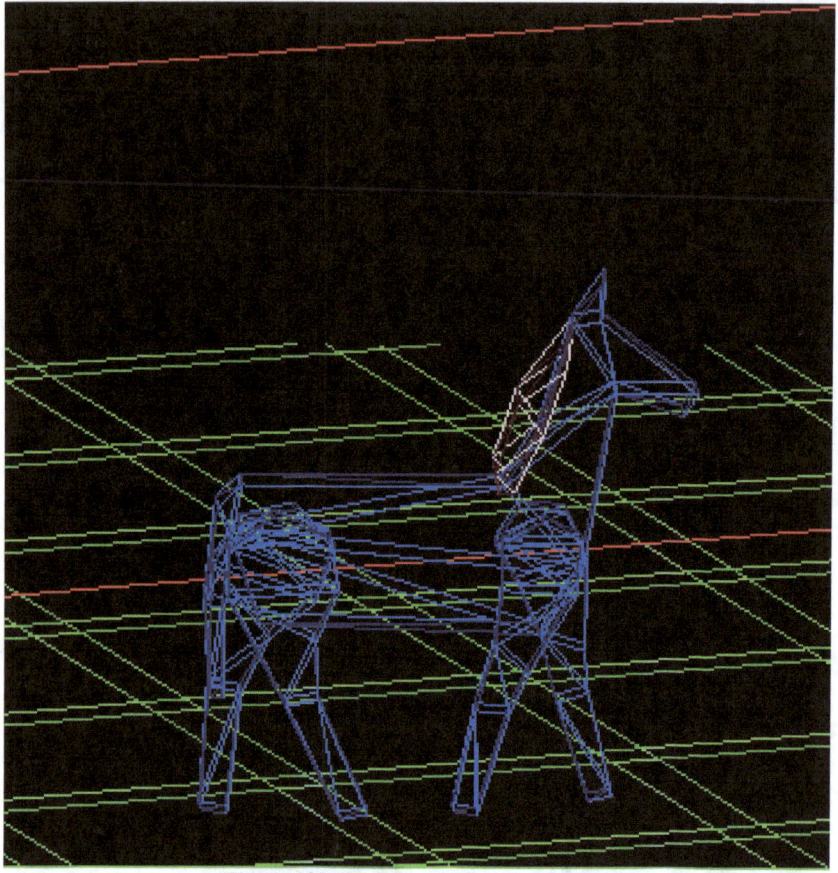

Figure 122. Pony Example (wire frame)

There are only two leg objects (front and rear). Each is drawn twice. The lateral displacement is always the same. The rotating motion is implemented by calling glRotatef() and passing the leg rotation angle, which is incremented as before with the crank angle. There is very little difference between the pony and steam engine examples—mostly the shape of the objects.

```
void RenderPony()
  {
  glColor(0.1F,0.1F,1.0F);
  glTriangles(body);
```

```
glColor(1.0F,0.5F,0.5F);
glTriangles(mane);
glColor(0.1F,0.1F,1.0F);
glPushMatrix();
glTranslatef(FrontLegPos[0],FrontLegPos[1],
  FrontLegPos[2]);
glRotatef(LegAngle,0.0,0.0,1.0);
glTriangles(fleg);
glPopMatrix();
glPushMatrix();
glTranslatef(FrontLegPos[0],FrontLegPos[1],
  -FrontLegPos[2]);
glRotatef(-LegAngle,0.0,0.0,1.0);
glTriangles(fleg);
glPopMatrix();
glPushMatrix();
glTranslatef(BackLegPos[0],BackLegPos[1],
  BackLegPos[2]);
glRotatef(-LegAngle,0.0,0.0,1.0);
glTriangles(rleg);
glPopMatrix();
glPushMatrix();
glTranslatef(BackLegPos[0],BackLegPos[1],
  -BackLegPos[2]);
glRotatef(LegAngle,0.0,0.0,1.0);
glTriangles(rleg);
glPopMatrix();
}
```

Chapter 41. Walking Motion

We next discuss walking motion. Our example, of course, will be an Imperial Walker. Before we can delve into articulating each leg, we must first identify the various parts, including the joints. These have been separated by colors in the figure below (author unknown):

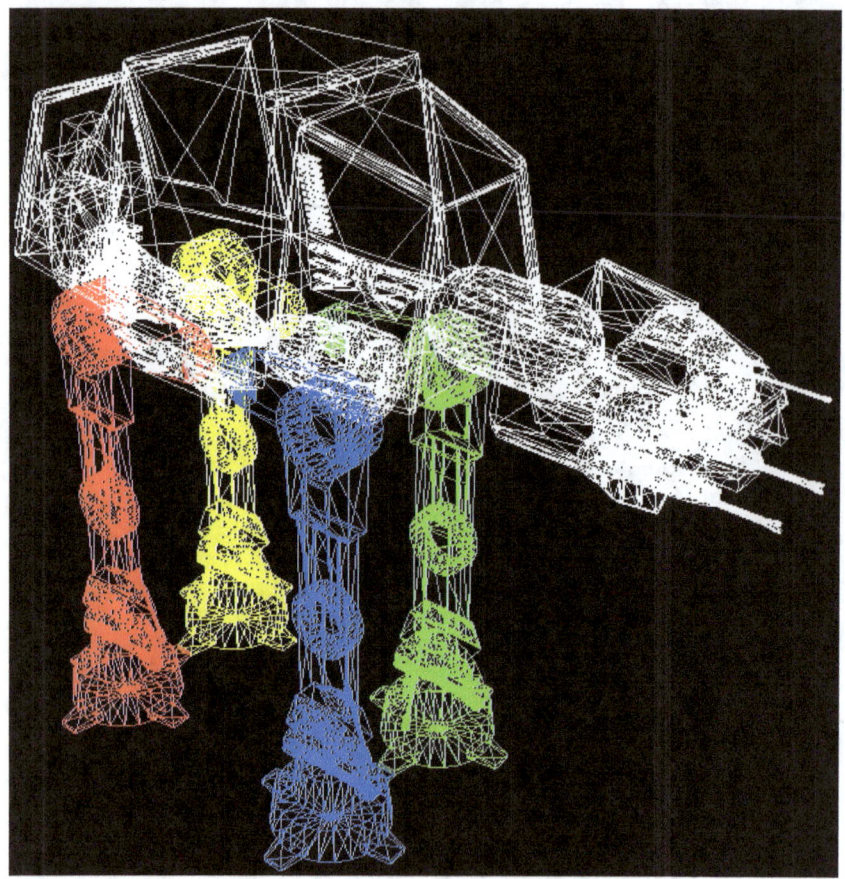

Figure 123. Parts of an Imperial Walker

You can readily find such models on the Web. These are usually in the form of VRML (Virtual Reality Markup Language) files or 3DS (AutoCAD® 3D Studio) files, which are rather inconvenient to work with unless you have very expensive software. These can be translated by TP2 (see Appendix S) into 3D elements or triangles, both simple text files that are convenient to work with (see pony.3dv and pony.tri in the Chapter 40). There are several file conversions (with source code) available in the utilities folder in the online archive. Separating out one leg, we see the details, including the points of rotation shown in red:

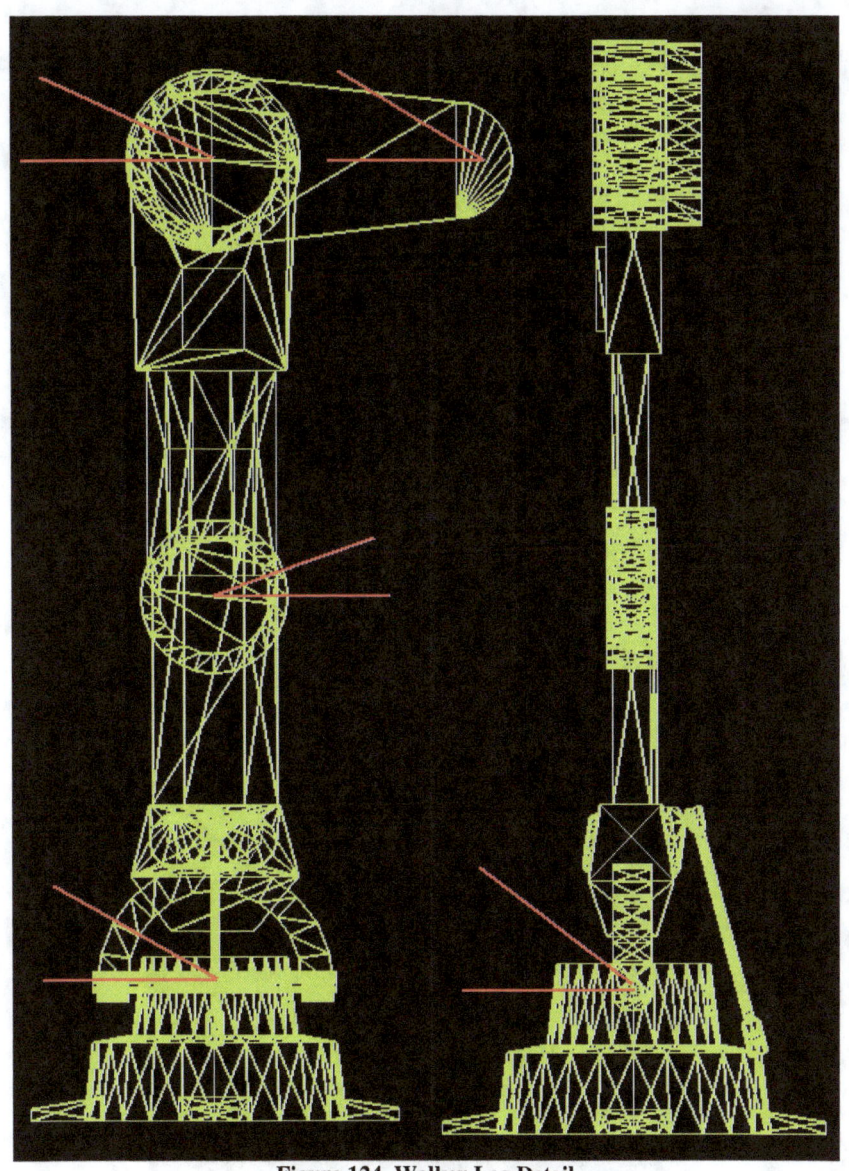

Figure 124. Walker Leg Detail

As with the steam engine and pony, we will first draw the parts that do not articulate, then apply appropriate translations and rotations (pushing the transformation onto the stack before and popping it off the stack afterward) draw a group of elements, then move on to the next group. In order for the hip joint to work properly, we must rotate two groups by equal and opposite angles and also displace the second, as shown below:

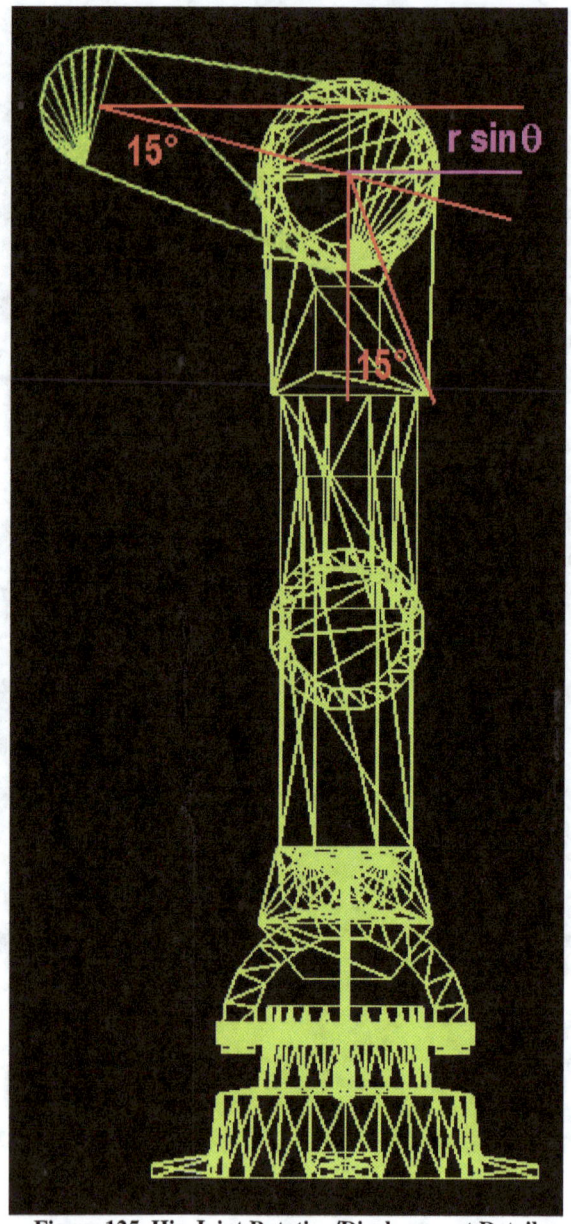

Figure 125. Hip Joint Rotation/Displacement Detail

The left, right, front, and rear legs can be drawn from the same group of elements with rotation and translation. First we split the legs into sections.

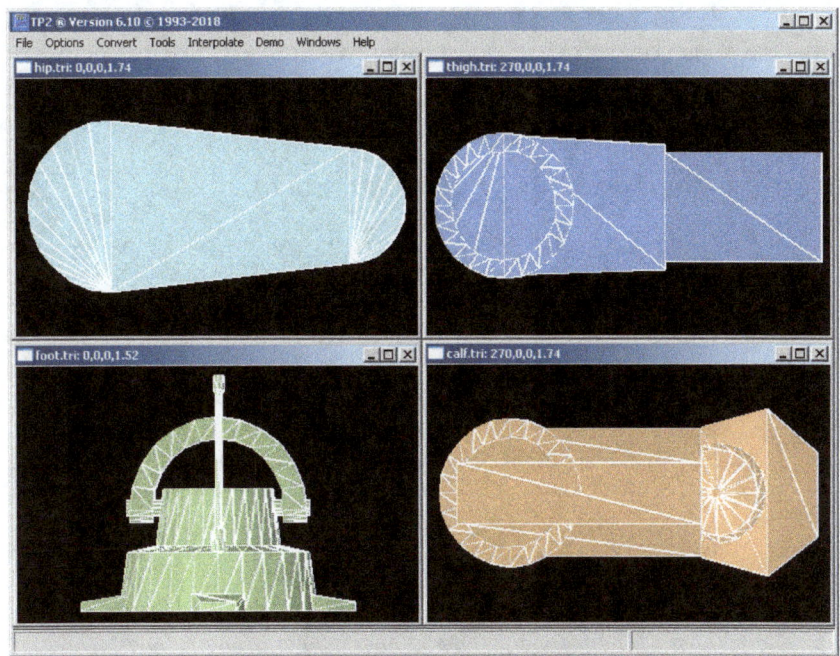

Figure 126. Walker Leg Split into 4 Groups

If the groups are not obvious from the source file (for example, 3DS or VRML), you can select individual elements with TP2 and split the groups manually. To do this, load the file and then select the option *selection of 3D objects*. When you click on each element, it will change colors. The default new color is red but you can change it with the *selection color* option.

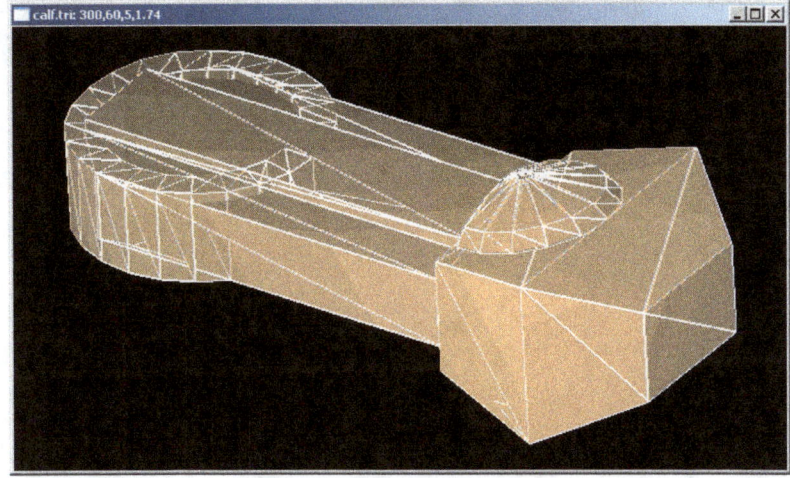

Figure 127. Walker Calf Group

You may also want to outline the elements. To do this, select *User Controls* from the *Windows®* menu, as shown below. You can also use the controls to pan and adjust the view.

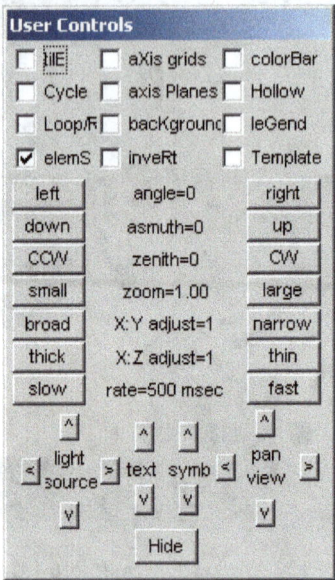

Figure 128. TP2 User Controls

In order to further discuss these groups, we will bring them into Excel® where they can be rotated and translated using simple functions. You will find two programs (3DVtoCSV and TRItoCSV) to facilitate this process in the utilities folder. Comma Separated Values (CSV) can be opened by Excel® and are a native format. Each of the element groups forming the leg has been converted to comma separated values and combined into a single spreadsheet, walker.xls that you will find in the examples\walker folder.

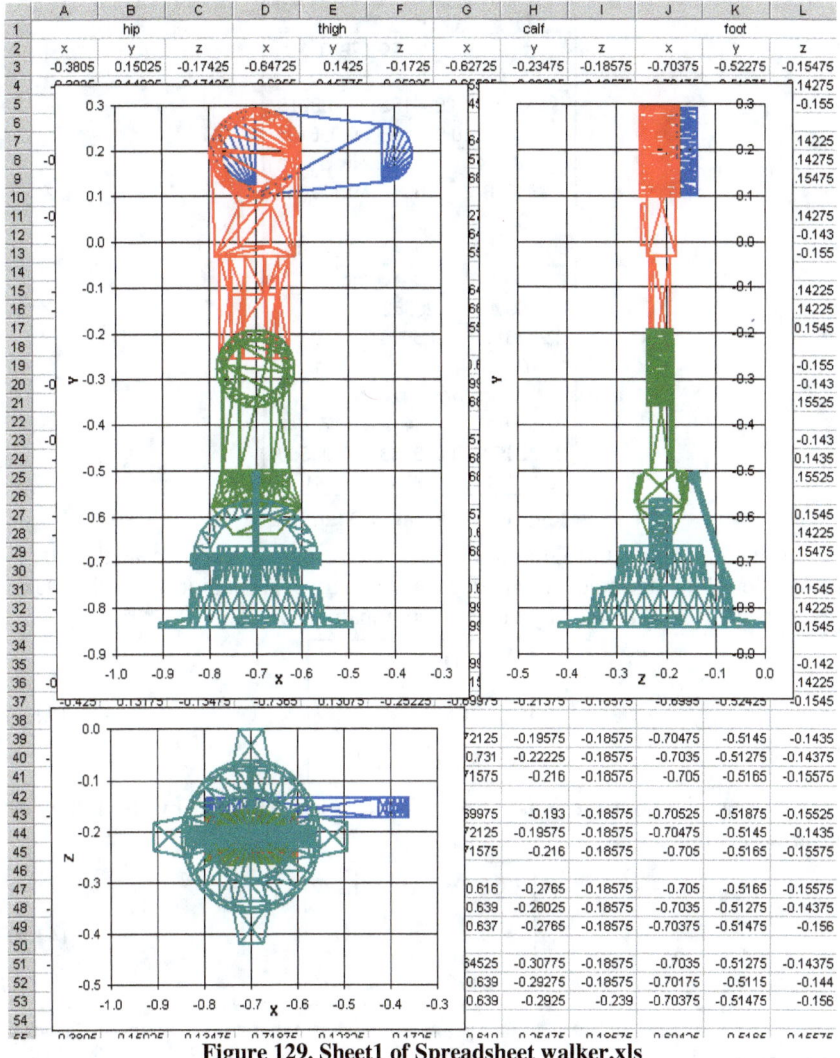

Figure 129. Sheet1 of Spreadsheet walker.xls

Rotations are most efficiently performed using matrix operations. These are covered in Chapter 4 in more detail and are implemented in Sheet2 of the spreadsheet walker.xls over to the right side, as shown in this next figure. The user-adjustable angles are in bold blue font.

M	N	O
5	x-rotation	
1	0	0
0	0.996195	-0.08716
0	0.087156	0.996195
10	y-rotation	
0.984808	0	0.173648
0	1	0
-0.17365	0	0.984808
15	z-rotation	
0.965926	-0.25882	0
0.258819	0.965926	0
0	0	1
combined rotation		
0.951251	-0.25489	0.173648
0.272453	0.958333	-0.08583
-0.14454	0.128958	0.98106

Figure 130. Rotation Matrices

Rotations about the three axes (xyz) are specified by three angles (θφψ) using the following three 3x3 matrices, one at a time. A rotation about the x-axis by an angle θ is performed by the following matrix operation:

$$\begin{vmatrix} 1 & 0 & 0 \\ 0 & \cos\theta & -\sin\theta \\ 0 & \sin\theta & \cos\theta \end{vmatrix} \qquad (41.1)$$

A rotation about the y-axis by an angle φ is performed by the following matrix operation:

$$\begin{vmatrix} \cos\varphi & 0 & \sin\varphi \\ 0 & 1 & 0 \\ -\sin\varphi & 0 & \cos\varphi \end{vmatrix} \qquad (41.2)$$

A rotation about the z-axis by an angle ψ is performed by the following matrix operation:

$$\begin{vmatrix} \cos\psi & -\sin\psi & 0 \\ \sin\psi & \cos\psi & 0 \\ 0 & 0 & 1 \end{vmatrix} \qquad (41.3)$$

The three rotations are combined using two calls to the Excel® matrix multiplication function (MMULT):

```
=MMULT(MMULT(M2:O4,M6:O8),M10:O12)
```

The rotation is applied using one call to MMULT and two calls to the transpose function (TRANSPOSE):

=TRANSPOSE(MMULT($M$14:$O$16,TRANSPOSE(Sheet1!A3:C3)))

The end result for θ=5°, φ=10°, and ψ=15° is:

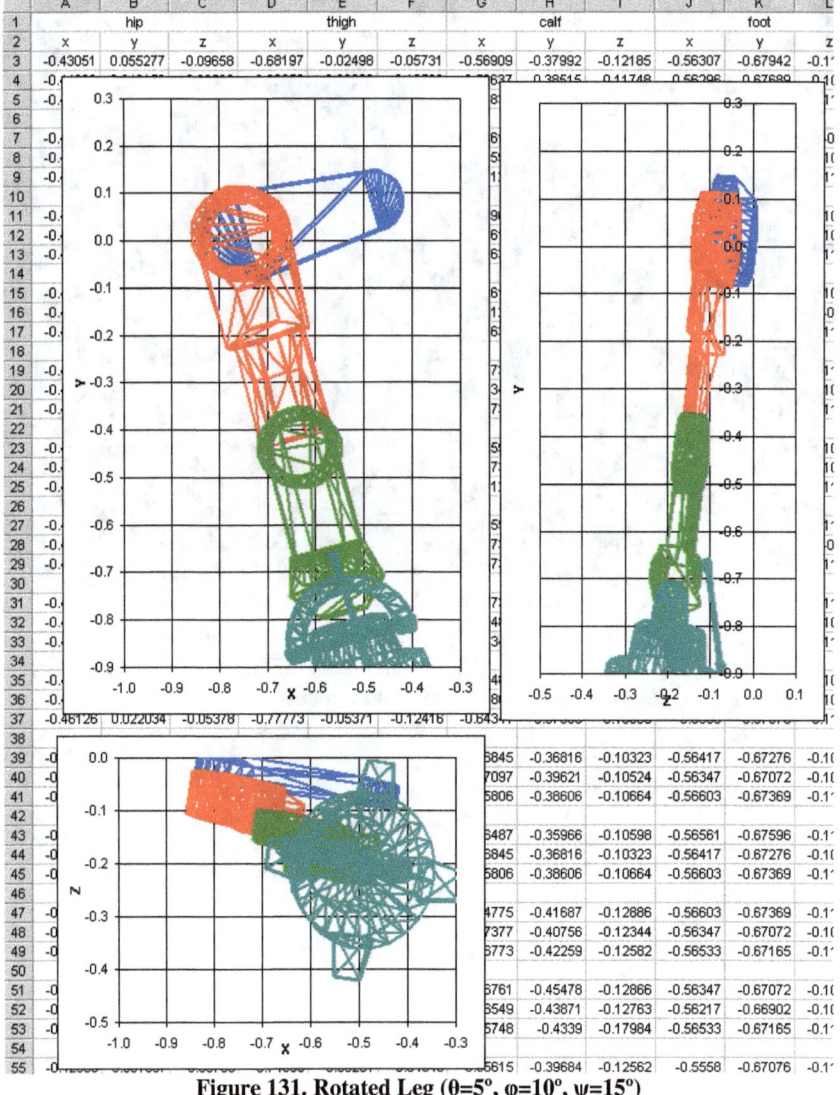

Figure 131. Rotated Leg (θ=5°, φ=10°, ψ=15°)

We start with the same basic program as in the pony example, only we read the walker elements from walker.tri, as shown in the next figure:

Figure 132. One-Legged Model in 3D Triangles

Rendering the entire walker using only one leg four times requires only a short section of code. The four data statements (dX,dZ,dW,yA) contain the adjustments to make 4 legs out of 1 group of elements.

```
void RenderWalker()
  {
  int i;
  float dX[4]={0.F,0.000F,-0.473F,-0.473F};
  float dZ[4]={0.F,0.309F, 0.000F,-0.309F};
  float dW[4]={0.F,0.423F, 0.000F,-0.423F};
  float yA[4]={0.F,0.F,180.F,180.F};
  glColor(1.F,0.F,0.F);
  glTriangles(body);
  for(i=0;i<4;i++)
     {
     glPushMatrix();
     glTranslatef(dX[i],0.F,dZ[i]);
     glRotatef(yA[i],0.F,1.F,0.F);
     glColor(0.F,1.F,1.F);
     glTriangles(hip);
     glPopMatrix();
     glPushMatrix();
```

```
        glTranslatef(dX[i],0.F,dW[i]);
        glRotatef(yA[i],0.F,1.F,0.F);
        glColor(0.F,1.F,1.F);
        glColor(0.F,1.F,0.F);
        glTriangles(thigh);
        glColor(1.F,1.F,0.F);
        glTriangles(calf);
        glColor(0.F,1.F,0.F);
        glTriangles(foot);
        glPopMatrix();
    }
}
```

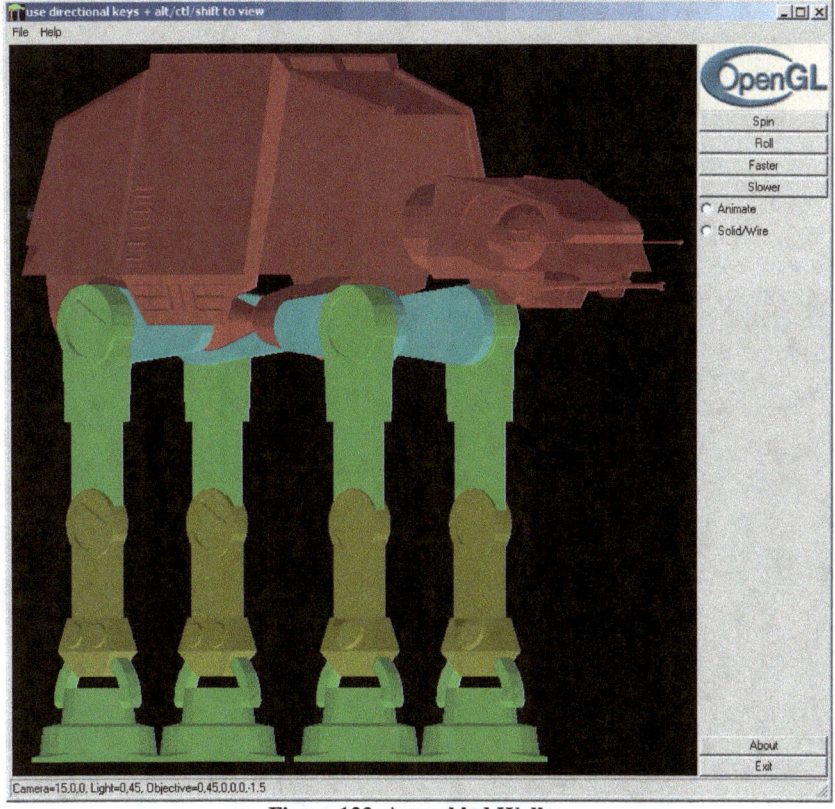

Figure 133. Assembled Walker

Hip Rotation

The cyan hip groups are rotated by some angle (Ahip), which can be different for each of the four hips. As each hip rotates through some angle, the group must be repositioned so as to maintain the pivot location on the body. The X and Y adjustments are given by:

```
hX=0.465*(cos((Ahip- 25)*PI/180)-cos( -25*PI/180));
```

```
hY=0.465*(cos((Ahip-115)*PI/180)-cos(-115*PI/180));
```

The inner radius is 0.465, the point of maximum horizontal displacement is 25°, and the point of maximum vertical displacement is 115°. This radius and angle come from the vector from the centroid (X=Y=Z) and the pivot point of the hip at the center of the smaller end that attaches to the body.

Thigh Rotation

The thigh group must be adjusted so that it follows the larger end of the hip as it rotates. The radius (0.275) is the distance between the two round sections on either end of the hip.

```
pX= 0.275*(cos(Ahip*PI/180)-1);
pY=-0.275* sin(Ahip*PI/180);
```

Rotating the thigh group produces displacements, which must be compensated for if the outer (second) hip joint is to remain intact. The radius (0.728) and angle (286°) arises from the vector between the centroid and knee.

```
tX= 0.728*(sin((Athigh-286)*PI/180)-sin(-286*PI/180));
tY=-0.728*(cos((Athigh-286)*PI/180)-cos(-286*PI/180));
```

We can assign a pair of keys to the hip and thigh rotation angles to conveniently control the display groups. Rotating the hips +90° and the thighs -90° produces the following:

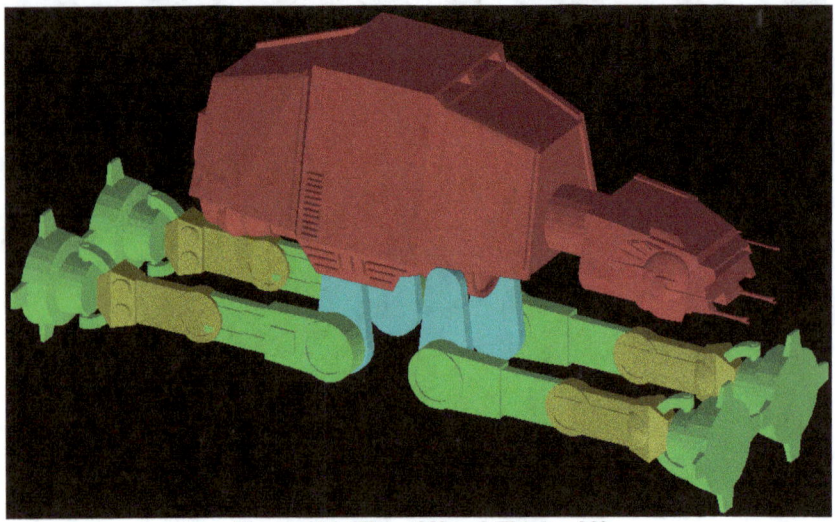

Figure 134. Hips +90° and Thighs -90°

Calf Rotation

The calf group must be adjusted so that it follows the lower thigh joint. Note that our rotations control the segments, not the joints. The thigh rotation angle doesn't impact the knee per se in this model because the joints are simple disks. It does, however, impact the calf group, which will require a rotation and two displacements, as before so that the knee joint remains intact. The radius is 0.753 and the angle is 249°.

```
cX= 0.753*(sin((Acalf-249)*PI/180)-sin(-249*PI/180));
cY=-0.753*(cos((Acalf-249)*PI/180)-cos(-249*PI/180));
```

Foot Rotation

And finally, the foot position must be adjusted to keep the ankle joint together. This is accomplished by the following code. The radius is 0.928 and the angle is 229°.

```
fX= 0.928*(sin((Afoot-229)*PI/180)-sin(-229*PI/180));
fY=-0.928*(cos((Afoot-229)*PI/180)-cos(-229*PI/180));
```

As we have assigned each of these angles a hot key (hip=CTL_UP/DOWN, thigh=CTL_LEFT/RIGHT, calf=ALT_PGUP/DN, foot=CTL_PGUP/DN), we can move the legs interactively.

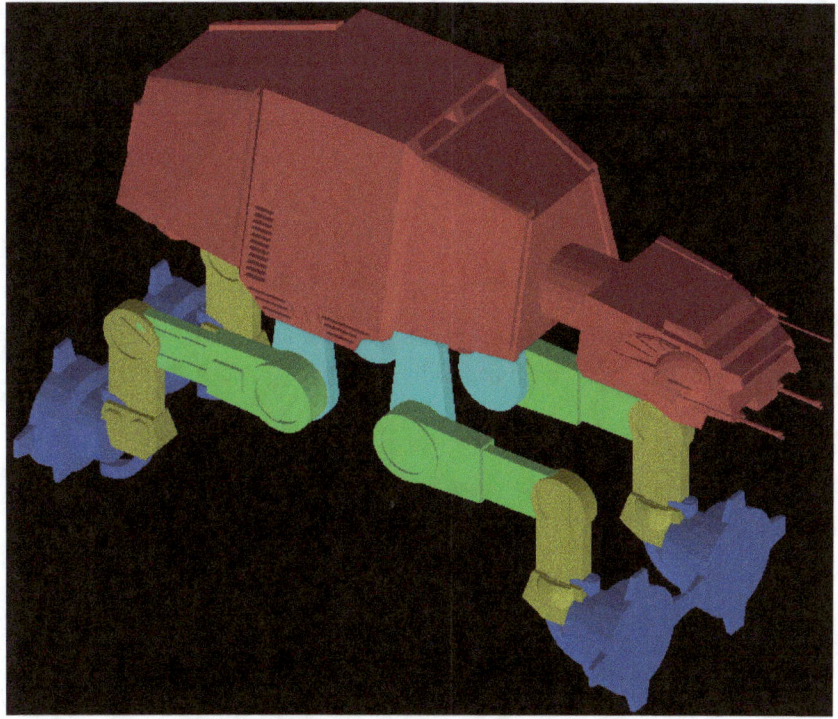

Figure 135. Hip=Calf=90° and Thigh=Foot=-90°

The interactive adjustments are simple, as illustrated by the following:

```
if(wParam==PUSH_CTL_DOWN)
  {
  Ahip[0]+=5.F;
  Ahip[1]+=5.F;
  Ahip[2]+=5.F;
```

```
Ahip[3]+=5.F;
glRepaint();
return(TRUE);
}
```

Coordinated Leg Motion

In order to achieve coordinated leg motion, we must vary the for angles for each leg separately over time. To do this, we merely set up a table that goes through a cycle consisting of one stride for a single leg. Each leg will go through the same motions, only there will be a time delay between each. Conceptually, this looks like the figure below:

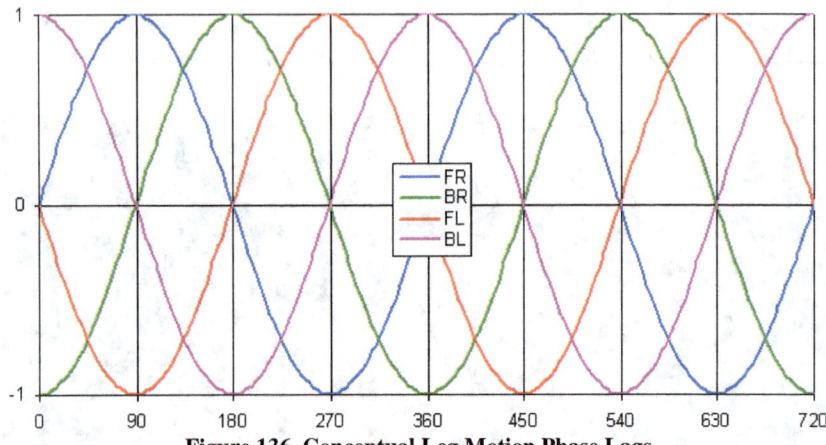

Figure 136. Conceptual Leg Motion Phase Lags

This pattern is easily implemented by a snippet of code:
```
Twalk+=5.;
for(i=0;i<4;i++)
  {
  Ahip[  i]=-(10* sin((Twalk-i*90)*PI/180)-5 );
  Athigh[i]= (20*(cos((Twalk-i*90)*PI/180)-1));
  Acalf[ i]= (20* cos((Twalk-i*90)*PI/180)    );
  Afoot[ i]=-Athigh[i]-Acalf[i];
  }
```

More complex patterns can be implemented in a similar fashion. One might even provide multiple gaits (walk, trot, canter, gallop). For this particular linkage, setting Afoot+Athigh+Acalf=0 will keep the foot parallel to the ground. The animation is progressed by simply incrementing the sequence angle, Twalk. The phase angle between the legs progressively lags by 90° (-i*90). More complicated sequences are, of course, possible. To conceptualize and implement more complex motions, it is often helpful to construct a physical model of the linkage, as illustrated below:

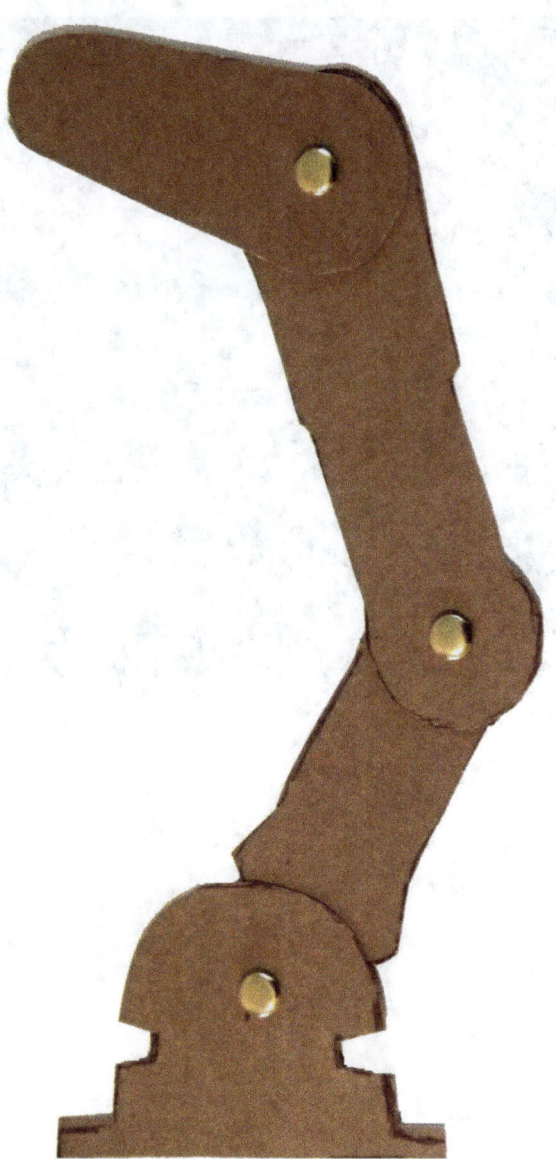

Figure 137. Adjustable Cardboard Leg Model

And finally, we have the walker galloping along at the touch of a button:

Figure 138. Walker Complete with Animation

Chapter 42. Skeletal Motion

The skeleton model (shown on page iv) was obtained from the Web, written in #VRML V2.0 by Thomas Baier (thomas.baier@stmuc.com) dated Apr 03 10:14:40 2002. We first break it up into groups and write these out as 3D triangles using wrlto3dv and 3dvtotri, which may be found in the utilities folder in the online archive accompanying this text. The end result can be displayed using TP2:

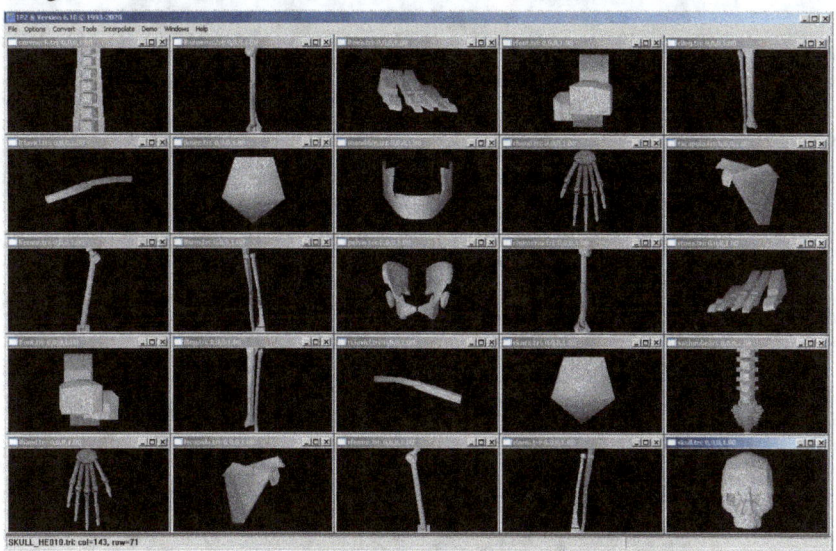

Figure 139. Skeletal Groups

There were only 5 groups to the walker (body, hip, thigh, calf, and foot) and so we had a separate section of code to read each one. There are 26 groups in the skeleton, which warrants a more flexible arrangement and referencing. One way to do this is with an index, which indicates the beginning of each group. The length of each group is the difference between the beginning of the group and the beginning of the next group. We can also assign an index to each group and use this to reference them. C will automatically assign indices:

```
enum{skull,mandible,cervneck,thorax,lclavicl,lscapula,
   lhumerus,llarm,lhand,rclavicl,rscapula,rhumerus,
   rlarm,rhand,pelvis,saclumbr,lfemur,lknee,llleg,
   lfoot,ltoes,rfemur,rknee,rlleg,rfoot,rtoes};
```

The model is stored in the following structure:

```
typedef struct{float x,y,z;}XYZ;
typedef struct{XYZ c,n,p,q,r;}TRI;
struct{int*i,n;TRI*t;}model;
```

203

The basic model is shown below in solid and wire frame:

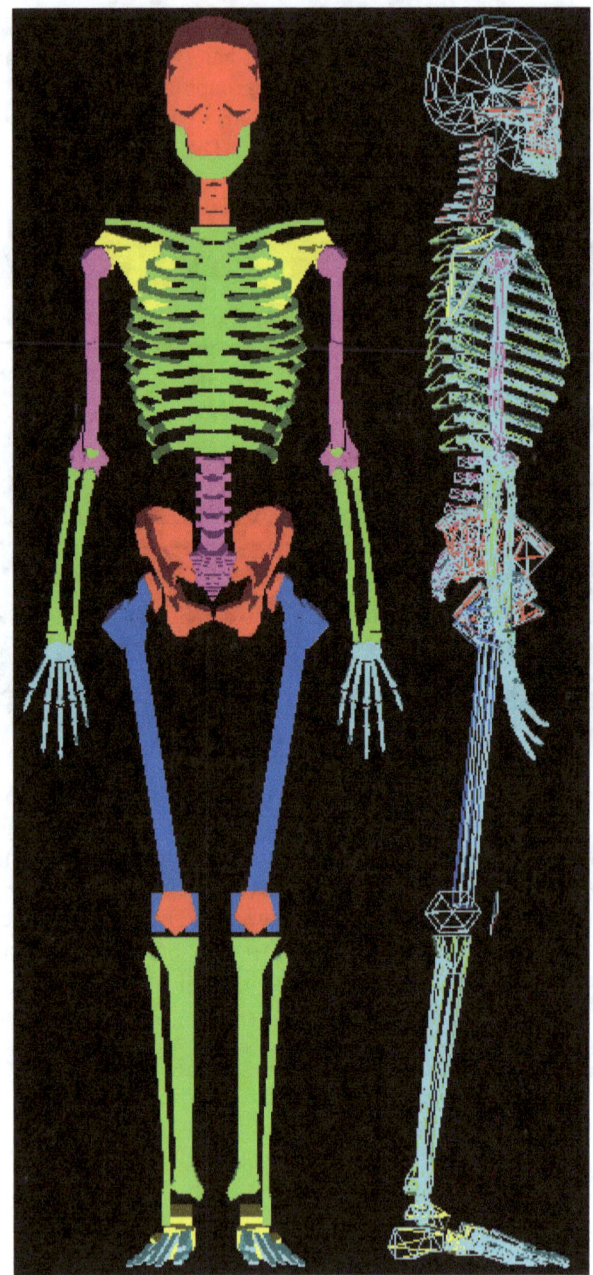

Figure 140. Basic Skeleton Model

The model is rendered by group, as shown below (before adding rotations for simplification):
```
void RenderSkeleton()
   {
   int g,n;
   float red[3]={1.F,0.F,0.F};
   float green[3]={0.F,1.F,0.F};
   TRI t;
   for(g=0;g<=rtoes;g++)
     {
     for(n=model.i[g];n<model.i[g+1];n++)
       {
       t=model.t[n];
       if(group<0)
         glMaterialfv(fill?GL_FRONT_AND_BACK:GL_FRONT,
           GL_AMBIENT_AND_DIFFUSE,(float*)&t.c);
       else if(g==group)
         glMaterialfv(fill?GL_FRONT_AND_BACK:GL_FRONT,
           GL_AMBIENT_AND_DIFFUSE,red);
       else
         glMaterialfv(fill?GL_FRONT_AND_BACK:GL_FRONT,
           GL_AMBIENT_AND_DIFFUSE,green);
       glBegin(GL_POLYGON);
       glNormal3f(t.n.x,t.n.y,t.n.z);
       glVertex3f(t.p.x,t.p.y,t.p.z);
       glVertex3f(t.q.x,t.q.y,t.q.z);
       glVertex3f(t.r.x,t.r.y,t.r.z);
       glEnd();
       }
     }
   }
```
Here we can color normally or make one group a different color (red) from all the rest (green). The group can be selected with a pair of hot keys:
```
if(wParam==PUSH_ALT_SPACE)
  {
  group--;
  if(group<-1)
    group=rtoes;
  glRepaint();
  return(TRUE);
  }
if(wParam==PUSH_CTL_SPACE)
  {
  group++;
  if(group>rtoes)
    group=-1;
  glRepaint();
  return(TRUE);
  }
```

The figure below shows the thorax red and the rest green:

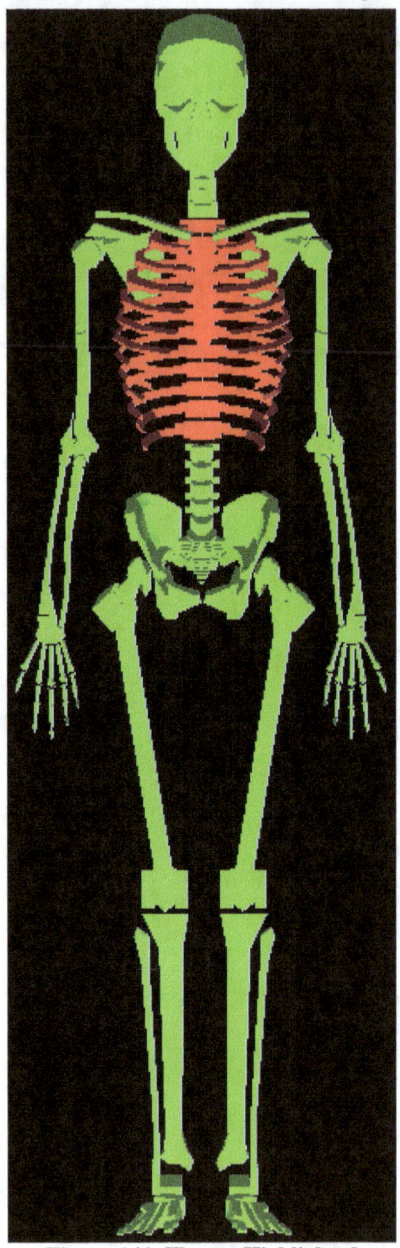

Figure 141. Thorax Highlighted

Simply hold down CTL or ALT and tap the spacebar to cycle through the groups. This illustrates how to add interactive features and also helps in formulating the articulation equations.

Shoulder Rotation

We assign the left and right shoulder rotations to hot keys alt-S and ctl-S, respectively .The shoulder vector is 25.35 in length at 91° making the corresponding adjustments:

```
if(g==lhumerus||g==llarm||g==lhand)
{
R=25.35;
A=91.;
dX=0.;
dY=( R*(sin((lShoulder-A)*PI/180)
 -sin(-A*PI/180)));
dZ=(-R*(cos((lShoulder-A)*PI/180)
 -cos(-A*PI/180)));
glTranslatef(dX,dY,dZ);
glRotatef(lShoulder,1.F,0.F,0.F);
}
if(g==rhumerus||g==rlarm||g==rhand)
{
R=25.35;
A=91.;
dX=0.;
dY=( R*(sin((rShoulder-A)*PI/180)
 -sin(-A*PI/180)));
dZ=(-R*(cos((rShoulder-A)*PI/180)
 -cos(-A*PI/180)));
glTranslatef(dX,dY,dZ);
glRotatef(rShoulder,1.F,0.F,0.F);
}
```

Note that we must apply these same adjustments to the lower arm and hand, as they are connected to the humerus.

Elbow Adjustments

In order to keep the elbow joint intact, we must adjust all of the groups attached to the humerus. The elbow vector is 11.8 in length and 93° making the corresponding adjustments:

```
if(g==llarm||g==lhand)
{
R=11.8;
A=93.;
dX=0.;
dY=( R*(sin((lElbow-A)*PI/180)-sin(-A*PI/180)));
dZ=(-R*(cos((lElbow-A)*PI/180)-cos(-A*PI/180)));
glTranslatef(dX,dY,dZ);
glRotatef(lElbow,1.F,0.F,0.F);
```

```
    }
    if(g==rlarm||g==rhand)
    {
    R=11.8;
    A=93.;
    dX=0.;
    dY=( R*(sin((rElbow-A)*PI/180)-sin(-A*PI/180)));
    dZ=(-R*(cos((rElbow-A)*PI/180)-cos(-A*PI/180)));
    glTranslatef(dX,dY,dZ);
    glRotatef(rElbow,1.F,0.F,0.F);
    }
```

Wrist Rotation

The wrist has two degrees of freedom and two rotation angles. We assign the left and right wrist rotations to hot keys alt-R and ctl-R, respectively .The wrist rotation vector is 10.5 in length at 85° making the corresponding adjustments:

```
    if(g==lhand)
    {
    R=10.5;
    A=85.;
    dX=(R*(sin((LWrist-A)*PI/180)
      -sin(-A*PI/180)));
    dY=0.F;
    dZ=(R*(cos((LWrist-A)*PI/180)
      -cos(-A*PI/180)));
    glTranslatef(dX,dY,dZ);
    glRotatef(LWrist,0.F,1.F,0.F);
    }
    if(g==rhand)
    {
    R=10.5;
    A=-85.;
    dX=(R*(sin((-RWrist-A)*PI/180)
      -sin(-A*PI/180)));
    dY=0.F;
    dZ=(R*(cos((-RWrist-A)*PI/180)
      -cos(-A*PI/180)));
    glTranslatef(dX,dY,dZ);
    glRotatef(-RWrist,0.F,1.F,0.F);
    }
```

We assign the left and right wrist flexing motions to hot keys alt-F and ctl-F, respectively.The wrist flex vector is 1.2 in length at 0° making the corresponding adjustments (same right and left):

```
            dY=-R*(sin((rWristF-A)*PI/180)-sin(-A*PI/180));
            dZ= R*(cos((rWristF-A)*PI/180)-cos(-A*PI/180));
            glTranslatef(0.F,dY,dZ);
            glRotatef(rWristF,1.F,0.F,0.F);
```

We can now position both arms and hands with combinations of ctl/alt SERF, as illustrated in this next figure:

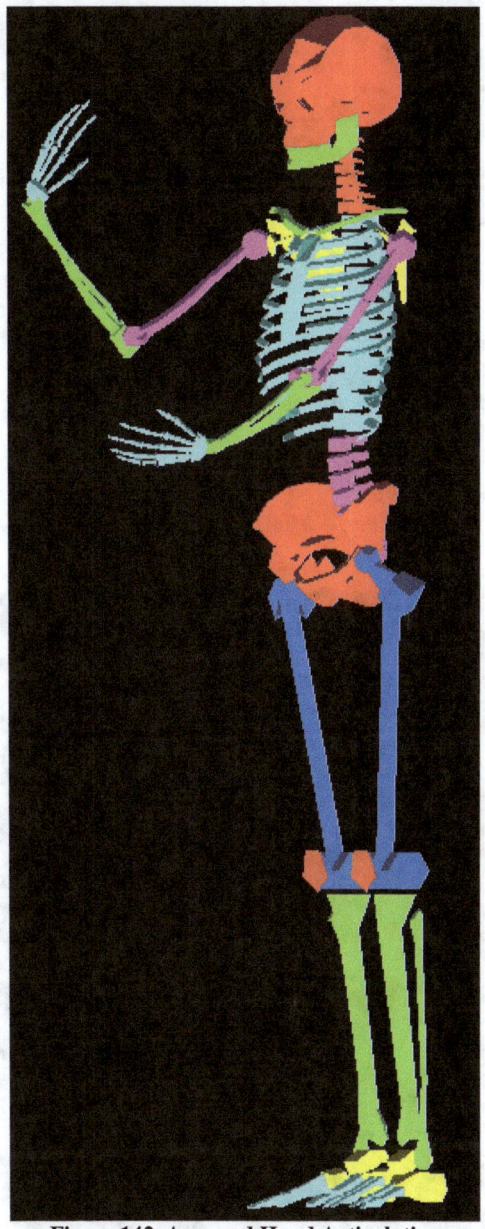

Figure 142. Arm and Hand Articulation

Jaw Motion

We will assign the alt-J hotkey to move the jaw. The radius in this case is 33.6 (see, for instance, the average Y coordinate in mandible.tri) and the angle is 90°, making the adjustments:

```
if(g==mandible)
  {
  R=33.6;
  A=90.;
  dY= R*(sin((Mandible-A)*PI/180)-sin(-A*PI/180));
  dZ=-R*(cos((Mandible-A)*PI/180)-cos(-A*PI/180));
  glTranslatef(0.F,dY,dZ);
  glRotatef(Mandible,1.F,0.F,0.F);
  }
```

We also limit the rotation from -45° to 0°:

```
if(wParam==PUSH_ALT_J)
  {
  Mandible-=5.F;
  if(Mandible<-44.F)
    Mandible=0.F;
  glRepaint();
  return(TRUE);
  }
```

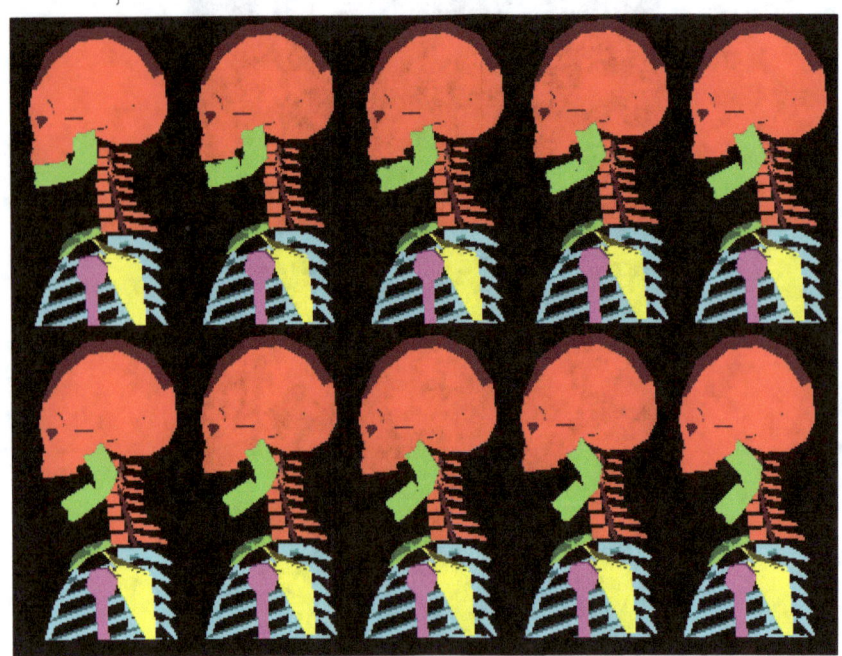

Figure 143. Jaw Rotation

Hip Rotation

We assign the hotkeys alt-H and ctl-H to the left and right hip rotation, respectively. The hip vector is 3.6 in length at 120° (see average X value of upper portion in lfemur.tri), making the adjustments:

```
if(g==lfemur||g==lpatella||g==lfibia||g==lfoot
   ||g==ltoes)
{
R=3.6;
A=120.;
dY=( R*(sin((lHip-A)*PI/180)-sin(-A*PI/180)));
dZ=(-R*(cos((lHip-A)*PI/180)-cos(-A*PI/180)));
glTranslatef(0.F,dY,dZ);
glRotatef(lHip,1.F,0.F,0.F);
}
if(g==rfemur||g==rpatella||g==rfibia||g==rfoot
   ||g==rtoes)
{
R=3.6;
A=120.;
dY=( R*(sin((rHip-A)*PI/180)-sin(-A*PI/180)));
dZ=(-R*(cos((rHip-A)*PI/180)-cos(-A*PI/180)));
glTranslatef(0.F,dY,dZ);
glRotatef(rHip,1.F,0.F,0.F);
}
```

We limit the hip rotation to -70° to +110°.

Knee Rotation

We assign the hotkeys alt-K and ctl-K to the left and right knee rotation, respectively. The knee vector is 20 in length at 20° (see average Y value of upper portion in llleg.tri), making the adjustments (same for left and right):

```
if(g==lfibia||g==lfoot||g==ltoes)
{
R=20.;
A=100.;
dY=(-R*(sin((-lKnee-A)*PI/180)-sin(-A*PI/180)));
dZ=( R*(cos((-lKnee-A)*PI/180)-cos(-A*PI/180)));
glTranslatef(0.F,dY,dZ);
glRotatef(-lKnee,1.F,0.F,0.F);
}
```

We limit the knee rotation to 0° to 120°.

Ankle Rotation

We assign the hotkeys alt-A and ctl-A to the left and right ankle rotation, respectively. The ankle vector is 38 in length at 97° (see average Y value of upper portion in llleg.tri), making the adjustments (same for left and right):

```
if(g==lfoot||g==ltoes)
{
```

```
R=38.;
A=97.;
dY=(-R*(sin((lAnkle-A)*PI/180)-sin(-A*PI/180)));
dZ=( R*(cos((lAnkle-A)*PI/180)-cos(-A*PI/180)));
glTranslatef(0.F,dY,dZ);
glRotatef(lAnkle,1.F,0.F,0.F);
}
```

We limit the ankle rotation to -60º to +40º. We can not pose the skeleton as desired using a combination of hot keys.

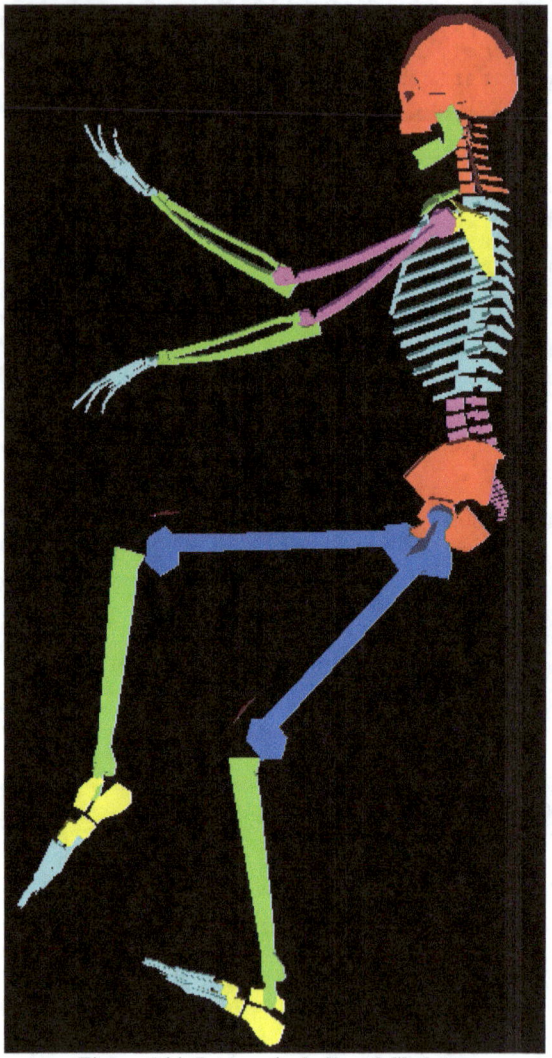

Figure 144. Interactively Posed Skeleton

Walking Motion

We can combine leg (and optionally arm) angles to approximate walking. While we could do something more elaborate, the same sort of algorithm used for the previous walker will do here.

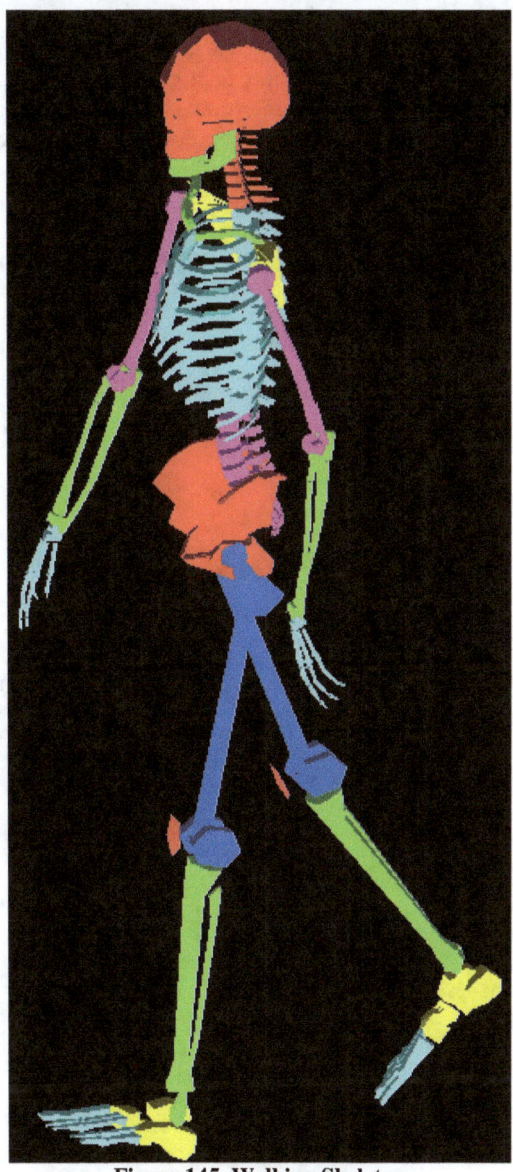

Figure 145. Walking Skeleton

Chapter 43. Rigid Wing Articulation

We will cover wing articulation in two steps: rigid and continuous. As hummingbird wings flex considerably less than all other birds, we will use a hummingbird for this first step. It was simple enough to distinguish between discrete parts of the previous models and identify these with different colors. We will be moving all the elements associated with the wings proportionately. It is more efficient to use nodes and elements than triangles, as the nodes appear in several elements. Displacing them before drawing makes more sense here than using OpenGL™ calls to perform this operation, as in the previous examples. The hummingbird model is read from humbird.3dv, which is located in the examples folder. A sample is listed below:

```
952 nodes
-0.00313818 -0.0117455 0.0049336
-0.00231971 -0.0114476 0.00516605
-0.00317203 -0.0121183 0.00493927
-0.00353294 -0.012288 0.00481474
-0.00252134 -0.0125129 0.00438231
-0.00354298 -0.0128829 0.00440458
etc.
1900 elements
500 502 501 RGB=0x8C8162
502 503 501 RGB=0xAB9D7B
502 504 503 RGB=0x928768
504 505 503 RGB=0xB09F82
506 505 504 RGB=0xB1A389
506 507 505 RGB=0xB2A48A
etc.
```

The model is read by the following code, which is similar to read3dv.c:

```
void ReadModel(char*fname)
  {
  char bufr[128],*ptr;
  int e,i,j,k,n;
  double x,y,z;
  FILE*fp;
  if((fp=fopen(fname,"rt"))==NULL)
    Abort(__LINE__,"can't open model file: %s",fname);
  if(!fgets(bufr,sizeof(bufr),fp))
    Abort(__LINE__,"unexpected end of file");
  if(sscanf(bufr,"%i",&nodes)!=1)
    Abort(__LINE__,"scan error on number of nodes");
  if(nodes<100)
    Abort(__LINE__,"expected at least 100 nodes but
    found %i",nodes);
  if((Node=calloc(nodes,sizeof(NODE)))==NULL)
    Abort(__LINE__,"can't allocate memory for nodes");
  for(i=0;i<nodes;i++)
    {
```

```c
      if(!fgets(bufr,sizeof(bufr),fp))
         Abort(__LINE__,"unexpected end of file");
      if(sscanf(bufr,"%lf%*[ ,\t]%lf%*[
,\t]%lf",&x,&y,&z)!=3)
         Abort(__LINE__,"scan error on x,y,z");
      Node[i].x=x;
      Node[i].y=y;
      Node[i].z=z;
      }
   if(!fgets(bufr,sizeof(bufr),fp))
      Abort(__LINE__,"unexpected end of file");
   if(sscanf(bufr,"%i",&elems)!=1)
      Abort(__LINE__,"scan error on number of elements");
   if(elems<100)
      Abort(__LINE__,"expected at least 100 elements but
      found %i",elems);
   if((Elem=calloc(elems,sizeof(ELEM)))==NULL)
      Abort(__LINE__,"can't allocate memory for
      elements");
   for(e=0;e<elems;e++)
      {
      if(!fgets(bufr,sizeof(bufr),fp))
         Abort(__LINE__,"unexpected end of file");
      if(sscanf(bufr,"%i%*[ ,\t]%i%*[
,\t]%i%n",&i,&j,&k,&n)!=3)
         Abort(__LINE__,"scan error on i,j,k");
      if(i<1||i>nodes)
         Abort(__LINE__,"no such node %i",i);
      if(j<1||j>nodes)
         Abort(__LINE__,"no such node %i",j);
      if(k<1||k>nodes)
         Abort(__LINE__,"no such node %i",k);
      Elem[e].i=i-1;
      Elem[e].j=j-1;
      Elem[e].k=k-1;
      ptr=bufr+n;
      while(strchr(" \t,",*ptr))
         ptr++;
      if(_memicmp(ptr,"rgb=",4)==0)
         ptr+=4;
      if(ptr[0]!='0'||ptr[1]!='x')
         Abort(__LINE__,"scan error on 0xRRGGBB following
      i,j,k");
      sscanf(ptr,"%i",&Elem[e].rgb);
      }
   fclose(fp);
   }
```

The GUI and associated procedures and objects are contained in humbird.c and humbird.rc and are similar to the codes for the walker and skeleton.

Figure 146. Hummingbird Windows® GUI

Figure 147. Hummingbird Wire Frame Elements

The hummingbird elements may also be viewed in the Excel spreadsheet humbird.xls, as shown below:

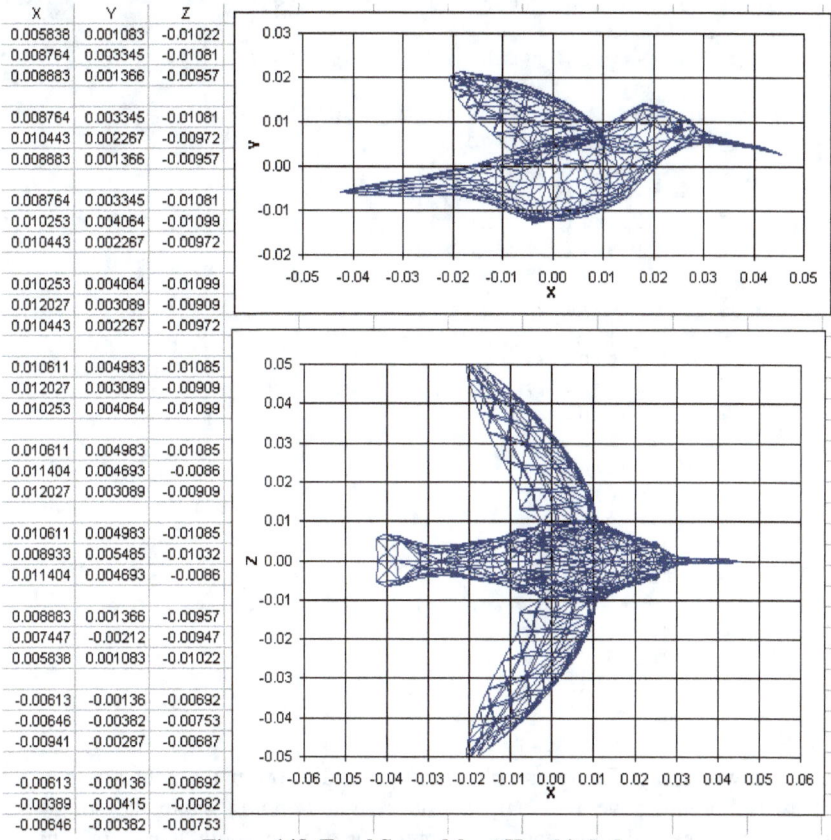

Figure 148. Excel Spreadsheet Humbird.xls

Here we see that the wings start at about z=±0.01 so that we can *flap* the wings by applying an increasing adjustment in y for z beyond this value. Each triangular element is drawn from the 3 nodes from the list along with the color for this particular element. In order to get the coloring, we must create an outward normal vector, which will change as the wings flap so that these must be recalculated at each step:

```
glBegin(GL_TRIANGLES);
s=2.5*sin(flap*M_PI/180.)-2.;
for(e=0;e<elems;e++)
  {
  i=Elem[e].i;
  j=Elem[e].j;
  k=Elem[e].k;
  n1=Node[i];
  n2=Node[j];
```

```
      n3=Node[k];
      if(fabs(n1.z)>0.01)
         n1.y+=0.375*(fabs(n1.z)-0.01)*s;
      if(fabs(n2.z)>0.01)
         n2.y+=0.375*(fabs(n2.z)-0.01)*s;
      if(fabs(n3.z)>0.01)
         n3.y+=0.375*(fabs(n3.z)-0.01)*s;
      glColor(Elem[e].rgb);
      P.x=(float)(n2.x-n1.x);
      P.y=(float)(n2.y-n1.y);
      P.z=(float)(n2.z-n1.z);
      Q.x=(float)(n3.x-n1.x);
      Q.y=(float)(n3.y-n1.y);
      Q.z=(float)(n3.z-n1.z);
      N=Normalize(CrossProduct(P,Q));
      x1=(float)n1.x;
      y1=(float)n1.y;
      z1=(float)n1.z;
      x2=(float)n2.x;
      y2=(float)n2.y;
      z2=(float)n2.z;
      x3=(float)n3.x;
      y3=(float)n3.y;
      z3=(float)n3.z;
      glNormal3f(N.x,N.y,N.z);
      glVertex3f(x1,y1,z1);
      glVertex3f(x2,y2,z2);
      glVertex3f(x3,y3,z3);
      }
   glEnd();
```

We will apply a more complex *flapping* and also *flex* the wings in the next chapter. For now, we will only consider rigid *flapping*. Note the somewhat bulky mixture of double and single precision floating-point numbers. This is unavoidable, for C presumes all floating-point numbers and constants to be doubles unless typed otherwise with a trailing F or (float) casting, while OpenGL™ assumes most floating-point numbers are single precision. This is a historical artifact because OpenGL™ was developed before Intel processors and the Windows® operating system became ubiquitous. Speed and storage were much greater concerns in the early days of OpenGL™. Intel FPUs (floating-point processing units) often process double precision reals faster than single precision ones and have an 80-bit native format. This was not true for other processors, especially those not having an FPU. I personally recall those days quite clearly and am glad to have left them behind. Three frames of the end result are shown in this next figure:

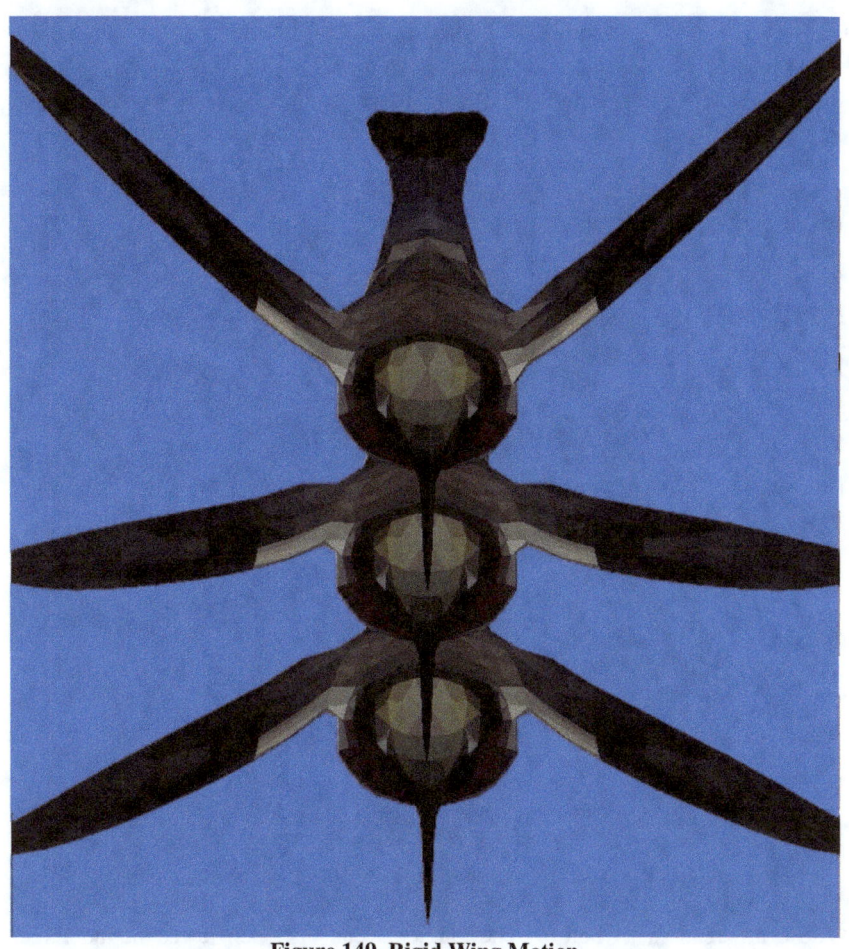

Figure 149. Rigid Wing Motion

Chapter 44. Flexed Wing Articulation

For this next step we will use a condor. As the hummingbird was fairly stubby, the wing stretching was not particularly noticeable. If we were to use the same formula with the condor, this would look unnatural. Therefore, we will bend (flex) the wings without stretching them. All of the associated files can be found in the examples\condor folder. The GUI is shown below:

Figure 150. Condor Windows® GUI

There were only 952 nodes and 1900 triangular elements in the humming bird model. The condor model consists of 5795 nodes and 11,664 elements. These are read in as before. The elements can also be viewed in the Excel spreadsheet condor.xls, which is shown on the next page. The wings extend outward from about $z > \pm 0.05$ and the tail, which we also want to flex, extends back from about $x < -0.15$. We can rigidly flap the tail with a simple motion, but the wings will be a little more complicated. We will not consider individual feathers until the next chapter.

Realistic wing flexing may be approximated by the deflection of a cantilever beam with distributed loading. The force of air is distributed over the wing, the wing is attached at the body, plus the bones are thicker toward the body and thinner toward the tips. Structural mechanics is beyond the scope of this text and so the reader is referred to the Web, where many resources, figures, and equations may be found. Such a beam is illustrated in this next figure:

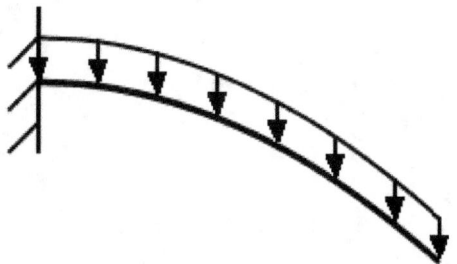

Figure 151. Uniformly Loaded Cantilever Beam

The deflection along any point, x, along the span of a uniformly loaded cantilever beam is given by the following expression:

$$\delta = \frac{wx^2}{24EI}\left(6L^2 - 4Lx + x^2\right) \quad (44.1)$$

where w is the loading (force per unit length), L is the length of the beam, E is the modulus of elasticity, and I is the area moment of inertia of the cross-section. The particulars are not important for our purposes, but we will utilize the parabolic shape: y=a+bx+cx².

In order to compensate for the stretching effect, we must calculate the arc length along the flexed wing. The calculus of arc lengths is also beyond the scope of this book. Length along an arc or curve is given by the following expression:

$$s = \int_p^q \sqrt{1 + \left(\frac{dy}{dx}\right)^2}\, dx \quad (44.2)$$

For our parabola dy/dx=b+2cx so that:

$$s = \int_p^q \sqrt{1 + (b + 2cx)^2}\, dx \quad (44.3)$$

This expression can be analytically integrated to yield:

$$s = \frac{2\alpha cq + \alpha b + \gamma - 2\beta cp - \beta b - \ln 2 - \ln(2cp + b + \beta)}{4c} \quad (44.4)$$

$$\alpha = \sqrt{1 + b^2 + 4bcq + 4c^2 q^2} \quad (44.5)$$

$$\beta = \sqrt{1 + b^2 + 4bcq + 4c^2 p^2} \quad (44.6)$$

$$\gamma = \ln(4cq + 2b + 2r) \quad (44.7)$$

Calculation of the arc length along a curve is illustrated in the Excel spreadsheet arc_length_calculus.xls in the equations folder of the online archive. A typical curve and associated calculations are shown below:

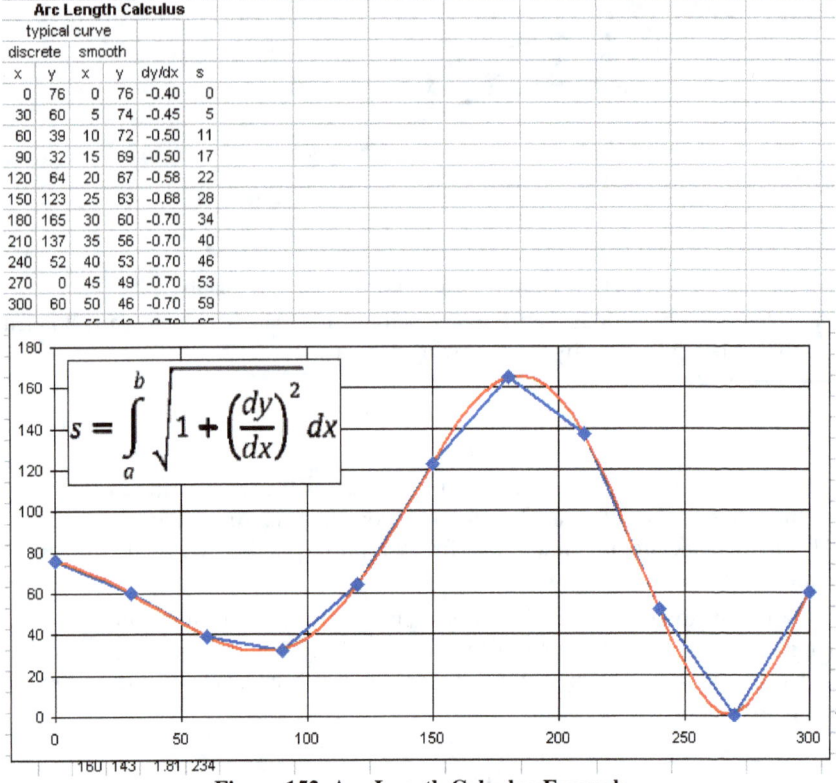

Figure 152. Arc Length Calculus Example

As the centerline of the condor model lies along y=z=0, the wing length plus body radius is effectively equal to:

$$L_W = \sqrt{y^2 + z^2} \qquad (44.8)$$

We can, therefore, simply adjust both coordinates (y and z) of each wing node by the ratio of the length before and after adjustment using the hypot() math function:

```
if(fabs(n1.z)>0.05&&n1.x>-0.155)
  {
  a=hypot(n1.y,n1.z);
  dz=fabs(n1.z)-0.05;
  b=0.375*(9.*s-3.);
  c=b/2.;
  dy=(b+c*dz)*dz;
  n1.y+=dy;
  r=hypot(n1.y,n1.z);
  n1.y*=a/r;
  n1.z*=a/r;
  }
```

The end result is shown in this next figure:

Figure 153. Flexed Wing Articulation

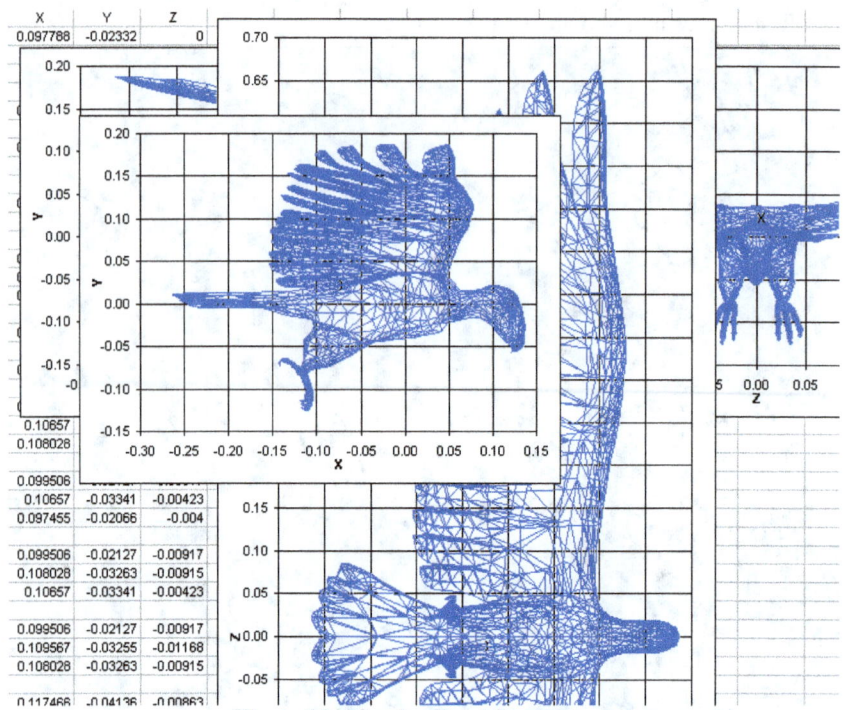

Figure 154. Condor Excel Spreadsheet

Chapter 45. Undulating Articulation

Before we get into finer objects such as hair, we will consider waving motion that is more complex than the basically one-dimensional wing flapping. To introduce this next topic, we begin with the TWAVE demo from the original OpenGL™ SDK. The associated files can be found on the Web. A cleaned-up version is provided in the examples\twave folder. This code eliminates superfluous items, uses standard variable types, and specifically targets the Windows® operating system. It can also be compiled without error using Visual Studio, which is a requirement for all of the code discussed in this text. The result is:

Figure 155. TWAVE OpenGL™ Demo

There are several waving flag demos available on the Web. Another is provided here in the examples\flag folder, which is built upon the program structure of the hummingbird and condor examples with elements from the TWAVE demo.

The Windows® GUI deploying the simplest undulation in the y and z directions is shown in this next figure:

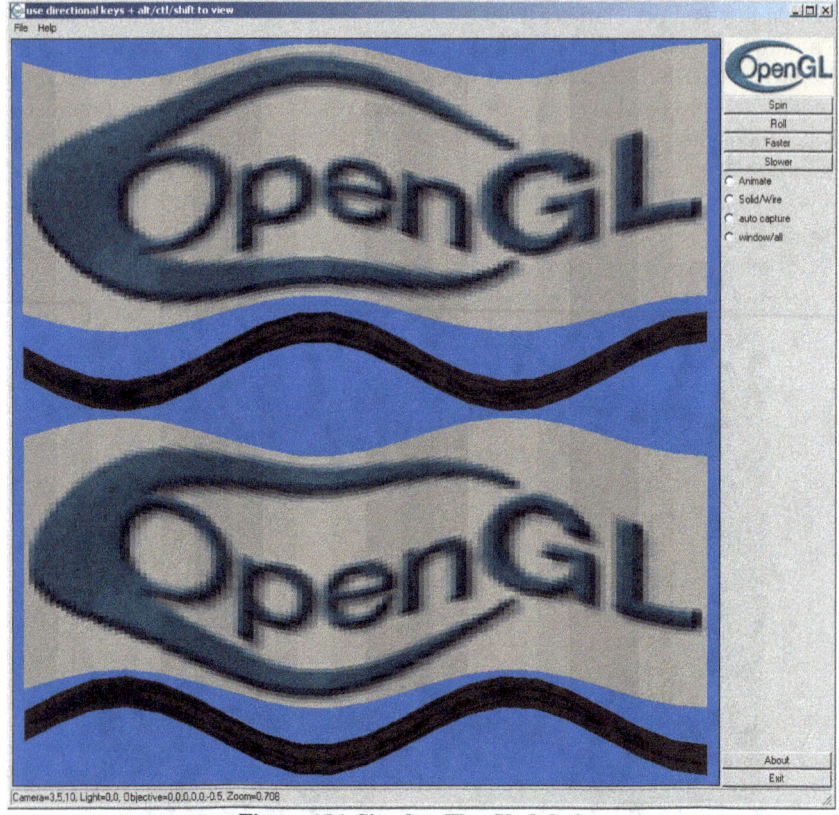

Figure 156. Simplest Flag Undulation

We also incorporate a texture (the OpenGL™ flag) in this example (also see Appendix C for more on textures). In order to achieve a more natural coloration of filaments (such as hair or fur), we will need to apply a texture.

Chapter 46. Modeling Hair

On our path to create realistic hair or fur, we begin with a few discrete hairs. The general effect we're reaching for is illustrated in this first figure:

Figure 157. Conceptualized Discrete Hairs

Actual individual hairs look like this:

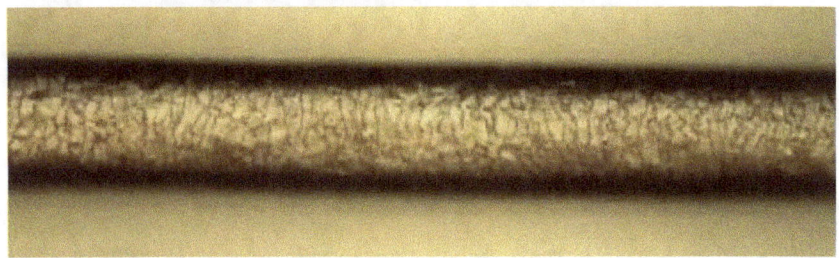

Figure 158. Individual Hair

Our model hairs will be elongated cones, which may bend along the centerline. A curved, shrinking ring of quadrangles (i.e., a *tube*) will form each hair. These are generated in the same way that the cylindrical flagpole and spherical knob were added to the example in the preceding chapter. The x and y location along with the radius are provided as a array. The number of sections along each tube is determined by the number of xyr triads. The code is listed below:

```c
#define X(i) XYR[3*(i)]
#define Y(i) XYR[3*(i)+1]
#define R(i) XYR[3*(i)+2]
void RenderTube(double*XYR,int L,int M)
  {
  int i,j,l,m;
  double A,B,*cosA,*cosB,Rm,Rx,*sinA,*sinB,Xm,Xx,Ym,Yx;
  VECTOR*N,*V;
  if(L<3)
    return;
  if(M<3)
    return;
  Rm=Rx=R(0);
  Xm=Xx=X(0);
  Ym=Yx=Y(0);
  for(l=1;l<L;l++)
     {
     if(R(l)<Rm)
        Rm=R(l);
     if(R(l)>Rx)
        Rx=R(l);
     if(X(l)<Xm)
        Xm=X(l);
     if(X(l)>Xx)
        Xx=X(l);
     if(Y(l)<Ym)
        Ym=Y(l);
     if(Y(l)>Yx)
        Yx=Y(l);
     }
  if(Rm>=Rx)
    return;
  if(Xm>=Xx)
    return;
  if(Ym>=Yx)
    return;
  cosA=calloc(L,sizeof(double));
  sinA=calloc(L,sizeof(double));
  for(l=0;l<L;l++)
     {
     i=max(0,l-1);
     j=min(L-1,l+1);
     A=atan2(X(i)-X(j),Y(j)-Y(i));
     cosA[l]=cos(A);
     sinA[l]=sin(A);
     }
  cosB=calloc(M,sizeof(double));
  sinB=calloc(M,sizeof(double));
  for(m=0;m<M;m++)
     {
```

```
      B=m*2.*M_PI/M;
      cosB[m]=cos(B);
      sinB[m]=sin(B);
      }
   N=calloc(L*M,sizeof(VECTOR));
   V=calloc(L*M,sizeof(VECTOR));
   for(i=l=0;l<L;l++)
      {
      for(m=0;m<M;m++,i++)
         {
         N[i].x=(float)(cosB[m]*cosA[l]);
         N[i].y=(float)(cosB[m]*sinA[l]);
         N[i].z=(float)(sinB[m]);
         V[i].x=(float)(X(l)+R(l)*N[i].x);
         V[i].y=(float)(Y(l)+R(l)*N[i].y);
         V[i].z=(float)(     R(l)*N[i].z);
         }
      }
   for(l=0;l<L-1;l++)
      {
      glBegin(GL_QUAD_STRIP);
      for(m=0;m<=M;m++)
         {
         i=M*l+m%M;
         j=M*(l+1)+m%M;
         glNormal3d(N[i].x,N[i].y,N[i].z);
         glVertex3d(V[i].x,V[i].y,V[i].z);
         glNormal3d(N[j].x,N[j].y,N[j].z);
         glVertex3d(V[j].x,V[j].y,V[j].z);
         }
      glEnd();
      }
   free(V);
   free(N);
   free(cosA);
   free(sinA);
   free(cosB);
   free(sinB);
   }
#undef R
#undef Y
#undef X
```

We begin with 400 brown hairs evenly spaced over a pink patch of appropriate size with a light blue background. The *scalp* has a slight curvature and extends slightly beyond the hairs. The files can be found in folder examples\hair.

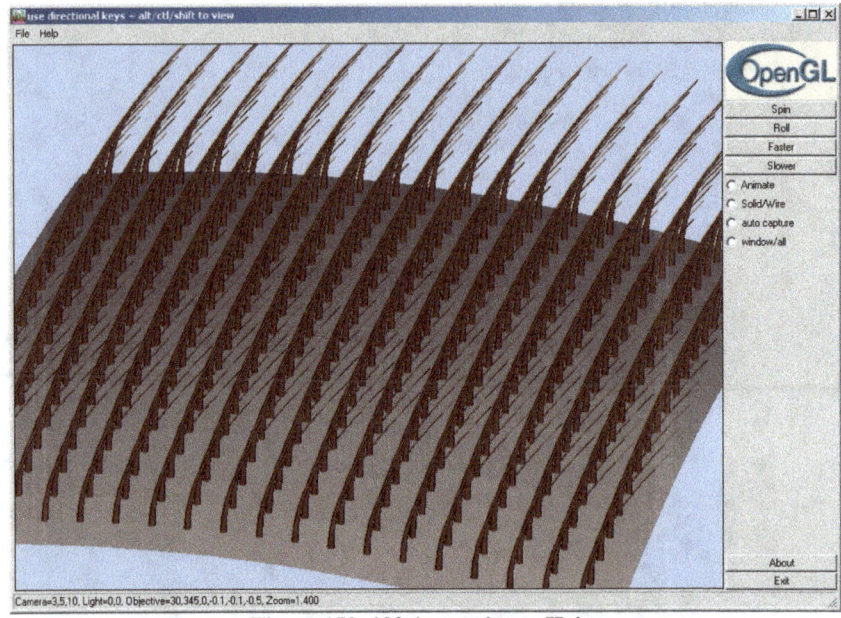
Figure 159. 100 Approximate Hairs

Next, we need a minimal head model with scalp elements identified.

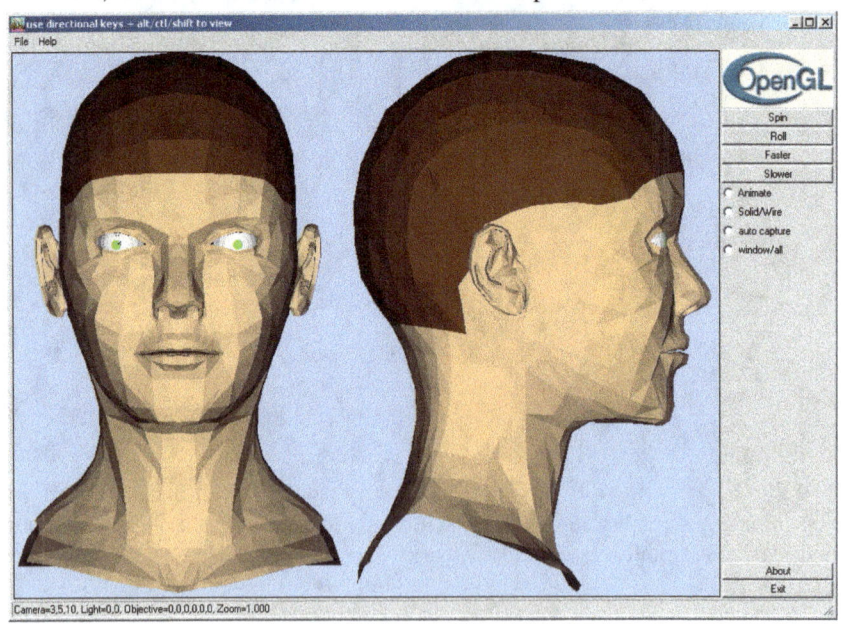
Figure 160. Minimal Head Model

This generic woman and also a generic man head can be found in the models folder of the online archive. We now want to attach one or more hairs to each of the triangular scalp elements. This is what one hair per element sticking upward looks like:

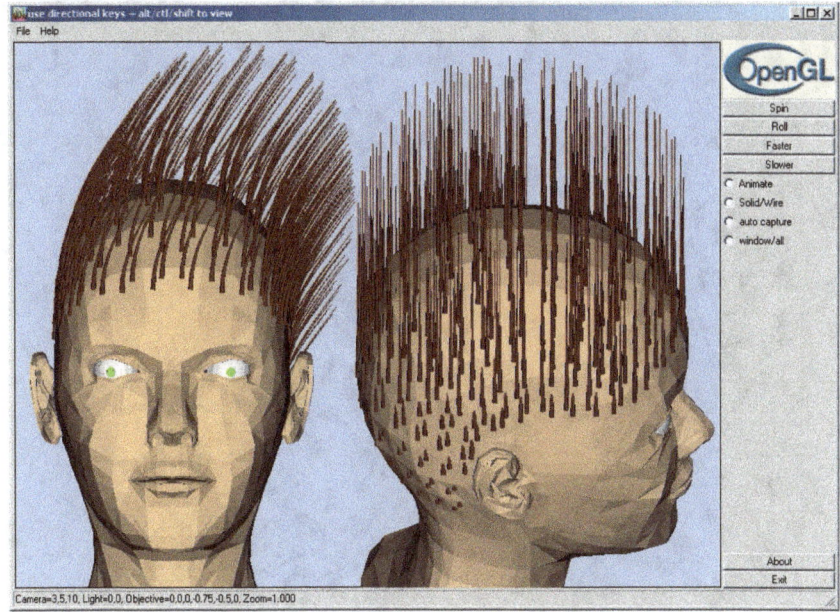

Figure 161. Without Localized Direction

Getting the direction (and eventually curvature) of the hairs will take more effort, as we shall see. Rendering spiked hair is quite simple,

```
void RenderHair(double u,double v,double w,double
   s,double x,double y,double z)
{
glLineWidth(5.F);
glBegin(GL_LINES);
glVertex3d(x,y,z);
glVertex3d((float)(x+0.5*s*u),(float)(y+0.5*s*v),
   (float)(z+0.5*s*w));
glEnd();
}
```

We are already calculating the outward normals, as these must be used for lighting. This gives us the initial direction of the hairs. We can use these to render spiked hairs sticking out in all directions, as shown in this next figure:

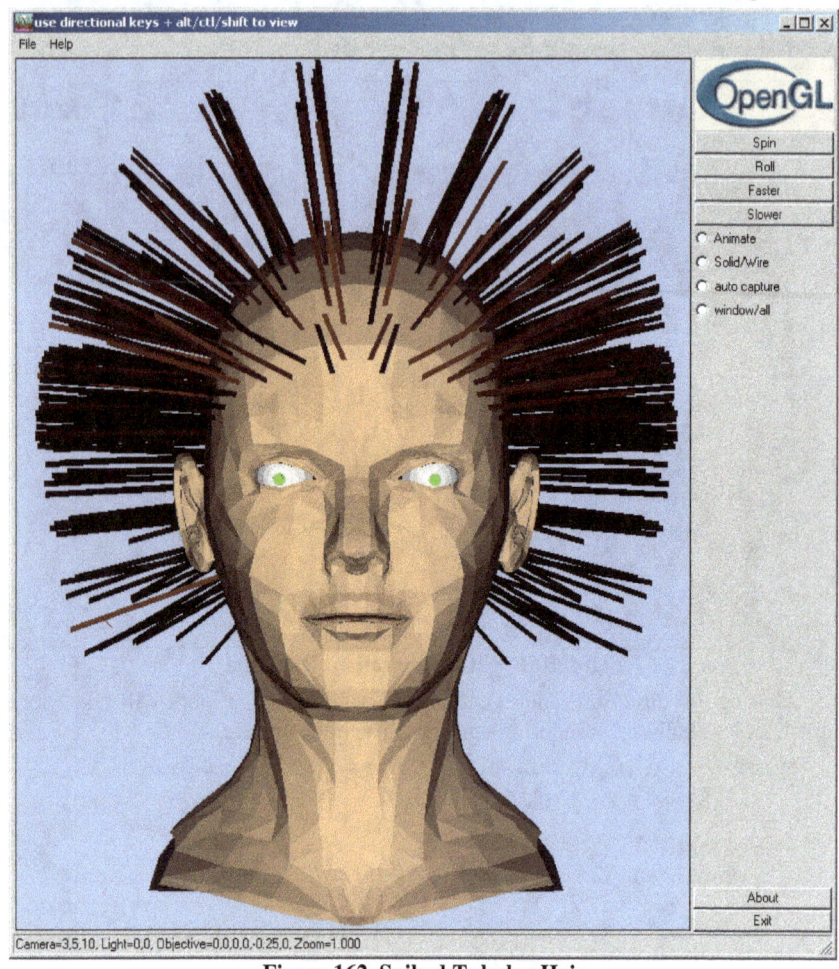

Figure 162. Spiked Tubular Hair

We can add a downward (or upward) gravity-like effect by arcing toward -y (down or +y up) proportional to the distance along the hair, s^2.

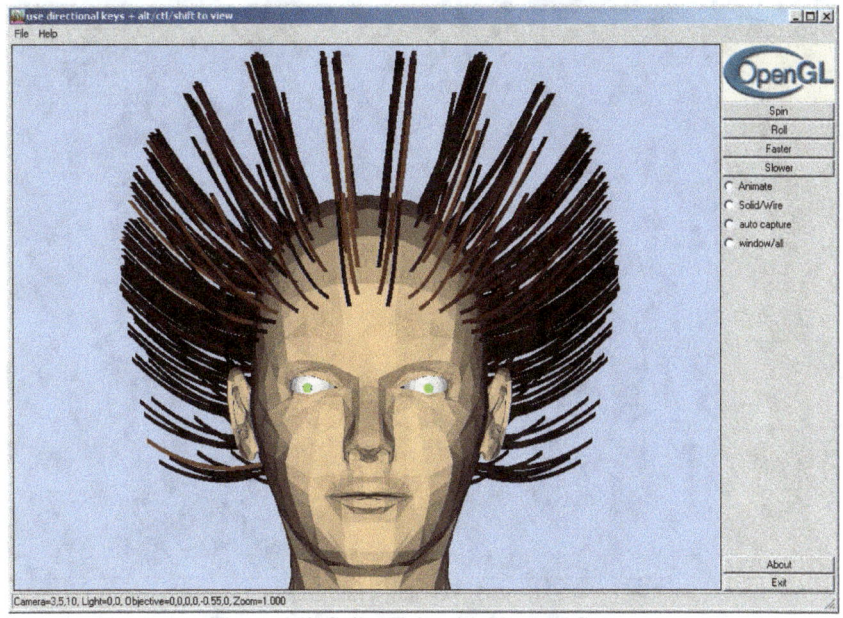

Figure 163. Spike Hair with Upward Sweep

We ultimately want to draw tapered tubes rather than simple lines (see Figures 42 and 44). Not only would these provide proper lighting effects but also textures. Rotation of each hair using calls to glRotatesf() so as to obtain the proper curvature is more problematic than it might seem. It is more effective to extrude each hair along a curved path line, as with the teapot spout and handle.

Figure 164. Classic OpenGL™ Teapot

Details of the tapered tubular hairs are shown in this next figure:

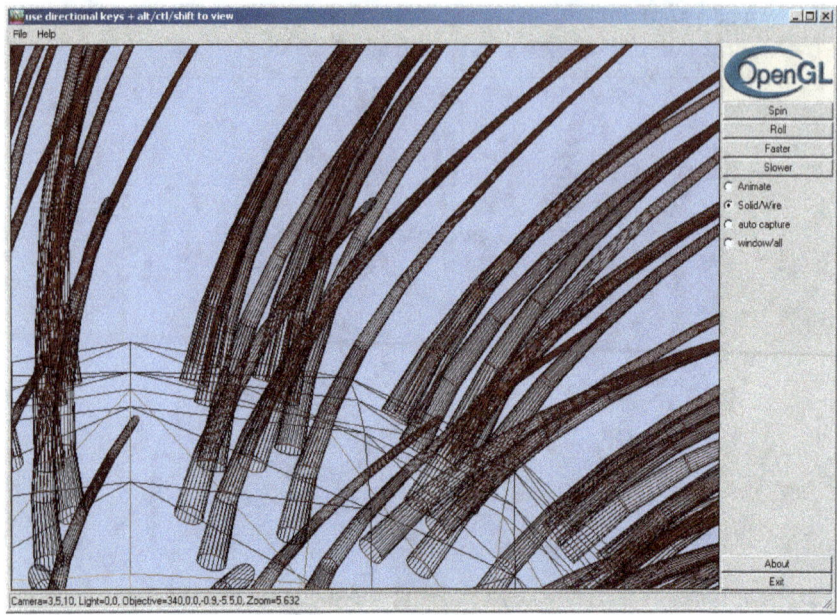

Figure 165. Tubular Hair Detail

The math we need is the same as the 3D coil demo built into TP2:

Figure 166. 3D Coil

Each ring in the coil lies in a plane perpendicular to the centerline. More specifically, these planes are defined by two orthogonal vectors, **u** and **v**. The cross product of these two vectors (**u**×**v**=**s**) lies along the centerline of the coil. If s is the parametric centerline and t is the distance along the centerline, then the vector **s** is given by:

$$\vec{s} = \begin{matrix} \dfrac{dx}{dt}\hat{i} \\ \dfrac{dy}{dt}\hat{j} \\ \dfrac{dz}{dt}\hat{k} \end{matrix} \qquad (46.1)$$

If the vectors **u** and **v** are normalized and φ is the angle around the centerline, then a circle of radius r in the perpendicular plane at the point (x,y,z) is given by:

$$\begin{aligned} x + r\left(u_x \cos\varphi + v_y \sin\varphi\right)\hat{i} \\ y + r\left(u_y \cos\varphi + v_y \sin\varphi\right)\hat{j} \\ z + r\left(u_z \cos\varphi + v_z \sin\varphi\right)\hat{k} \end{aligned} \qquad (46.2)$$

The angle in the xy plane, θ, is given by:

$$\tan\theta = -\frac{\left(\dfrac{dx}{dt}\right)}{\left(\dfrac{dy}{dt}\right)} \qquad (46.3)$$

If we require **u** to be in the xy plane, we have:

$$\begin{aligned} u_x &= \sin\theta \\ u_y &= \cos\theta \\ u_z &= 0 \end{aligned} \qquad (46.4)$$

As **u** and **v** are perpendicular, their dot product is equal to zero:

$$u_x v_x + u_y v_y + u_z v_z = 0 \qquad (46.5)$$

Combining these relationships yields the second vector, **v**:

$$v_x = -\frac{dz}{dt}\cos\theta$$

$$v_y = \frac{dz}{dt}\sin\theta \tag{46.6}$$

$$v_z = \begin{cases} \dfrac{dx}{dt}\dfrac{1}{\cos\theta} \\ \dfrac{dy}{dt}\dfrac{-1}{\sin\theta} \end{cases}$$

With these equations, we can now draw a tapering *tube* beginning at a given point arbitrarily meandering in three dimensions. There is also a small program (coil.c) in the models folder that creates a single tube and illustrates the mathematics in a minimal context. The complex *tube* is rendered with the following code that first calculates the position of all the nodes, then rolls them out as quad strips for each section along the centerline. The outward normals are calculated for each section of the quad strip as it's being added.

```
typedef struct{float r,t,x,y,z;}RTXYZ;
void RenderComplexTube(RTXYZ*rtxyz,int n,int m)
    {
    int i,i1,i2,i3,j,k;
    float a,c,dxdt,dydt,dzdt,phi,s,theta;
    VECTOR p,u,v,*w;
    w=calloc(n*m,sizeof(VECTOR));
    for(k=i=0;i<n;i++)
       {
       if(i==0)
          {
          i1=i;
          i2=i+1;
          }
       else if(i==n-1)
          {
          i1=n-2;
          i2=n-1;
          }
       else
          {
          i1=i-1;
          i2=i+1;
          }
       dxdt=(rtxyz[i2].x-rtxyz[i1].x)/
          (rtxyz[i2].t-rtxyz[i1].t);
       dydt=(rtxyz[i2].y-rtxyz[i1].y)/
          (rtxyz[i2].t-rtxyz[i1].t);
       dzdt=(rtxyz[i2].z-rtxyz[i1].z)/
          (rtxyz[i2].t-rtxyz[i1].t);
```

```
    theta=(float)(-atan2(dydt,dxdt));
    phi=(float)atan2(hypot(dxdt,dydt),dzdt);
    u.x=(float)sin(theta);
    u.y=(float)cos(theta);
    u.z=0.F;
    if(fabs(cos(theta))>fabs(sin(theta)))
        v.z=(float)(dxdt/cos(theta));
    else
        v.z=(float)(-dydt/sin(theta));
    v.x=(float)(-dzdt*cos(theta));
    v.y=(float)(dzdt*sin(theta));
    a=(float)sqrt(v.x*v.x+v.y*v.y+v.z*v.z);
    v.x/=a;
    v.y/=a;
    v.z/=a;
    for(j=0;j<m;j++,k++)
       {
       c=(float)cos(j*2.*M_PI/m);
       s=(float)sin(j*2.*M_PI/m);
       w[k].x=(float)(rtxyz[i].x
          +rtxyz[i].r*(s*u.x+c*v.x));
       w[k].y=(float)(rtxyz[i].y
          +rtxyz[i].r*(s*u.y+c*v.y));
       w[k].z=(float)(rtxyz[i].z
          +rtxyz[i].r*(s*u.z+c*v.z));
       }
    }
for(i=0;i<n-1;i++)
   {
   glBegin(GL_QUAD_STRIP);
   for(j=0;j<=m;j++)
      {
      i1=m*i+(j%m);
      i2=m*(i+1)+(j%m);
      i3=m*(i+1)+((j+1)%m);
      u.x=w[i2].x-w[i1].x;
      u.y=w[i2].y-w[i1].y;
      u.z=w[i2].z-w[i1].z;
      v.x=w[i3].x-w[i1].x;
      v.y=w[i3].y-w[i1].y;
      v.z=w[i3].z-w[i1].z;
      p=Normalize(CrossProduct(u,v));
      glNormal3d(p.x,p.y,p.z);
      glVertex3f(w[i1].x,w[i1].y,w[i1].z);
      glVertex3f(w[i2].x,w[i2].y,w[i2].z);
      }
   glEnd();
   }
free(w);
}
```

The end result is shown in this next figure, which has the hair shape from Figure 44 and the curvature from Figure 46:

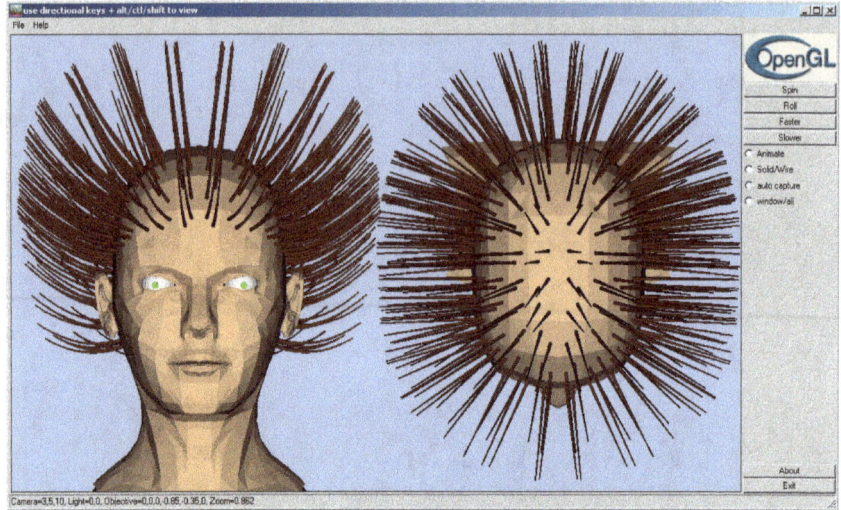

Figure 167. Complex Tube Hairs

The complex hair is then reduced to the following brief code:

```
void RenderComplexHair(double u,double v,double w,double
    s,double x,double y,double z)
  {
  int i,n;
  double g,l,r;
  RTXYZ rtxyz[11];
  l=0.5*s;
  g=hypot(u,w)*l/2.;
  n=sizeof(rtxyz)/sizeof(RTXYZ);
  r=0.01;
  for(i=0;i<n;i++)
     {
     rtxyz[i].t=(float)(i/(n-1.));
     rtxyz[i].r=(float)(r);
     rtxyz[i].x=(float)(x+i*u*l/(n-1));
     rtxyz[i].y=(float)(y+i*v*l/(n-1)+i*i*g/(n-1)/(n-1));
     rtxyz[i].z=(float)(z+i*w*l/(n-1));
     r*=0.9;
     }
  RenderComplexTube(rtxyz,n,16);
  }
```

The next step toward realism is adding more thinner hairs. We first increase from one to three per scalp element and divide the diameter by two. The end result, which is starting to look a little more reasonable, is shown below:

238

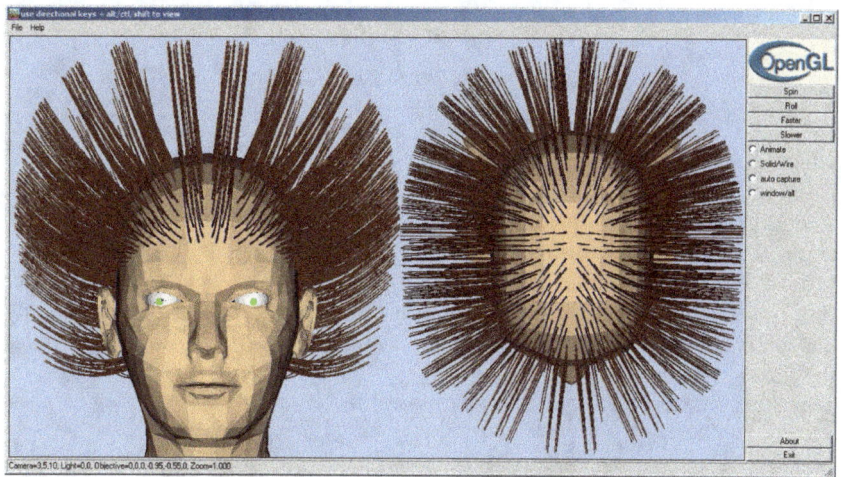

Figure 168. Three Complex Tube Hairs per Element

Next 7 hairs and one-fourth the diameter…

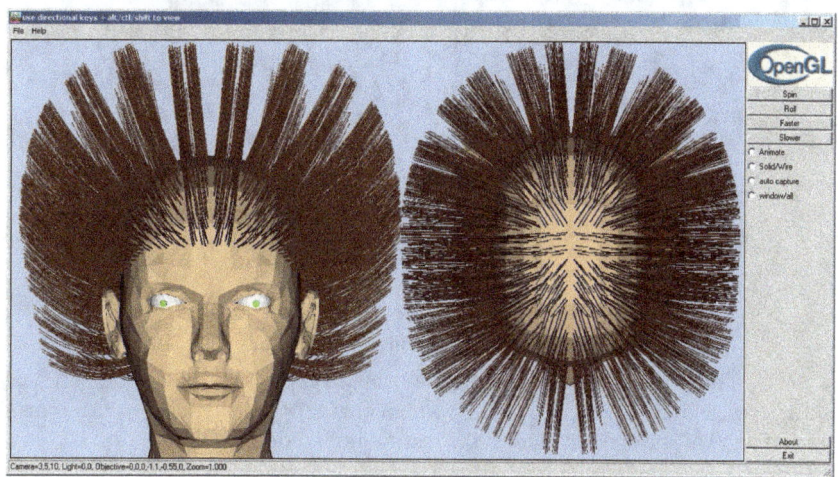

Figure 169. Seven Complex Tube Hairs per Element

These would be more realistic were they somewhat randomly spaced. We will eventually get there after considering various motions and color effects. At this level of detail, the rendering time is from one to two seconds, depending on the processor. While real-time animation has been practical up until this point with the other examples, it is not practical at this level of detail. That is why we have built in the capability of *auto capture* to store sequential frames as individual files that can be combined to create an animated GIF.

The number of hairs per elements should be proportional to the area. The area of a triangle in 3D is given by Heron's formula:

$$a = \sqrt{s(s-a)(s-b)(s-c)}$$
$$s = \frac{a+b+c}{2}$$
(46.7)

where a, b, c are the lengths of the three sides. The side lengths are calculated using the Pythagorean theorem. The average area per scalp element is 0.00643. The largest is 0.01541, about 2.4 times the average. The smallest is 0.00178, about 0.28 times the average. Evenly spacing our previous density would be about 2 hairs in the smallest element and 17 in the largest or about one hair per 0.001 area unit. Increasing from an average of 7 to 21, spacing these randomly and proportional to element area, yields a slightly better result but also triples the time to render.

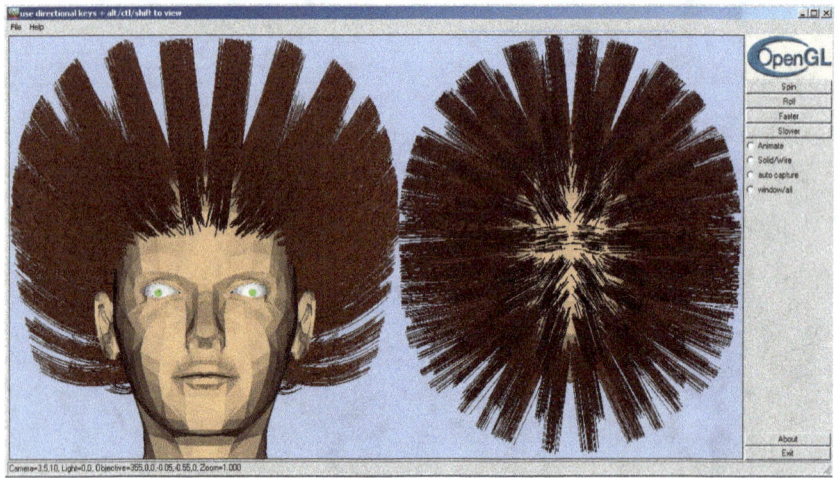

Figure 170. Twenty-One Randomly Spaced Hairs per Element

We are approaching a minimal acceptable density. We can still see clumping. Adding a random x and z component to the gravity term will diminish this effect. This next figure shows the addition of random x and y.

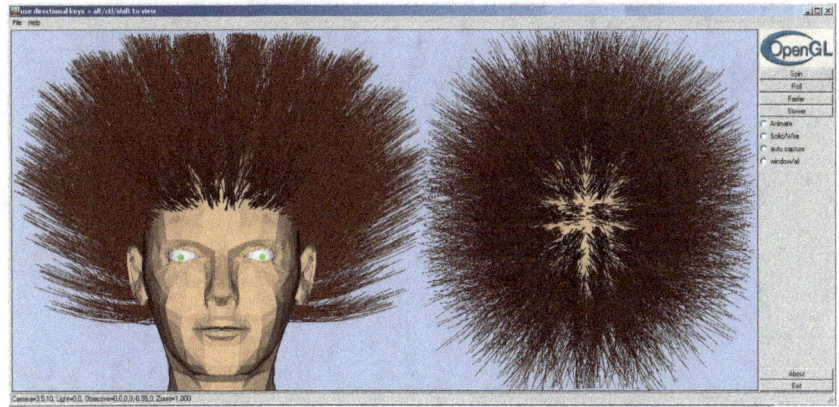

Figure 171. Twenty-One Randomly Spaced Hairs with Random XY

We still need at least three times greater density and also random lengths. With this step we achieve a somewhat realistic frizz.

Figure 172. Sixty-Three Average Hairs per Element with Random XYL

The rendering time is now six to twelve seconds and so we now introduce delayed painting. This was covered in the two previous texts in this series. Basically, we draw some of the elements and set a flag. We also add another timer. When this timer is called, if the current rendering is complete and the flag is set, then all of the elements are redrawn and the flag is reset.

The temporary rendering pending a full repaint is shown in this next figure:

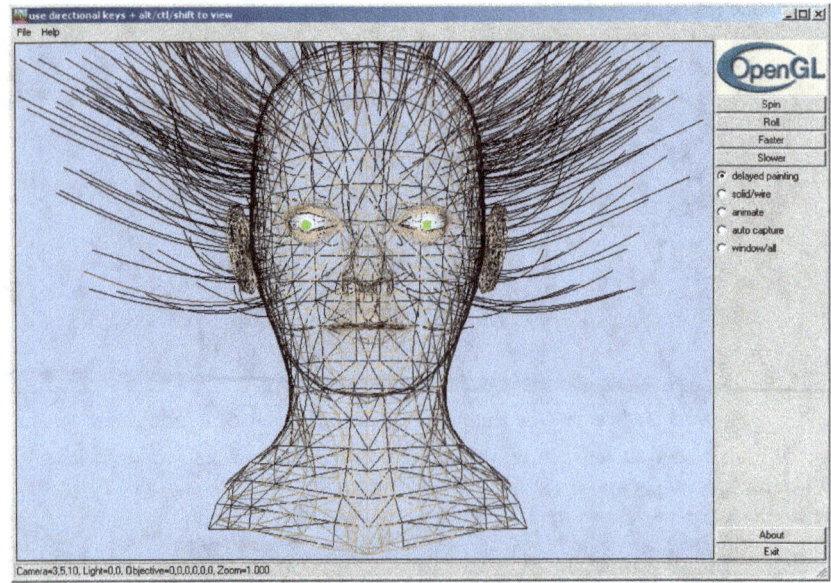

Figure 173. Partial Rendering with Pending Repaint

We next want to replace the frizz with down swept hair. This means the top hairs must be displaced laterally (in ±x) and into the screen (-z) so that they don't fall back into the head. We also want to deploy normal gravity (-y).

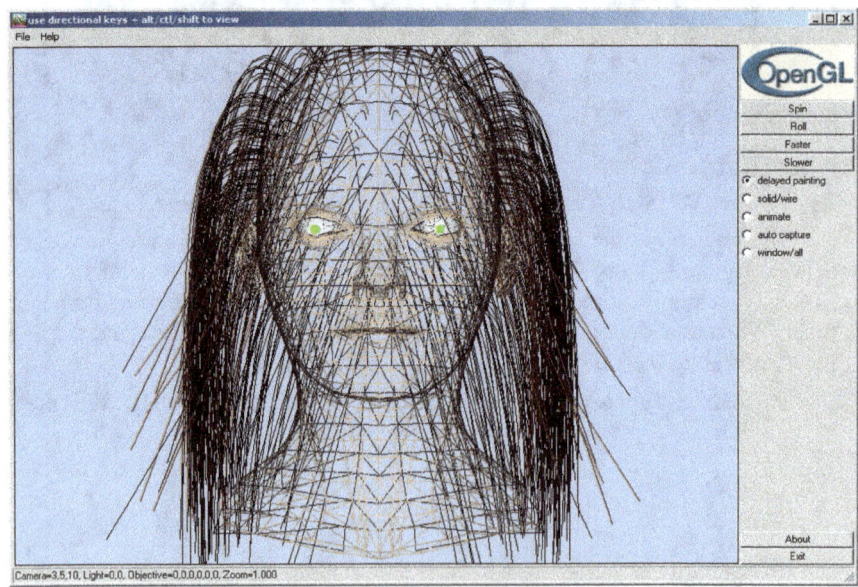

Figure 174. Partial Rendering with Downward Gravity

While this next full rendering won't make the cover of *Vogue*, it is a reasonable approximation of hair.

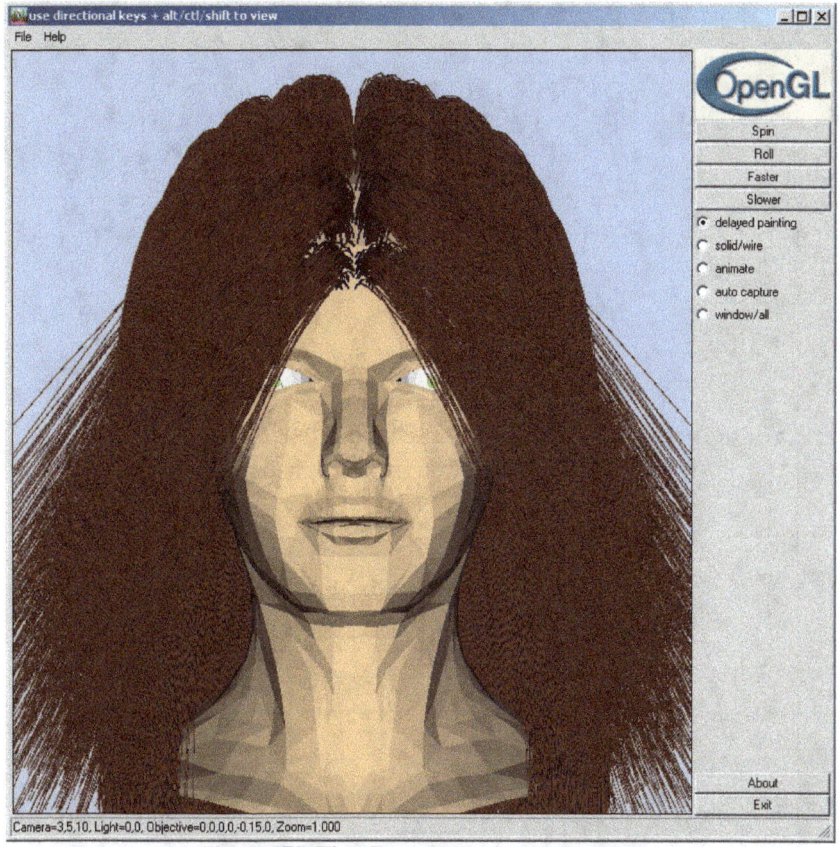

Figure 175. First Reasonable Approximation

The hairs must randomly *jittered* along the part to make it less pronounced. This can be accomplished by adding small random adjustments to each component of the normal vector.

```
if(hypot(x,z)<0.1)
  {
  u+=xrand()/10.;
  v+=xrand()/10.;
  w+=xrand()/10.;
  }
```

Another way to control the path of the hairs from the scalp out would be to define a *hoop* and use this as a sort of *target*. Such a hoop is shown in the next two figures.

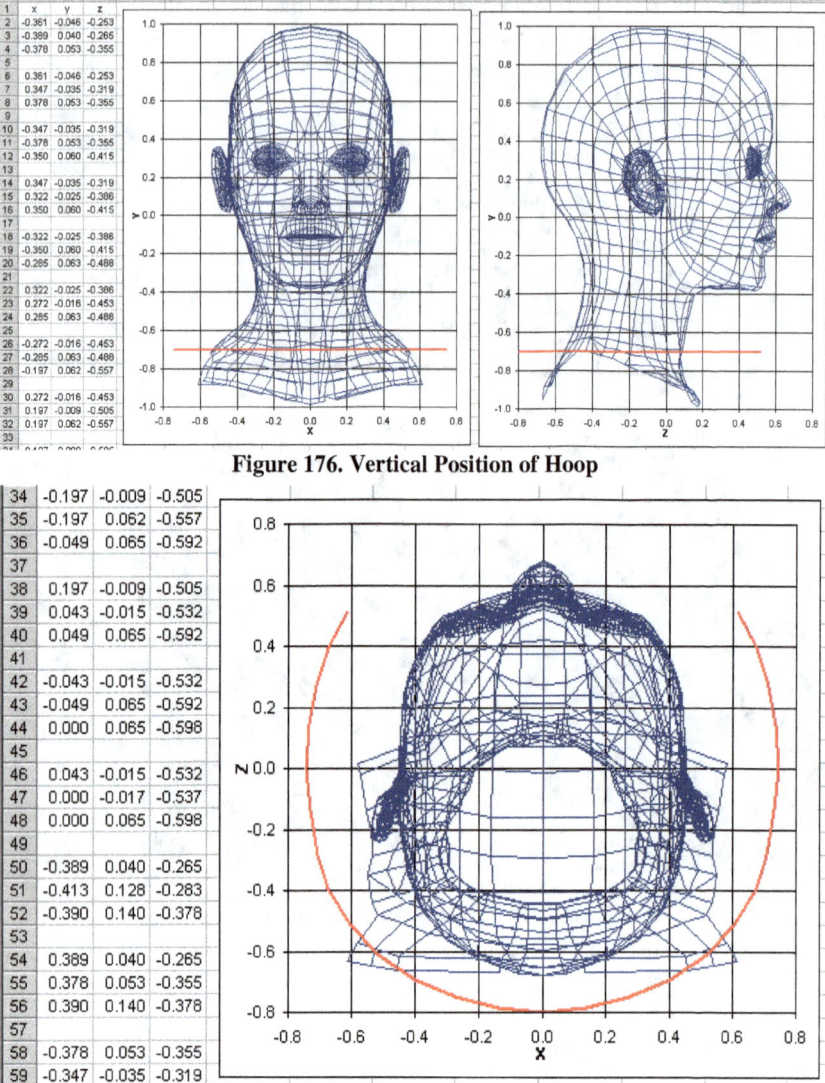

Figure 176. Vertical Position of Hoop

Figure 177. Hoop in the X-Z Plane

We can pick the closest point on the hoop and bend the hair toward it. To add realism, we can also jitter the destination in xyz.

```
if(style_option==2)
  {
  for(j=i=0;i<m;i++)
    {
    rr=hypot3d(x-hoop[i].x,y-hoop[i].y,z-hoop[i].z);
    if(i==0)
```

```
        rm=rr;
      else if(rr<rm)
        {
        rm=rr;
        j=i;
        }
      }
    if(j>0)
      i=j-1;
    else
      i=1;
    q=drand();
    h.x=(float)(q*hoop[i].x+(1.-q)*hoop[j].x);
    h.y=(float)(q*hoop[i].y+(1.-q)*hoop[j].y);
    h.z=(float)(q*hoop[i].z+(1.-q)*hoop[j].z);
    h.x+=(float)(xrand()/50.);
    h.y+=(float)(xrand()/50.);
    h.z+=(float)(xrand()/50.);
```

The piecewise approximation of this path is calculated linearly:

```
    for(i=0;i<n;i++)
      {
      t=i/(n-1.);
      rtxyz[i].t=(float)t;
      rtxyz[i].r=(float)r;
      if(i<n/2)
        {
        rtxyz[i].x=(float)(x+i*u*l/(n-1));
        rtxyz[i].y=(float)(y+i*v*l/(n-1));
        rtxyz[i].z=(float)(z+i*w*l/(n-1));
        }
      else
        {
        q=(n-1-i)*2./n;
        rtxyz[i].x=(float)(q*rtxyz[n/2-1].x+(1.-q)*h.x);
        rtxyz[i].y=(float)(q*rtxyz[n/2-1].y+(1.-q)*h.y);
        rtxyz[i].z=(float)(q*rtxyz[n/2-1].z+(1.-q)*h.z);
        }
      r*=0.9;
      }
```

To spread the bangs away from the eyes, we add:

```
    for(i=1;i<n;i++)
      if(rtxyz[i].z>=0.4)
        if(rtxyz[i].y<=0.45)
          if(fabs(rtxyz[i].x)<0.5)
            rtxyz[i].x=(float)sign(0.5,rtxyz[i].x);
```

This leaves a jointed unrealistic path between two points, starting perpendicular to the scalp element and ending near the hoop. In order to achieve a smooth curve, we add some level of smoothing, in this case 3 passes.

```
for(j=0;j<3;j++)
  {
  for(i=1;i<n-1;i++)
    {
    rtxyz[i].x=(rtxyz[i-1].x+rtxyz[i+1].x)/2.F;
    rtxyz[i].y=(rtxyz[i-1].y+rtxyz[i+1].y)/2.F;
    rtxyz[i].z=(rtxyz[i-1].z+rtxyz[i+1].z)/2.F;
    }
  }
```

When pre-drawing (delayed painting enabled), we use line segments. When making the final pass, we draw the complex tubes.

```
if(partial_paint)
  {
  glBegin(GL_LINE_STRIP);
  for(i=0;i<n;i++)
    glVertex3d(rtxyz[i].x,rtxyz[i].y,rtxyz[i].z);
  glEnd();
  }
else
  RenderComplexTube(rtxyz,n,16);
```

These various options are selected by parameters at the top of the code:

```
#define thick_lines      1
#define simple_tubes     2
#define complex_tubes    3
#define rendering        3
int downswept_hairs   = 1;
int hairs_per_element=63;
int randomize_gravity= 1;
int randomize_lengths= 1;
int style_option      = 2;
```

We can also change the colors, for instance of the pupils.

```
  else
  if(style_option==1&&(Elem[e].rgb==pink||Elem[e].rgb==
  green))
    glColor(brown);
  else if(style_option==2&&Elem[e].rgb==pink)
    glColor(0xFFDFBF);
  else if(style_option==2&&Elem[e].rgb==green)
    glColor(blue);
  else
    glColor(Elem[e].rgb);
```

The end result for Style Option 1 is shown in this next figure:

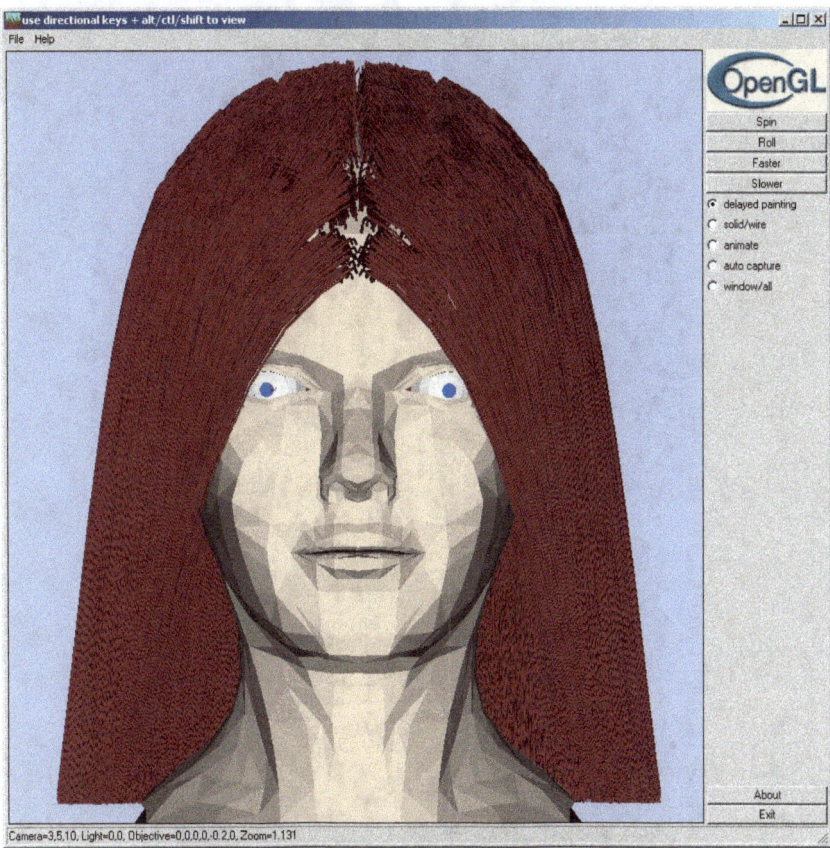

Figure 178. Style Option 1 with Hoop and Parted Bangs

We can change a few parameters to produce a different appearance, changing the skin tone and pupil coloration:

```
if(Elem[e].rgb==brown)
  {
  if(style_option==1)
    glColor(black);
  else if(style_option==2)
    glColor(dark_red);
  else
    glColor(brown);
```

This combination is Style Option 2:

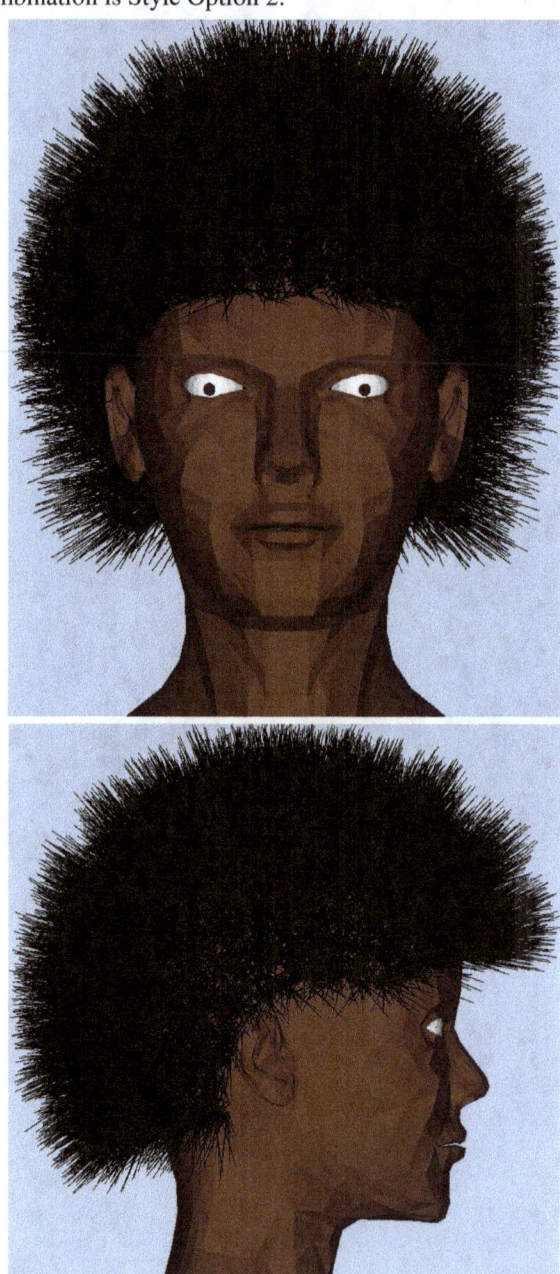

Figure 179. Style Option 2

Appendix A: Example Details & Setup

There are over fifty fully functional examples included in the online archive:

http://www.dudleybenton.altervista.org/software/3D Rendering/3D_Rendering_in_Windows.zip

Each one is complete and will unpack into a separate folder. The examples have been precompiled and will run on any version of Windows®. There is also an Excel® spreadsheet listing the examples in the top-level folder.

Name/Folder	Engine	Extra	Colors	Level	Anim.	Features
Accnot	OpenGL		24-bit	1	0	simple example using built-in shapes
Alpha3D	OpenGL	GLAUX	24-bit	4	0	illustrates intermixing of opaque and alpha blending; also mouse click input
Atlantis	OpenGL	GLUT	24-bit	3	1	animation objects (fish swimming around)
Blender	OpenGL	GLUT	24-bit	3	1	fade, animations, text (with anti-aliasing)
Blue Pony	OpenGL	Mesa	24-bit	3	2	animation, bitmap images, extrusion of parts (2D to 3D)
Bounce	OpenGL	Mesa	24-bit	3	1	bouncing checkered sphere
Chess	OpenGL	GLUT	24-bit	3	1	animation, chess pieces, chess board movements
Cube Map	OpenGL	Mesa	24-bit	2	1	rotating sphere inside rotating cube with checkerboard textures
Dino Ball	OpenGL	GLUT	24-bit	3	1	extrusion (2D to 3D), click and drag to rotate
Dino Draw	OpenGL	GLUT	24-bit	3	1	extrusion (2D to 3D), animation, click to activate
Dino Shade	OpenGL	GLUT	24-bit	4	1	extrusion (2D to 3D), animation, shadows, reflections
Dino Spin	OpenGL	GLUT	24-bit	3	1	extrusion (2D to 3D), animation, click to activate, text
DOF not	OpenGL	GLAUX	24-bit	2	0	depth-of-field illustration with 5 teapots
Earth & Moon	OpenGL	Mesa	24-bit	2	1	rotating spheres covered with photographs
Field3D	WinAPI	none	N/A	4	3	create 3D fields from data and display in slices

flange	WinAPI	none	24-bit	2	1	simple sort and paint back to front
Fog	OpenGL	GLAUX	24-bit	2	0	illustrates 3 types of fog; also mouse click input
Gears	OpenGL	Mesa	24-bit	3	1	three rotating gears
GearTrain	OpenGL	Mesa	24-bit	3	1	more complex gears
GL Puzzle	OpenGL	GLUT	24-bit	2	1	buttons, mouse menus, animation
Ideas	OpenGL	GLUT	24-bit	4	1	animation, shapes interacting with planes, lighting, changing viewpoint
IsoSurf	OpenGL	Mesa	24-bit	3	0	arbitrary surface, lighting, rotation, keyboard input
Knight's Tour	OpenGL	none	24-bit	4	3	animation, textures, controls, logic, interaction
Long Ago	WinAPI	none	N/A	1	1	familiar scrolling yellow text, star field simulation, Star Wars Theme
Lorenz	OpenGL	GLUT	24-bit	2	1	animated spheres and lines
Material	OpenGL	GLAUX	24-bit	2	0	12 spheres with different surface/light interaction
Morph3D	OpenGL	Mesa	24-bit	2	2	transforming geometric shapes, animation, keyboard input
Move Light	OpenGL	GLAUX	24-bit	2	3	click the mouse to move the light source around a torus
Occlude	OpenGL	Mesa	24-bit	2	1	occlusion test
Olympic Rings	OpenGL	none	24-bit	2	1	animated toruses forming olympic logo
Origami	OpenGL	GLUT	24-bit	3	2	continuous shape changing while animating with rotating viewpoint
Planet Up	OpenGL	GLAUX	24-bit	1	1	Earth & Moon as wireframe spheres; press arrow keys to rotate/orbit
Point Burst	OpenGL	GLUT	24-bit	3	1	little spheres bursting forth and bouncing into view
Reflect	OpenGL	Mesa	24-bit	3	1	rotating reflective torus shows an image
Reflect Dino	OpenGL	GLUT	24-bit	4	1	extrusion (2D to 3D), animation, reflections
Reflect2	OpenGL	Mesa	24-bit	3	1	rotating cylinder and cone produce reflection

Name	API	Library	Color	a	b	Description
Roller Coaster	OpenGL	GLUT	24-bit	4	1	animation, complex object building, changing viewpoint (following coaster)
scclrlt	OpenGL	GLAUX	24-bit	1	0	color light source with stock shapes
scene	OpenGL	GLAUX	24-bit	1	0	white light source with stock shapes
Shapes	OpenGL	none	24-bit	3	3	create and display various geometric shapes using OpenGL
Sky Fly	OpenGL	GLUT	24-bit	4	3	interactive fly over with terrain and clouds
SpinCube	WinAPI	none	N/A	2	1	rotating cube screen saver displays BMP, GIF, or JPG
Stonehenge1	OpenGL	GLAUX	24-bit	3	3	fog, rain, lighting, animated tour
Stonehenge2	OpenGL	none	24-bit	3	3	more advanced rendering and controls
Stonehenge3	My3D	none	24-bit	4	3	fog, lighting, rotations, textures, buttons
surface	WinAPI		24-bit	2	2	simple sort and paint; use keys to rotate and zoom
Tea Amb	OpenGL	GLAUX	24-bit	1	0	three options for ambient lighting
Teapot	OpenGL	Mesa	24-bit	3	0	rotating teapot with shadow, moving light, and textures
Teapots	OpenGL	none	24-bit	2	0	surface effects (shiny, dull, plastic, metallic, etc.)
TexGen	OpenGL	GLAUX	24-bit	2	0	illustrates how to generate and apply a texture
Tprim	OpenGL	GLAUX	24-bit	1	0	illustrates drawing primitives (lines, polygons, etc.)
tselect	OpenGL	GLAUX	24-bit	2	3	illustrates how to select objects with the mouse
View3D	My3D	none	8-bit	4	3	automatic capture to GIF, import AutoCAD 3D Studio files
View3DS	OpenGL	none	24-bit	4	3	load 3D Studio models and display them using OpenGL
VRML View	WinAPI	none	24-bit	2	2	reads and displays VRML files
Win3D	Win3D	none	N/A	2	1	hidden line/surface removal; interference; 3D font; no source code

Note1: GLAX is the OpenGL auxiliary library

Note2: GLUT is the OpenGL utilities library

Note3: Mesa is Brian Paul's additions to OpenGL

Note4: My3D is rendering engine I developed, completely independent of OpenGL

Note5: All copyright notices are in the respective source code files.

Unpack the archive into a folder of your choice. You may need to copy the include files (*.h) from the gl folder into the include folder associated with your compiler and the library files (*.lib) into the lib folder. There are three different versions of these files in separate subfolders by year of issue. I have put the most common at the top level. You will know immediately whether you need to copy these files, as the compiler will display a message that it can't find one or more of the include files and exit.

I build everything from a command prompt (which, incidentally is not a DOS box). This may or may not work with what you use to write code, presumably some sort of text editor. I don't recommend Visual Studio®. It's very expensive and completely unnecessary. Each of the examples is in a separate folder, containing everything you need to build it. There is a small batch file, _compile.bat, in each folder to compile that example. These batch files depend on your having already set up a folder containing the Microsoft® compiler (for details see Appendix T).

Appendix B. Working with Pixel Contexts

The term *pixel context* is tossed about in OpenGL™ literature as if it were intuitive or had meaning in a broad context. It doesn't, particularly in the context of Windows® programming. The Windows® APIs use completely different terminology and the documentation doesn't mention pixel contexts. While the terminology is unfamiliar, the concepts are not.

In order to paint anything in Windows® you must have a handle to a *device context*. When this device context is in memory, it's called a *compatible* device context. In order to paint on the display without flicker, you must first build the image in memory and then BitBlt it onto the display. Color images in memory are called DIB sections in Windows®. You must select the DIB section into the memory device context. The combination of a memory device context and a DIB section (plus a few other things, including a Z-buffer) is called a pixel context.

OpenGL™ only works with pixel contexts. You can see what pixel contexts are available by calling DescribePixelFormat(). You select the one you want by calling SetPixelFormat(). You prepare it for use with OpenGL™ by calling wglCreateContext() and distinguishing this one context from many by calling wglMakeCurrent(). When it comes time to paint it onto the display, you call SwapBuffers(), which just *paints* them rather than actually *swapping* them.

Pixel contexts, along with these virtually undocumented Windows® API calls, are defined in wingdi.h and ntgdi.h. Other than facilitating OpenGL™ rendering, it's not clear why these even exist in the Windows® context or why they are linked in gdi32.lib and implemented in gdi32.dll. Whatever the reason, this is what they are and you must utilize them to do anything with OpenGL™.

You must first get a pixel context before doing anything with OpenGL™. You don't get to *request* (or *specify*) a particular pixel context; rather, you must *select* one from a list that will work for you intend to do. You get a list of available formats by calling DescribePixelFormat(). The following is a typical list of such formats:

index	OpenGL	double buffer	RGBA	need palette	system palette	color bits	depth bits	stencil bits	generic	accelerated	score	stencil score
1	1	0	1	0	0	32	24	0	0	0	0	0
2	1	0	1	0	0	32	24	0	0	0	0	0
3	1	0	1	0	0	32	24	8	0	1	0	0
4	1	0	1	0	0	32	24	8	0	0	0	0
5	1	0	1	0	0	32	0	0	0	0	0	0
6	1	0	1	0	0	32	0	0	0	0	0	0
7	1	1	1	0	0	32	24	0	0	0	80	0
8	1	1	1	0	0	32	24	0	0	0	80	0
9	1	1	1	0	0	32	24	8	0	1	88	88
10	1	1	1	0	0	32	24	8	0	0	80	80
11	1	1	1	0	0	32	0	0	0	0	64	0
12	1	1	1	0	0	32	0	0	0	0	64	0
13	1	1	1	0	0	32	24	0	0	0	80	0
14	1	1	1	0	0	32	24	0	0	0	80	0
19	0	1	1	0	0	32	24	0	0	0	0	0
90	0	1	1	0	0	32	24	8	0	0	0	0
91	1	0	1	0	0	32	32	8	1	1	0	0
92	1	0	1	0	0	32	16	8	1	0	0	0
93	1	1	1	0	0	32	32	8	1	1	90	90
94	1	1	1	0	0	32	16	8	1	0	82	82
95	1	0	1	0	0	32	32	8	1	1	0	0
96	1	0	1	0	0	32	16	8	1	0	0	0
97	1	1	1	0	0	32	32	8	1	0	82	82
98	1	1	1	0	0	32	16	8	1	0	82	82
99	1	0	0	0	0	32	32	8	1	1	0	0
100	1	0	0	0	0	32	16	8	1	0	0	0
101	1	1	0	0	0	32	32	8	1	1	0	0
102	1	1	0	0	0	32	16	8	1	0	0	0
105	1	0	1	0	0	24	32	8	1	0	0	0
106	1	0	1	0	0	24	16	8	1	0	0	0
107	1	0	0	0	0	24	32	8	1	0	0	0
108	1	0	0	0	0	24	16	8	1	0	0	0
111	1	0	1	0	0	16	32	8	1	0	0	0
112	1	0	1	0	0	16	16	8	1	0	0	0
113	1	0	0	0	0	16	32	8	1	0	0	0
114	1	0	0	0	0	16	16	8	1	0	0	0
125	1	0	0	1	1	4	32	8	1	0	0	0
126	1	0	0	1	1	4	16	8	1	0	0	0

This table has been abbreviated for space, but still illustrates the process you must go through in order to select an appropriate pixel context. First of all, some of the available formats don't even support OpenGL™. These are eliminated immediately. Ones that don't support double buffering or require a palette can also be eliminated. OpenGL™ depends on RGBA, so formats that don't support this can also be eliminated. The color depth should be at least 24 and will paint faster if this matches the depth of the display device context.

The depth bits are used for the Z-buffer and must be at least 16. Generic doesn't matter. Accelerated may draw faster, but is not always available, depending on hardware and drivers. If you want to use stenciling, that can be included in the criteria. I calculate a score for each and pick the one with the highest score. If none of the available formats score above zero, exit the program. The following code snippet implements this selection process:

```
HDC GetBestPixelFormat(HDC hDC,int stencil)
{
int i,j,n,s,sx;
PIXELFORMATDESCRIPTOR pfd;
if((n=DescribePixelFormat(hDC,1,0,NULL))<1)
return(NULL);
j=sx=-1;
for(i=1;i<=n;i++)
{
DescribePixelFormat(hDC,i,
   sizeof(PIXELFORMATDESCRIPTOR),&pfd);
if(!(pfd.dwFlags&PFD_SUPPORT_OPENGL))
  continue;
if(!(pfd.dwFlags&PFD_DOUBLEBUFFER))
  continue;
if(pfd.iPixelType!=PFD_TYPE_RGBA)
  continue;
if(pfd.dwFlags&PFD_NEED_PALETTE)
  continue;
if(pfd.dwFlags&PFD_NEED_SYSTEM_PALETTE)
  continue;
if(pfd.cColorBits<24)
  continue;
if(pfd.cDepthBits<16)
  continue;
if((1<<pfd.cStencilBits)<stencil)
  continue;
s=pfd.cDepthBits/16;
if(pfd.dwFlags&PFD_GENERIC_ACCELERATED)
  s+=2;
if(pfd.cColorBits==GetDeviceCaps(hDC,BITSPIXEL))
  s+=8;
else if(pfd.cColorBits>=24)
  s+=4;
if(s<sx)
```

```
    continue;
  sx=s;
  j=i;
  }
  if(j<0)
  return(NULL);
  DescribePixelFormat(hDC,j,
    sizeof(PIXELFORMATDESCRIPTOR),&pfd);
  if(!SetPixelFormat(hDC,j,&pfd))
  return(NULL);
  return(hDC);
  }
```

A pixel context must be selected and implemented. This is a three-step process, as illustrated in the following code snippet:

```
  if((pDC=GetBestPixelFormat(hPlot))==0)
    Abort(__LINE__,"can't find best pixel context\nerror
    code %i",GetLastError());
  if((rDC=wglCreateContext(pDC))==0)
    Abort(__LINE__,"can't create OpenGL context\nerror
    code %i",GetLastError());
  if(!wglMakeCurrent(pDC,rDC))
    Abort(__LINE__,"can't make OpenGL context
    current\nerror code %i",GetLastError());
```

You will also need to declare the following variables:

```
HDC pDC;    /* plot window device context */
HGLRC rDC;  /* OpenGL rendering context */
int pFS;    /* pixel format selector */
PIXELFORMATDESCRIPTOR pFd;
```

The rendering process also has several steps:

```
  glClearDepth(1);
  glClearColor(0,0,0,0);
  glClearStencil(0);
  glClear(GL_COLOR_BUFFER_BIT|
    GL_DEPTH_BUFFER_BIT|GL_STENCIL_BUFFER_BIT);
insert rendering instructions here
  guFinish();
  SwapBuffers(pDC);
```

Appendix C. Working with Textures

Textures are 32-bit (DWORD) bitmaps ordered: RGBA. These don't have a header, as is the case with a Windows BITMAP (i.e., BITMAPINFOHEADER structure). Instead, the dimensions are specified in a call to the rendering engine:

```
glTexImage2D(GL_TEXTURE_2D,0,3,bi->biWidth,
    bi->biHeight,0,GL_BGR_EXT,
    GL_UNSIGNED_BYTE,(BYTE*)bits);
```

The RGBA bits are entered by row and in the same order (bottom up) as a Windows® BITMAP. The width and height must both be a power of two, though not necessarily the same (i.e., 2, 4, 8, 16, 32, 64, 128, 256, 512, or 1024). Texture bitmaps can be quite large, considering there is no compression. Neither Windows® nor OpenGL™ recognize JPEGs as such. If you want to keep the texture as a JPEG, you must also provide your own code to unpack it. Such a code (jpeg6b.c) can be found in the online archive accompanying this and several other of my texts. The JPEGS can easily be handled as resources and loaded when a program starts up. The following is a typical section of a resource file (*.RC):

```
#undef RT_RCDATA
#define RT_RCDATA 0xA

Agate          RT_RCDATA   "agate.jpg"
BlackGranite   RT_RCDATA   "blackgranite.jpg"
Lapis          RT_RCDATA   "lapis.jpg"
Malachite      RT_RCDATA   "malachite.jpg"
Marble         RT_RCDATA   "marble.jpg"
Oak            RT_RCDATA   "oak.jpg"
Pedauk         RT_RCDATA   "pedauk.jpg"
Purpleheart    RT_RCDATA   "purpleheart.jpg"
Walnut         RT_RCDATA   "walnut.jpg"
WhiteGranite   RT_RCDATA   "whitegranite.jpg"
Yew            RT_RCDATA   "yew.jpg"
Kewazinga      RT_RCDATA   "kewazinga.jpg"
```

Note the redefinition of constant RT_RCDATA, which is used for user-defined unstructured binary objects. Some versions of Visual Studio contain a bug. If you don't redefine this constant in the resource file, you will not be able later to load the resource. The other types (e.g., ICON, BITMAP, DIALOG) appear to work well enough. It is also not necessary to redefine RT_RCDATA in the source code (*.C). Preparation of 24-bit images is a simple reordering (don't forget that Windows® bitmaps are aligned on DWORD boundaries, while OpenGL™ bitmaps aren't).

```
wide=4*((bm->biWidth*24+31)/32);
add=wide-3*bm->biWidth;
for(h=0;h<bm->biHeight;h++)
    {
    for(w=0;w<bm->biWidth;w++)
```

```
        {
        r=*bits++;
        g=*bits++;
        b=*bits++;
        *stib++=b;
        *stib++=g;
        *stib++=r;
        }
    bits+=add;
    }
```

Preparation of palette-based (8 bit or less) bitmaps is straightforward:

```
if(bHead->biBitCount<=8)
   {
   map=allocate(__LINE__,bHead->biWidth*bHead-
   >biHeight*3,1);
   pal=((BYTE*)bHead)+sizeof(BITMAPINFOHEADER);
   pix=pal+bHead->biClrUsed*sizeof(DWORD);
   if(bHead->biBitCount==8)
      {
      for(h=i=j=0;h<bHead->biHeight;h++)
         {
         for(w=0;w<bHead->biWidth;w++)
            {
            k=pix[i++];
            map[j++]=pal[4*k];
            map[j++]=pal[4*k+1];
            map[j++]=pal[4*k+2];
            }
         }
      }
```

Appendix D. Working with Resources

Windows® resource objects can be anything from lists (including meshes) to bitmaps to surfaces (such as topography). These are defined in the resource file (*.RC), compiled with the resource compiler (to produce a file named *.res), and embedded in the executable (*.exe) by the linker. Like object modules (*.obj) these can be deleted once the executable has been created, as they serve no further purpose (see the several batch files _compile.bat in the online archive). Each resource has a type (ICON, BITMAP, DIALOG, or user-defined: RT_RCDATA). Loading a resource is a four-step process:

1) Find the resource (locates the resource)
2) Load the resource (doesn't actually load the resource)
3) Lock the resource (actually loads the resource)
4) Get the resource size (tells you how big it is)

This is illustrated by the following code snippet:

```
typedef struct{DWORD size;void*data;}RESOURCE;
RESOURCE LoadTexture(char*type,char*rname)
  {
  HGLOBAL rLoad;
  HRSRC rFind;
  static RESOURCE res;
  if((rFind=FindResource(hInst,rname,RT_RCDATA))==NULL)
    Abort(__LINE__,"can't find resource %s\nWindows
    error code %li",rname,GetLastError());
  if((rLoad=LoadResource(hInst,rFind))==NULL)
    Abort(__LINE__,"can't load resource %s\nWindows
    error code %li",rname,GetLastError());
  if((res.data=LockResource(rLoad))==NULL)
    Abort(__LINE__,"can't lock resource %s\nWindows
    error code %li",rname,GetLastError());
  res.size=SizeofResource(hInst,rFind));
  return(res);
  }
```

As the RESOURCE structure is larger than the EAX register on an Intel processor, you must make the variable res static; otherwise, returning will generate a stack overflow (a fatal protection fault). The JPEG format is very efficient for storing images and saves a lot of space. These are very convenient and easy to unpack after loading (see jpeg6b.c in the online archive). The GIF format is also compact and easy to implement (see gif89a.c in the online archive). There are many other compression algorithms, which could be used to reduce the size of other data structures. I often use Lempel-Ziv/Arithmetic compression for this task.

You could load a bitmap resource directly using the API call LoadBitmap(); however, this returns a handle to the bitmap and not the bitmap itself. From the handle, you would need to follow this up with a call to GetObject() in order to get a pointer to the actual bitmap, which is actually a DIBSECTION (device independent bitmap). If you store a BMP file as a binary resource the file header will be at the front of the data block, so you must skip over this in order to get a pointer to the bitmap itself, as illustrated in the following code snippet:

```
BITMAPINFOHEADER*LoadBMP(char*name)
  {
  return((BITMAPINFOHEADER*)(((BYTE*)GetResource(
    hInst,name,RT_RCDATA))+sizeof(BITMAPFILEHEADER)));
  }
```

You first hard type the pointer to a BYTE* then add the size of the file header (14 bytes) then hard type the result to the desired pointer. This presumes that you stored the bitmap in the resource file as:

```
name RT_RCDATA "image.bmp"
```

Appendix E. Working with Lists

In Chapter 28 we saw that a *list* could be used to streamline definition and rendering of a sphere with a texture. This is a very simple list and is created with three steps:

1) Get an assigned integer
2) Fill the list
3) Close the list

For the Earth example, this becomes:

```
gEarth=glGenLists(1);
glNewList(gEarth,GL_COMPILE);
gluSphere(Quadric,2.,24,24);
glEndList();
```

Lists can be quite useful. While they don't necessarily speed up rendering, they can simplify implementation, at least from code appearance. One example would be to define each of the chess pieces as a list if polygons. You could then refer to each one in the rendering process by the single integer assigned by OpenGL™ by calling glGenLists(). The Olympic ring demo, gear demo, blue pony, and dino examples use this method. Several of the teapot examples also build a list.

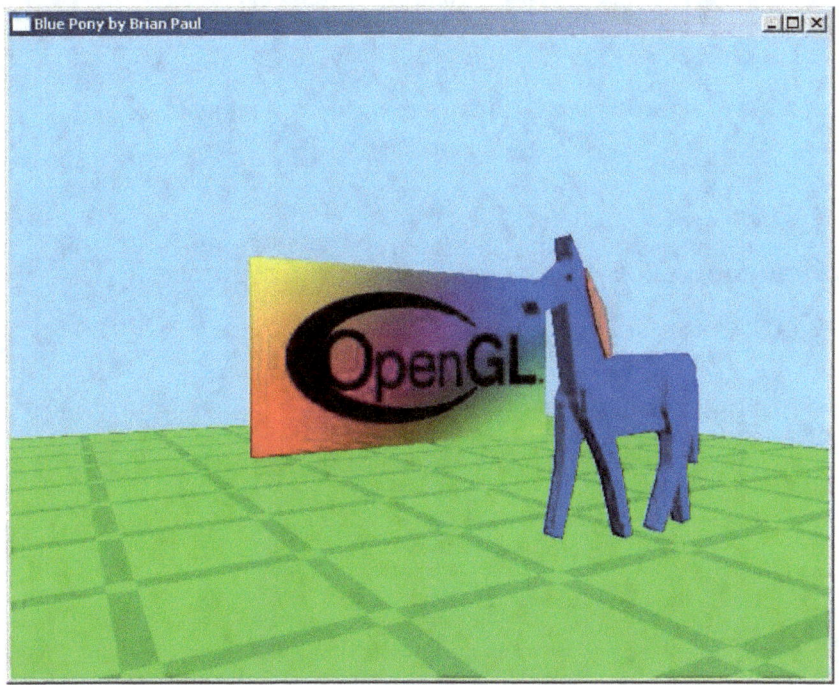

The list used in the blue pony demo (written by Brian Paul) is shown below:

```c
void MakePony(void)
  {
  Pony=glGenLists(1);
  glNewList(Pony,GL_COMPILE);
  glMaterialfv(GL_FRONT,GL_AMBIENT_AND_DIFFUSE,blue);
  ExtrudePart(sizeof(PonyVerts)/sizeof(GLfloat)/2,
    PonyVerts,PonyDepth);
  glMaterialfv(GL_FRONT,GL_AMBIENT_AND_DIFFUSE,black);
  glNormal3f(0.0,0.0,1.0);
  glBegin(GL_POLYGON);
  glVertex3f(EyePos[0]-EyeSize,EyePos[1]-EyeSize,
    EyePos[2]);
  glVertex3f(EyePos[0]+EyeSize,EyePos[1]-EyeSize,
    EyePos[2]);
  glVertex3f(EyePos[0]+EyeSize,EyePos[1]+EyeSize,
    EyePos[2]);
  glVertex3f(EyePos[0]-EyeSize,EyePos[1]+EyeSize,
    EyePos[2]);
  glEnd();
  glNormal3f(0.0,0.0,-1.0);
  glBegin(GL_POLYGON);
  glVertex3f(EyePos[0]-EyeSize,EyePos[1]+EyeSize,
    -EyePos[2]);
  glVertex3f(EyePos[0]+EyeSize,EyePos[1]+EyeSize,
    -EyePos[2]);
  glVertex3f(EyePos[0]+EyeSize,EyePos[1]-EyeSize,
    -EyePos[2]);
  glVertex3f(EyePos[0]-EyeSize,EyePos[1]-EyeSize,
    -EyePos[2]);
  glEnd();
  glEndList();
  Mane=glGenLists(1);
  glNewList(Mane,GL_COMPILE);
  glMaterialfv(GL_FRONT,GL_AMBIENT_AND_DIFFUSE,
    pink);
  ExtrudePart(sizeof(ManeVerts)/sizeof(GLfloat)/2,
    ManeVerts,ManeDepth);
  glEndList();
  FrontLeg=glGenLists(1);
  glNewList(FrontLeg,GL_COMPILE);
  glMaterialfv(GL_FRONT,GL_AMBIENT_AND_DIFFUSE,
    blue);
  ExtrudePart(sizeof(FrontLegVerts)/sizeof(GLfloat)/2,
    FrontLegVerts,LegDepth);
  glEndList();
  BackLeg=glGenLists(1);
  glNewList(BackLeg,GL_COMPILE);
  glMaterialfv(GL_FRONT,GL_AMBIENT_AND_DIFFUSE,blue);
  ExtrudePart(sizeof(BackLegVerts)/sizeof(GLfloat)/2,
    BackLegVerts,LegDepth);
```

```
glEndList();
}
```

In order to facilitate motion, the pony is broken into four pieces: pony, mane, front leg, and back leg, using four calls to glGenLists(). Each list is a combination of several polygons, defined in data statements elsewhere in the code. The colors (blue, black, and pink) are also defined elsewhere in data statements. The Olympic ring, dino, gear, and blue pony demos (along with many others) can be found in the online archive accompanying *3D Rendering in Windows®*. The gears in that demo are implemented as lists. Consider the following code:

```
/* make the gears */
gear1=glGenLists(1);
glNewList(gear1,GL_COMPILE);
glMaterialfv(GL_FRONT,GL_AMBIENT_AND_DIFFUSE,red);
gear(1.0,4.0,1.0,20,0.7);
glEndList();
gear2=glGenLists(1);
glNewList(gear2,GL_COMPILE);
glMaterialfv(GL_FRONT,GL_AMBIENT_AND_DIFFUSE,green);
gear(0.5,2.0,2.0,10,0.7);
glEndList();
gear3=glGenLists(1);
glNewList(gear3,GL_COMPILE);
glMaterialfv(GL_FRONT,GL_AMBIENT_AND_DIFFUSE,blue);
gear(1.3,2.0,0.5,10,0.7);
glEndList();
```

and then drawn referencing the respective lists:

```
glPushMatrix();
glTranslatef(-3.0,-2.0,0.0);
glRotatef(angle,0.0,0.0,1.0);
glCallList(gear1);
glPopMatrix();
glPushMatrix();
glTranslatef(3.1,-2.0,0.0);
glRotatef(-2.0*angle-9.0,0.0,0.0,1.0);
glCallList(gear2);
glPopMatrix();
glPushMatrix();
glTranslatef(-3.1,4.2,0.0);
glRotatef(-2.0*angle-25.0,0.0,0.0,1.0);
glCallList(gear3);
glPopMatrix();
glPopMatrix();
glutSwapBuffers();
```

The dinosaur is also defined and then rendered as a list:

Appendix F. Working with Collections

A mesh is a user-defined collection of polygons having the same shape, most often triangles. These are defined by a structure:

```
typedef struct{float x1,x2,x3,y1,y2,y3,z1,z2,z3;DWORD
    color;}MESH;
```

It is most convenient to define a terminating characteristic rather than keep track of a count for each mesh. Meshes may be terminated by an obvious outlying value, such as FLT_MAX, or by an impossible color, such as –1 (which is 0xFFFFFFFF). As colors span RGB, only the first 24 bits on an Intel processor (Big Endian) are used, namely 0x00FFFFFF. If there is any non-zero value in the high byte, this flags the end of the mesh.

```
if((color&0xFF000000)!=0)
```

A section of the fire extinguisher mesh from Chapter 23 is listed below:

```
MESH FireExtinguisher[]={
{ 0.07F,0.75F, 0.00F, 0.01F,0.73F, 0.06F, 0.04F,0.73F,
    0.08F,red},
{ 0.07F,0.75F, 0.00F,-0.01F,0.73F,-0.03F,-0.02F,0.73F,
    0.00F,red},
{ 0.07F,0.75F, 0.00F,-0.02F,0.73F, 0.00F,-0.01F,0.73F,
    0.03F,red},
etc.
{-0.03F,0.71F, 0.07F, 0.03F,0.71F, 0.11F, 0.03F,0.82F,
    0.11F,black},
{-0.02F,0.71F,-0.07F,-0.05F,0.82F, 0.00F,-0.02F,0.82F,-
    0.07F,black},
{-0.13F,1.00F,-0.01F,-0.17F,0.97F,-0.02F,-0.18F,0.99F,-
    0.01F,black},
etc.
{ 0.00F,0.00F, 0.00F, 0.00F,0.00F, 0.00F, 0.00F,0.00F,
    0.00F,-1}};
```

Many of the objects in the demos found in the online archive are meshes. As you look through the examples, you will find most of these in files like: name.h. These are included by the compiler and become static data statements that are placed accordingly in the executable image and readily accessed by the code, often without requiring any additional processing, other than being passed to the rendering engine.

It is customary for these to be centered about (0,0,0) and oriented toward the viewer. When drawing the scene, precede the mesh with the desired displacement glTranslatef() and rotation glRotatef(). In most cases the translation will precede the rotation, but not always, depending on the desired effect. Controlling the order of these two calls can add considerable complexity to your scene with very little coding effort.

The forklift used in the MSRE example is a single mesh, which is rendered as shown below:

Appendix G. Working with Topography

The Sandy Run model is all about topography. It was created to simulate and visualize an actual flooding event that resulted from a minivan being washed down an embankment during a torrential rain. The minivan was temporarily stuck under a railroad trestle, backing water up into the adjacent downtown area long enough to fill the basement of two buildings and cause considerable damage. The part played by the minivan wasn't discovered right away because a tow truck had removed it and some time elapsed between before anyone realized that it had been parked upstream of the trestle and was removed from the downstream area. Matching paint scrapings along the walls of the trestle confirmed this was the cause of the temporary flooding.

The Sandy Run demo is based on actual topography. The ETTP and Manhattan Project Museum demo also contain actual topography. This information was supplied in the form of contours. The surface was created by triangularization (i.e., 2D meshing) of the contours.

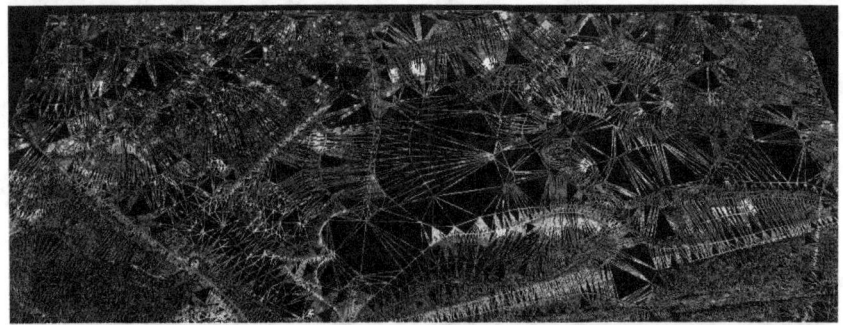

A closer view of the mesh is shown in this next figure:

Flooding is accomplished by drawing a blue flood plane and allowing it to intersect with the 3D surface of the topography. The water surface was calibrated based on measurements and observations, including eyewitness accounts of when the water reached specific locations. The aerial view is painted on top of the topography as a texture.

The surface is simply a collection of 3D triangles. The XZ locations are provided by the mesh generator and the Y location of the points comes from the contour values. The ETTP topography triangles and building outlines (hexahedra) are shown in this next figure:

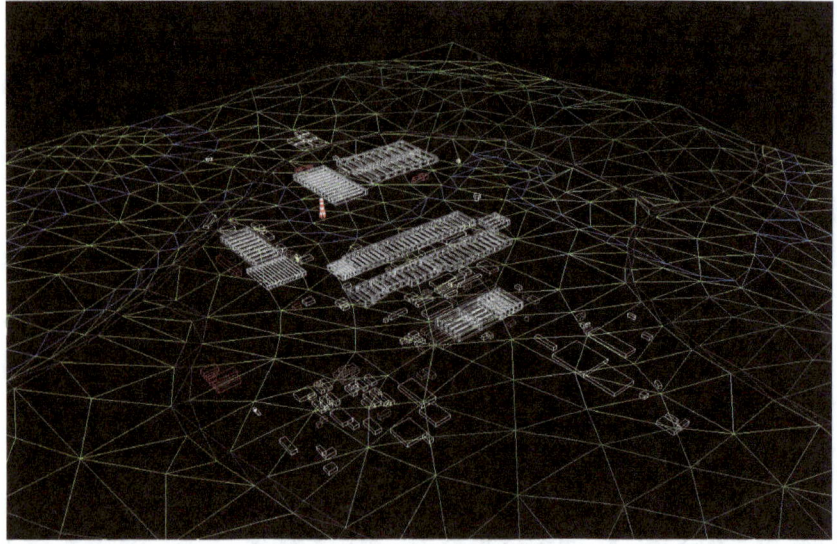

Appendix H. Selection of Objects

In a Windows® GUI, when the user clicks either button on the mouse, this send a message to the procedure assigned to that window. If it has no procedure (e.g., is a simple STATIC object), the message is sent to the procedure of the parent. There are four *click* messages:

```
WM_LBUTTONUP
WM_LBUTTONDOWN
WM_RBUTTONUP
WM_RBUTTONDOWN
```

These come with the mouse position combined in lParam, with the X position in the low part and Y position in the high part. These two parts are signed short (16-bit) integers. The location can be used with an inside polygon test to determine which object is being selected. There is also a

```
WM_MOUSEMOVE
```

message produced by dragging the mouse. You must save the initial position (i.e., DOWN message) and the final position (i.e., UP message) to create a rectangle followed by an inside polygon test. This presumes you know where the objects are displayed on the screen. If you have displayed the objects with Windows® API calls or with some custom software, as discussed in the *other* section of the first book in this series, *3D Rendering in Windows® with and without OpenGL™*, then this may be the case. If, however, you are using the OpenGL™ rendering engine, you will not know where the objects end up on a pixel-by-pixel basic. For that, we use *stenciling*.

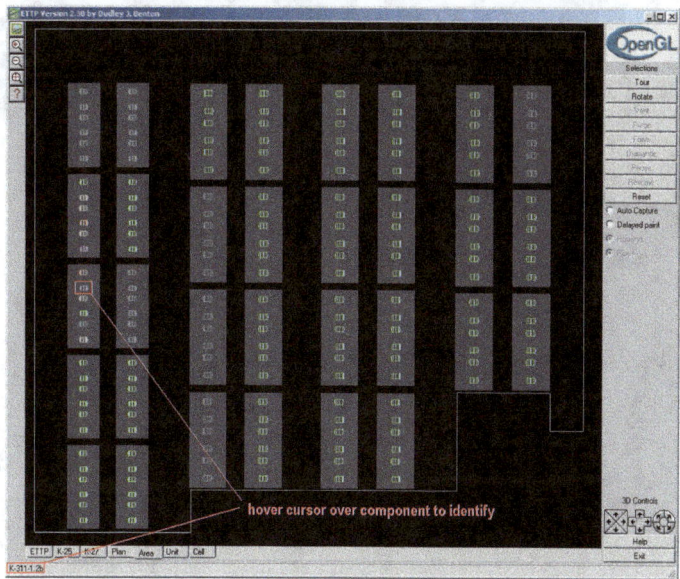

Figure 180. Use Cursor to Identify and Select Objects

Appendix I. OpenGL™ Stenciling

The OpenGL™ rendering engine provides something called *stenciling*. While this feature has multiple uses, we will consider only one of those here. Stenciling is like a fourth dimension of color. Stencil bits are listed in the table in Appendix B. If you want to use stenciling, you must select a pixel context that provides this feature. While some systems may provide more than 8 stencil bits, I have never seen this on a Windows® machine. This means that there can be no more than 256 distinct objects. Besides selecting the right context, there are a few commands that must come at the beginning of the rendering process:

```
glClearStencil(0);
glEnable(GL_STENCIL_TEST);
glStencilOp(GL_KEEP,GL_KEEP,GL_REPLACE);
glStencilFunc(GL_ALWAYS,0,-1);
```

The index (0-255) for each object is set before rendering with this call:

```
glStencilFunc(GL_ALWAYS,index,-1);
```

The index is retrieved by passing the XY location within the rendering window with this call:

```
glReadPixels(x,y,1,1,GL_STENCIL_INDEX,
  GL_UNSIGNED_INT,&index);
```

Stenciling is used here in the Knight's Tour example to identify the pieces and squares, for example, see "white king's rook" in the lower left hand corner.

Figure 181. Use of Stenciling to Identify Objects in OpenGL™

This code is implemented in several examples included in this series of three books, including View3D in *3D Articulation*; ETTP, knight, MSRE, museum, SandyRun, and SWSA5 in *3D Models in Motion*; and knight, stonehenge2, and View3DS in *3D Rendering*.

While OpenGL™ 's stenciling works well enough to identify a few objects, it doesn't help when you need to select a few elements from among thousands. There is no limit to the number of 3D elements displayed or selected using TP2 but your only option is to save the modified model out to a new file and manipulate the results with some other software such as a text editor. Another option is presented in Appendix K.

Appendix J. Rendering: How Long Does It Take?

Most of the examples accompanying this text render quite rapidly. The complex hair example takes several seconds, especially with the more complex options (e.g., style 1 or 2). There are some sections of code that might seem tedious (e.g., creating and smoothing polygons with the *hoop* hair style) so that you might wonder if these could be streamlined so as to decrease the rendering time. You might even think of saving the polygons and outward normals in arrays. After all, calculating the normals takes a cross product plus at least one hypotenuse. In one sweep through the normalization function is called over four million times. Wouldn't it be worth it to minimize this effort?

We can explore these questions with code profiling, as described at the bottom of Appendix T. You will find a batch file (_trace.bat) in the examples hair folder that will work with either the Synamtec™ or Digital Mars™ compilers to produce a *profiled* executable. The source code (hair.c) contains conditional compilation statements to implement the necessary differences, including disabling delayed painting and exiting after the first rendering. After the program finishes, there will be two files (trace.def and trace.log), which contain the profiling results. These are summarized in the table on the next page.

In this table we see 4,194,080 calls to Normalize(), which calls CrossProduct() so that it is also called 4,194,080 times. We see that the function taking the longest time for a single call is GetBestPixelFormat(), but it is only called once. Tree time is sum of the function plus everything that it calls so that the tree time for main program is the total runtime.

Consider the function times and the percentage column in particular. Tree time for RenderComplexTube() accounts for 84% of the total time. Tree time for Normalize() and CrossProduct() contribute only a little more than 4% each. The function itself is not burdensome. The rendering engine calls:

```
glBegin(GL_QUAD_STRIP);
glNormal3d(p.x,p.y,p.z);
glVertex3f(w[i1].x,w[i1].y,w[i1].z);
glEnd();
```

are not profiled so we can't tell directly how long these take. We could, however, comment out the lines and run the program again. This exercise would be unnecessary because it is clear that most of the RenderComplexTube() time is spent inside the OpenGL™ rendering engine.

What does all this mean? The rendering part is by far the most time-consuming. Streamlining the code is somewhat pointless. Storing the polygons and normals in arrays is also pointless. After all that effort, you would hardly notice any difference in the time to render.

Table J1. Rendering Hair Once with Style Option 1

num calls	tree time μs	func time μs	func time %	per call μs	function name
24,648	30,010,214	27,216,402	84.14033%	1,104	RenderComplexTube
24,648	32,046,887	1,760,312	5.44206%	71	RenderHair
4,194,080	1,419,116	1,419,116	4.38724%	0	Normalize
4,194,080	1,377,402	1,377,402	4.25828%	0	CrossProduct
666,678	220,414	220,414	0.68142%	0	hypot3d
1	157,050	156,890	0.48503%	156,890	GetBestPixelFormat
1	32,166,691	102,810	0.31784%	102,810	RenderHead
148,731	46,636	46,636	0.14418%	0	xrand
1	11,714	11,714	0.03621%	11,714	ReadModel
4,314	11,484	9,994	0.03090%	2	glColor
24,648	7,732	7,732	0.02390%	0	drand
1	7,745	5,326	0.01647%	5,326	CreateWindows
394	2,801	2,433	0.00752%	6	AreaTriangle
6,286	1,943	1,943	0.00601%	0	sign
2	32,168,574	1,723	0.00533%	861	glRepaint
37	1,645	1,636	0.00506%	44	MainProc@16
4,321	1,492	1,492	0.00461%	0	floatColor
4	32,169,149	537	0.00166%	134	PositionWindows
1	32,346,458	521	0.00161%	521	main
6	426	423	0.00131%	70	CreatePushButton
3	292	292	0.00090%	97	Register
5	276	273	0.00084%	54	CreateRadioButton
72	474	160	0.00049%	2	QuickSortIndices
2	158	158	0.00049%	79	WindowText
16	32,169,149	48	0.00015%	3	PlotProc@16
16	39	38	0.00012%	2	LogoProc@16
1	302	9	0.00003%	9	RegisterClasses
1	6	6	0.00002%	6	GetResource
1	8	2	0.00001%	2	LoadBitmapResource
1	10	2	0.00001%	2	LoadBitmaps
9,292,999		32,346,442	100.00000%		

Appendix K. Splitting a Model Mathematically

It can be quite tedious to split a model into left, right, front, and back legs or other such categories by selecting one element at a time. Some models (VRML, for example, skeleton.wrl in the model folder of the online archive) may be already split into parts and have clear separators in the file:

```
geometry DEF LFEMUR010_FACES    IndexedFaceSet
geometry DEF LHAND010_FACES     IndexedFaceSet
geometry DEF LHUMERUS010_FACES  IndexedFaceSet
geometry DEF LKNEE010_FACES     IndexedFaceSet
geometry DEF MANDIBLE010_FACES  IndexedFaceSet
geometry DEF PELVIS010_FACES    IndexedFaceSet
```

while most others may not. Another option for splitting models is mathematically. This process involves tests such as less than or greater than and also inside polygon calculations. To illustrate this we will use the T-Rex model, which may be found in the examples\T-Rex folder. The complete model (zip file) is included in the online archive accompanying *3D Models in Motion*. It can be rendered with View3D, which may be found in the online archive accompanying the present text. It is shown in the figure below:

Figure 182. T-Rex Rendered by View3D

View3D will import the model from the zip file (as 3DS) and export it to 3DV format, which is far less convoluted and also not arcane binary. This format can be read in and written out using read3dv.c, which may be found in the utilities folder. We will process this model with split.c, which may be found in the examples\T-Rex folder. To assist in defining boundaries and polygons, we will also convert the model to an excel spreadsheet using 3dvtocsv.c, which may be found in the utilities folder. The result is in T-Rex.xls, shown below:

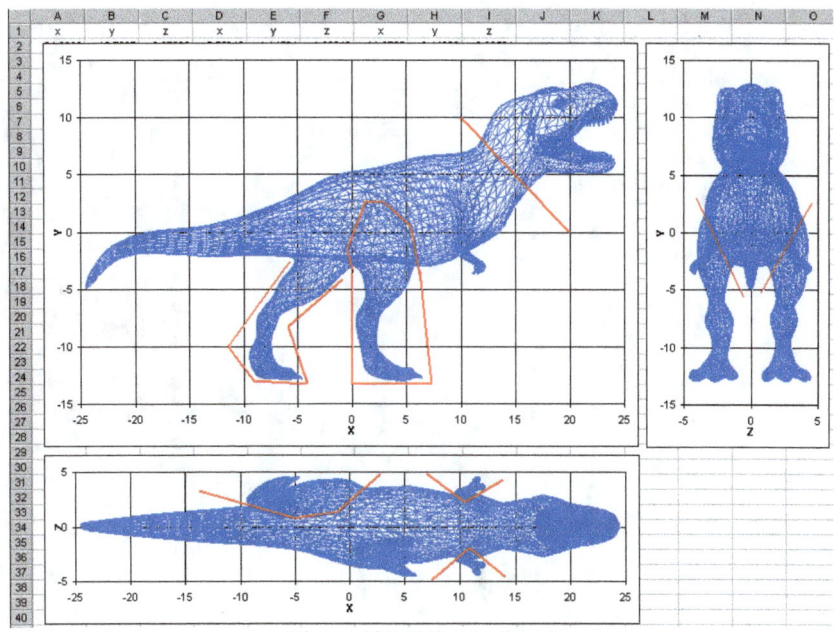

Figure 183. T-Rex in Excel

We read the model, process, and write it back out:

```
int main(int argc,char**argv,char**envp)
  {
  model=Read3DV("T-Rex.3dv");
  Split();
  Write3DV(&model,"split.3dv");
  return(0);
  }
```

We begin with the simplest test, that indicated by the downward-sloping diagonal line through the neck, y=20-x. If the centroid of an element (xc,yc,zc) is above this line, we change the color:

```
        for(e=0;e<model.elems;e++)
          {
          i=model.elem[e].i;
          j=model.elem[e].j;
          k=model.elem[e].k;
          x1=model.node[i].x;
          y1=model.node[i].y;
          z1=model.node[i].z;
          x2=model.node[j].x;
          y2=model.node[j].y;
          z2=model.node[j].z;
          x3=model.node[k].x;
          y3=model.node[k].y;
          z3=model.node[k].z;
```

```
xc=(x1+x2+x3)/3.;
yc=(y1+y2+y3)/3.;
zc=(z1+z2+z3)/3.;
if(yc>20.-xc)
   model.elem[e].color=0xFF0000;
else
   model.elem[e].color=0x00FF00;
}
```
The result is:

Figure 184. Element Centroids with y>20-x

To select just the eyes, we apply the following test
```
r=hypot(xc-19.26,yc-11.26);
if(r<0.35&&fabs(zc)>1.18)
```

Figure 185. Element Centroids with r<0.35 and |zc|>1.18

The PolyEdit utility (available free at the same location as the online archive accompanying this text) is 2D but can be quite useful too.

Figure 186. PolyEdit Showing Right Leg Selection Polygon

A 3D inside polygon test would be rather useless, as a point satisfying the criteria would have to lie *exactly* in the plane formed by two perpendicular vectors, which is unlikely. A 2D inside polygon test is quite useful, especially when combined with a second criteria along the third axis. The code is listed below:

```c
typedef struct{double x,y;}XY;
int InsidePolygon(XY*p,int n,double x,double y)
  {
  int above1,above2,i,right;
  double x1,x2,y1,y2;
  x2=p[n-1].x;
  y2=p[n-1].y;
  above2=y2>y?1:0;
  for(right=i=0;i<n;i++)
    {
    x1=x2;
    y1=y2;
    x2=p[i].x;
    y2=p[i].y;
    above1=above2;
    above2=y2>y?1:0;
    if(above1==above2)
      continue;
    if(x1>x&&x2>x)
      right++;
    else if(y1<y2)
      {
      if((x-x1)*(y2-y1)<(x2-x1)*(y-y1))
        right++;
      }
    else if(y1>y2)
      {
      if((x-x1)*(y2-y1)>(x2-x1)*(y-y1))
        right++;
      }
    }
  return(right&1);
  }
```

Note that the polygon is *not* closed. The polygon displayed in the preceding figure is:

```
XY poly[]={
  {  0.241,-10.490},
  {  0.948,-12.159},
  {  2.025,-13.213},
  {  3.563,-13.561},
  {  7.295,-13.152},
  {  6.671,-11.892},
  {  5.759,-11.205},
  {  4.265,-10.774},
  {  3.486, -9.338},
  {  3.691, -7.279},
  {  5.288, -5.670},
  {  6.282, -3.360},
  {  6.210, -1.174},
```

```
    {  5.657,   0.292},
    {  4.559,   1.265},
    {  3.420,   1.828},
    {  2.206,   2.012},
    {  1.101,   1.495},
    {  0.282,   0.540},
    {-0.189,  -1.473},
    {-0.036,  -2.971},
    {  0.594,  -3.679},
    {  0.903,  -5.217},
    {  0.147,  -7.000},
    {-0.136,  -9.009}};
```

The test is:
```
    if(InsidePolygon(poly,sizeof(poly)/sizeof(poly[0]),
      xc,yc)&&yc<-zc)
      model.elem[e].color=0xFF0000;
    else
      model.elem[e].color=0x00FF00;
```

The result is:

Figure 187. Leg Polygon Selection

Appendix L. Texture-Linked Models

Some models (e.g., 3DS) consist of a set of elements plus one or more textures. The textures are often JPGs, but not always. There are many formats within the TIF specification so that reading any one of these would be quite tedious. It is more efficient to use PaintShop™ or PhotoShop™ to convert any TIFs to JPGs and repackage. I have found several models online that have the wrong name embedded in the 3DS file for the texture. I have been able to fix these with a binary editor, using a shorter file name or padding the tail with zeroes if necessary. One model referred to the same texture with two different names so that the same image was included twice—quite wasteful.

Not only are some of the texture references misspelled in 3DS files found on the web, there is often no file extension (e.g., JPG or TIF) so that this must be assumed or supplied externally. View3D tries BMP, GIF, and JPG. Also, 3DS does not necessarily conform to OpenGL™ standards, particularly in the area of textures. Therefore, some textures must be *adjusted* (i.e., resized) before the models can be rendered with OpenGL™. This may also require changing the texture-to-vertex mapping. A resizing adjustment is always linear so that the coordinates can be easily modified (x'=a*x+b, y'=c*y+d). The coefficients (abcd) can be calculated with Excel. After that, read the model in (read3ds.c) and write it back out with the modified coordinates.

View3D expects the elements and textures to be contained within a single ZIP file and any textures to be stored in JPG format. You can repackage these if necessary so as to display them. View3D unzips the archive if necessary and places the files in the temporary folder. The location of the temporary folder in Windows® can be seen in Control Panel/System/Advanced Settings/Environment Variables or by opening a command prompt and typing> set.

Programmatic access to ZIP files is provided by the code (ziplib.c) and header (ziplib.h), both located in the utilities folder of the online archive accompanying the current text. Extracting the files accomplished by:

```
void ExtractFiles(char*archive)
  {
  int i,n;
  size_t uncomp_size;
  void*bufr;
  mz_zip_archive zip;
  mz_zip_archive_file_stat stat;
  if(_access(archive,0))
    return;
  memset(&zip,0,sizeof(zip));
  if(mz_zip_reader_init_file(&zip,archive,0)==0)
    return;
  n=(int)mz_zip_reader_get_num_files(&zip);
  for(i=0;i<n;i++)
    {
```

```
      if(mz_zip_reader_is_file_a_directory(&zip,i))
        continue;
      if(!mz_zip_reader_file_stat(&zip,i,&stat))
        {
        mz_zip_reader_end(&zip);
        goto error;
        }

      if((bufr=mz_zip_reader_extract_file_to_heap(&zip,stat
      .m_filename,&uncomp_size,0))==NULL)
        goto error;
      if(uncomp_size!=stat.m_uncomp_size)
        goto error;
      this_file.comp_size=(size_t)stat.m_comp_size;

      if(FileCreate(stat.m_filename,bufr,(size_t)stat.m_unc
      omp_size,stat.m_time)<0)
        goto error;
      free(bufr);
      }
error:
  mz_zip_reader_end(&zip);
  }
```

The sheep model in the View3DS folder is texture-linked:

Figure 188. Texture-Linked Sheep Model

Appendix M. Element Orientation

It is most often assumed that polygons are navigated in a counterclockwise direction. This presumption is as old as compass points:

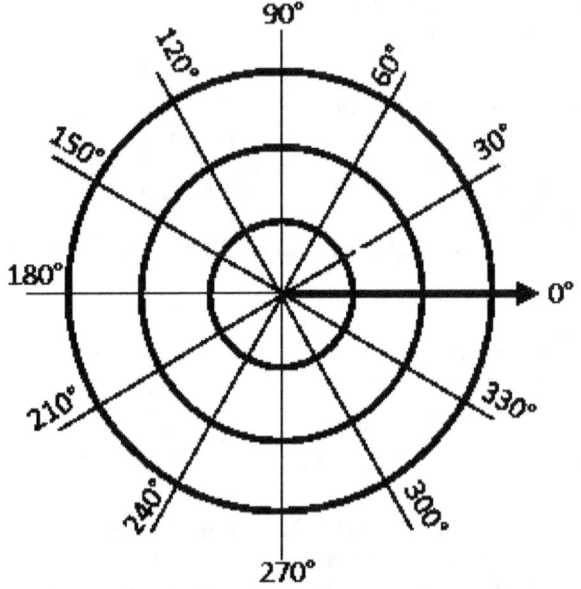

Figure 189

Figure 190. Counterclockwise Angles

Not all 3D models conform to this presumed orientation. You can select the orientation in OpenGL™

```
glFrontFace(GL_CCW);
glFrontFace(GL_CW);
```

but this won't fix the specified outward normals, only the automatically calculated one.

```
glEnable(GL_AUTO_NORMAL);
glDisable(GL_AUTO_NORMAL);
```

If the model appears unreasonably dark, the elements are probably backwards (i.e., clockwise). You can read the model in and write it back out with the opposite vertex order using the code found in the utilities folder of the online archive.

Appendix N: Painting without Flicker

The long ago example illustrates how to draw text that appears to be moving away from you as well as stars that you appear to be approaching. It also illustrates how to play a WAV file. Drawing the scrolling text without flicker requires two device contexts: 1) the display (or desktop) that you're painting onto, 2) the context where you draw stars and text. To eliminate flicker, use the BitBlt() API function to paint the final result onto the desktop.

Figure 191. Example of Painting without Flicker

There are two versions of this example. The first is 8 bits/pixel color so that each pixel is defined by a single byte. This facilitates distorting the text. The second example is 24 bits/pixel color and uses StretchBlt() to distort the text. The first illustrates byte-by-byte bitmap manipulations and the second illustrates the use of multiple device contexts and the GdiTransparentBlt() function to copy the text onto the stars.

Appendix O: Spinning Cube

The spinning cube demo was part of the earliest Microsoft® Software Developer Kits. The problem is, it was very poorly written and didn't work properly. It also would only read BMP files. I have completely rewritten it and added GIF and JPG formats. If you need functions to load, manipulate, and change any of these three image formats, you will find them in the Spin Cube folder.

Figure 192. Updated Spin Cube Screen Saver

This example uses a memory device context to build the image and BitBlt() to paint. It also keeps track of the part of the display that is changed, so that the minimum area is repainted. It uses the PlgBlt() to shear the images into parallelograms corresponding to the cube.

The setup also doesn't work in the SDK example. It's a little tricky to get a screen saver to run inside the preview window, as illustrated below. It's also necessary to set options and make adjustments, which requires a dialog and message processing. All of this is included in the revised edition of Spin Cube.

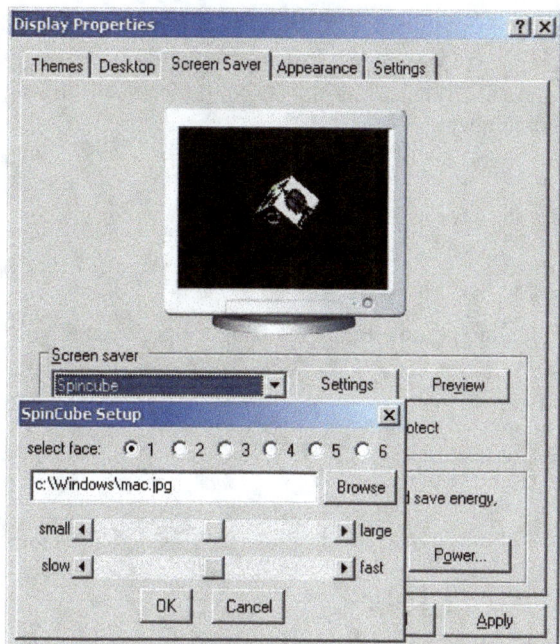

Figure 193. Spin Cube Options Dialog

Appendix P: Random Numbers

Random numbers are often used in rendering to create surfaces and simulated textures. The standard library (stdio.h) uses the following algorithm to produce random numbers:

```
short int rand(void)
  {
  static unsigned long int r=1;
  r=r*1103515245UL+12345UL;
  return((unsigned short int)(r/0x10000UL)&0x7FFF);
  }
```

Park & Miller[8] suggest the following simple algorithm:

```
short int random()
  {
  static long int seed=1;
  seed=(16807*seed)%2147483647;
  return(seed/2147483647);
  }
```

Marsaglia[9] has provided the following, considerably more complicated algorithm:

```
#define PHI 0x9e3779b9

static uint32_t Q[4096],c=362436;

void init_rand(uint32_t x)
  {
  int i;
  Q[0]=x;
  Q[1]=x+PHI;
  Q[2]=x+PHI+PHI;
  for(i=3;i<4096;i++)
    Q[i]=Q[i-3]^Q[i-2]^PHI^i;
  }

uint32_t rand_cmwc(void)
  {
  uint64_t t,a=18782LL;
  static uint32_t i=4095;
  uint32_t x,r=0xfffffffe;
  i=(i+1)&4095;
  t=a*Q[i]+c;
  c=(t>>32);
  x=t+c;
```

---

[8] "Random Number Generators: Good Ones Are Hard to Find," Park, S. K, and Miller, K. W., *Communications of the ACM*, Volume 31 Issue 10, Oct. 1988, pp. 1192-1201.

[9] Marsaglia, G. "Random Number Generators", *Journal of Modern Applied Statistical Methods*, Vol. 2., 2003.

```
if(x<c)
    {
    x++;
    c++;
    }
Q[i]=r-x;
return(Q[i]);
}
```

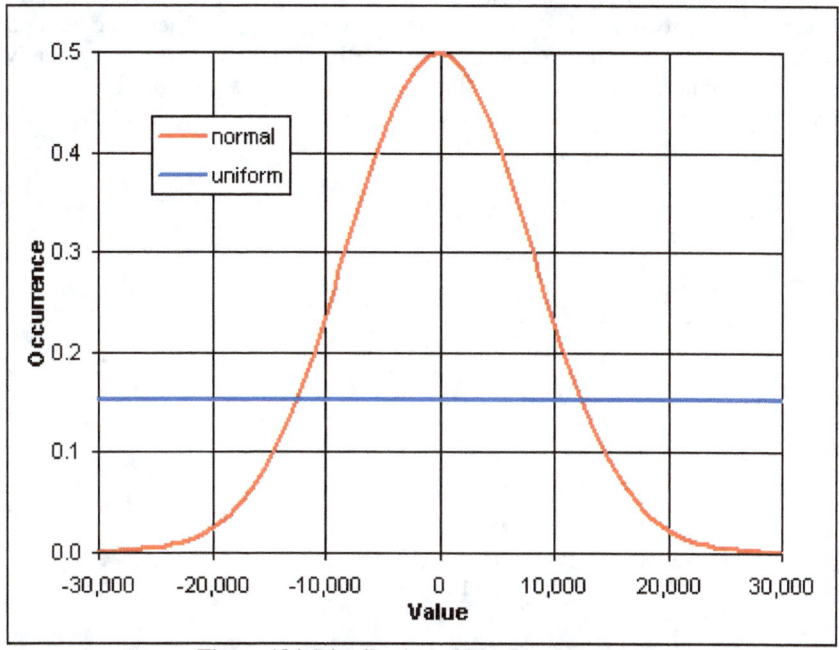

Figure 194. Distribution of Random Numbers

The Sky Fly example includes an advanced random number generator (random.c), developed at the University of California, Berkley. There are numerous less complicated random number generators that could be used with fully adequate results, which is why I replaced the Berkley algorithm with the following, much simpler one:

```
long random()
    {
    union{short s[2];long l}u;
    u.s[0]=rand();
    u.s[1]=rand();
    return(u.l);
    }
```

This same technique could be used to further randomize the result:

```
long random()
    {
```

```
int i;
union{BYTE b[4];long l;}u;
for(i=0;i<4;i++)
   u.b[i]=(BYTE)(((unsigned)rand())%256);
return(u.l);
}
```

These algorithms produce uniformly distributed random numbers, rather than normally distributed (a.k.a., Gaussian) random numbers. The difference between these two is illustrated in the preceding figure. There are several algorithms for converting uniformly distributed random numbers into normally distributed random numbers. The simplest is listed below for both integer and real numbers:

```
short int rnorm()
   {
   short int i;
   long l;
   for(l=i=0;i<12;i++)
      l+=rand();
   i=(short int)(l/12);
   return(i);
   }
double rdist(double avg,double std)
   {
   int i;
   double r;
   r=0.;
   for(i=0;i<12;i++)
      r+=rand()/32767.;
   return(avg+std*(r/6.-1.));
   }
```

Appendix Q. Hot Key Rotation

It is most convenient to control the view of 3D objects with the directional plus other control keys and to do so in steps. While many programs allow the user to select an item and then rotate it by dragging the mouse, this often results in ambiguous motions and irregular intervals. For example, angles in steps of 5° are usually adequate, as are displacements in steps of 5% of the display dimensions. This is easily accomplished in a Windows® GUI by defining what are called *accelerators*. These are listed in the resource (.rc) file. A sample is listed below and a complete list can be found in keys.rc in the utilities folder.

```
FAST ACCELERATORS
  BEGIN
    "A",PUSH_ALT_A,VIRTKEY,ALT
    "B",PUSH_ALT_B,VIRTKEY,ALT
    "C",PUSH_ALT_C,VIRTKEY,ALT
    "A",PUSH_CTL_A,VIRTKEY,CONTROL
    "B",PUSH_CTL_B,VIRTKEY,CONTROL
    "C",PUSH_CTL_C,VIRTKEY,CONTROL
    "A",PUSH_CTL_ALT_A,VIRTKEY,CONTROL,ALT
    VK_F1,PUSH_F1,VIRTKEY
    VK_F4,PUSH_ALT_F4,VIRTKEY,ALT
    VK_LEFT,PUSH_SHIFT_LEFT,VIRTKEY,SHIFT
    VK_RIGHT,PUSH_SHIFT_RIGHT,VIRTKEY,SHIFT
  END
```

The commands are defined in another file (keys.h), a sample is listed below:

```
#define PUSH_ALT_A      0x0F00
#define PUSH_ALT_B      0x0F01
#define PUSH_ALT_C      0x0F03
#define PUSH_ALT_F4     0x0F0D
```

These must be loaded in WinMain() and placed inside the main message loop, as shown below:

```
int WINAPI WinMain(HINSTANCE hCurrent,HINSTANCE
    hPrevious,char*lCommand,int nShow)
{
HACCEL acc;
acc=LoadAccelerators(hInst,"FAST");
while(GetMessage(&msg,NULL,0,0))
  if(!TranslateAccelerator(msg.hwnd,acc,&msg))
    if(!TranslateMessage(&msg))
      DispatchMessage(&msg);
```

When the user presses one of these keys, a corresponding message is sent to the main procedure, where it can be processed, as illustrated below:

```
LRESULT WINAPI MainProc(HWND hWnd,DWORD wMsg,WPARAM
    wParam,LPARAM lParam)
{
if(wMsg==WM_COMMAND)
  {
```

```
if(wParam==PUSH_UP)
  {
  Objective.a-=5;
  if(Objective.a<0)
    Objective.a=355;
  InvalidateRect(hPlot,NULL,FALSE);
  return(TRUE);
  }
if(wParam==PUSH_DOWN)
  {
  Objective.a+=5;
  if(Objective.a>355)
    Objective.a=0;
  InvalidateRect(hPlot,NULL,FALSE);
  return(TRUE);
  }
if(wParam==PUSH_LEFT)
  {
  Objective.c+=5;
  if(Objective.c>355)
    Objective.c=0;
  InvalidateRect(hPlot,NULL,FALSE);
  return(TRUE);
  }
if(wParam==PUSH_RIGHT)
  {
  Objective.c-=5;
  if(Objective.c<0)
    Objective.c=355;
  InvalidateRect(hPlot,NULL,FALSE);
  return(TRUE);
  }
```

The call to `InvalidateRect()` forces the plot window to be repainted, which causes the scene to be rendered again by the OpenGL™ engine.

```
LRESULT WINAPI PlotProc(HWND hWnd,DWORD wMsg,WPARAM
  wParam,LPARAM lParam)
  {
  if(wMsg==WM_CLOSE)
    return(FALSE);
  if(wMsg==WM_CREATE)
    return(FALSE);
  if(wMsg==WM_DESTROY)
    return(FALSE);
  if(wMsg==WM_PAINT)
    {
    HDC hDC;
    PAINTSTRUCT ps;
    hDC=BeginPaint(hWnd,&ps);
    if(pDC)
```

```
    {
    if(hDC!=pDC)
        Abort(__LINE__,"OpenGL device context not
preserved");
        glRepaint(TRUE);
        }
    EndPaint(hWnd,&ps);
    return(FALSE);
    }
if(wMsg==WM_SIZE)
    {
    PositionWindows();
    glRepaint(TRUE);
    return(FALSE);
    }
return(DefWindowProc(hWnd,wMsg,wParam,lParam));
}
```

In the GUI employed for these examples, the directional keys control scene rotations. Adding the alt key controls scene translation (i.e., pan). Adding the ctl key controls the light positioning. Pressing ctl-Z resets the scene, which was a useful combination implemented in early versions of AutoCAD.

Appendix R: GLUT® & Windows®

The OpenGL™ ™ Utilities Library, or GLUT®, is a convenient addition to the basic library, but it there are subtleties that you need to know when using this on the Windows® operating system. Windows® applications work with handles and device contexts, but the GLUT® functions do not provide these. If you want to build a fully functional Windows® application, you will need at least some of these essentials.

If you use glutInit(), glutInitWindowPosition(), glutInitWindowSize(), and glutMainLoop() to begin an application, as is the case in all of the Mesa examples, you will first need the handle to the instance. There are two ways of getting this: 1) as the first argument in WinMain(), or 2) the API function GetModuleHandle().

```
HINSTANCE hInst;
int WINAPI WinMain(HINSTANCE hInstance,HINSTANCE
   hPrev,char*lpszLine,int nShow)
{
  hInst=hInstance;
```

or

```
  hInst=GetModuleHandle(NULL);
```

The main procedure of a Windows® application is supposed to be WinMain(), not main(), although the latter will work and give you an extraneous console window. WinMain() does not come with the command line arguments, but these are available through global variables:

```
extern int __argc;
extern char**__argv;
extern char**_environ;
```

GLUT® creates a top-level window, but you need this to be a child window within the structure of your program. To accomplish this, you must first let GLUT® create its window. That way it will be the only active window. Use the GetActiveWindow() API call to get the handle to the GLUT® window. Then create your own top-level window using CreateWindow(). Finally, use the API function SetParent() to make the GLUT® window a child of your window.

You may also need the device context of the GLUT® window. Use the API functions GetDC() followed by ReleaseDC() to get this device context. You must release it so that OpenGL™ ™ can work with it. Do not use the API functions CreateDC() and DeleteDC(), as this device context has already been created.

If you need a handle to the bitmap in the device context created by GLUT®, first create a compatible bitmap from the device context. Then select this into the device context using the API function SelectObject(). This function will return the handle of the bitmap that was selected into the device context. Select it back into the device context and then destroy the compatible bitmap. This process is illustrated in the following code snippet:

```
HBITMAP GetGlutBitmap(HDC glutDC)
{
HBITMAP compHB,glutHB;
compHB=CreateCompatibleBitmap(glutDC,32,32);
glutHB=SelectObject(glutDC,compHB);
SelectObject(glutDC,glutHB)
DeleteObject(compHB);
return(glutHB);
}
```

Appendix S. Format Conversions Using TP2

I developed TPLOT in 1980 while working on my doctorate to graphically display the data I was collecting in the laboratory. It originally only worked on one device: Tektronix 4010. That's where the "T" in TPLOT came from. Over the years I added many devices and continued to use TPLOT as I worked in industry. TPLOT was written in FORTRAN, which became increasingly problematic, as operating systems evolved. In the summer of 1993, I began work on the second generation of TPLOT, which I named TP2. This new code was written in C, which opened up many more devices, but it was still not technically a Windows® application. That change didn't come until the spring of 1998. There have been dozens of revisions and additions since then. TP2 is available free online:

http://dudleybenton.altervista.org/software/index.html

Perhaps the biggest difference between TP2 and similar graphic utilities is file types. For instance, the file extension doesn't mean anything to Tecplot™[10]. That is, the same data could be stored in a file with any extension. For Tecplot™ the data structure is defined by various headers and there can be multiple types of data in the same file. For TP2 the data structure is identified by the file extension, as indicated below, and there can be only one data structure in a file.

filename.extention

In order to control how the data is presented in Tecplot™ you also need a layout file (usually, but not necessarily, filename.lay). TP2 displays data based on the type, which is indicated by the file extension. Tecplot™ will display 3D data as 3D or 2D with or without contours, shading, slicing, etc. TP2 will always display 3D data in 3D, unless you are specifically slicing at a plane. TP2 recognizes many more data structures than Tecplot™ (27 in all), each one having a different file extension. TP2 also has a layout (file extension TP2) and can display data from multiple files and of multiple structures, but this isn't mandatory, as with Tecplot™.

Surfaces and Volumes

Both Tecplot™ and TP2 handle 2D surfaces and 3D volumes. The display is similar, but the data structures are different. Tecplot™ requires the file to contain every x,y,z for 2D or x,y,z,w for 3D. One of the main motivations for developing TP2 was efficiency and compactness, including the smallest possible file sizes. If the surface or volume is complete (i.e., rectangular), whether or not the spacing is uniform, there is a definite pattern so that it is superfluous to enter

---

[10] Tecplot™ is a powerful and versatile tool for visualization of many different types of data, but particularly fluid flow, as this software arose from and was motivated by early CFD research. The developers of this software had connections with NASA and were deeply involved with aerodynamics. This excellent product can be found at their web site: https://www.tecplot.com/

all of the points except for z in 2D and w in 3D. That's how TP2 works. Surfaces are defined by a 2D table (file extension TB2) and volumes are defined by a 3D table (file extension TB3). The data are entered as a list of x's, then y's, then z's, then w's—not each and every x,y,z,w.

Finite Elements

Finite elements (triangles, quadrangles, tetrahedra, bricks, etc.) are very similar in Tecplot™ and TP2. The file structure consists of a list of nodes followed by a list of element indices. For TP2 2D finite elements have a file extension of 2DV and 3D finite elements have the extension 3DV.

Velocity Vectors

Velocity vectors are handled differently. In Tecplot™ the velocity components (typically u, v, and w) can be in any column, but are defined along with spatial coordinates (x, y, and z). With TP2 2D velocity vectors consist of x, y, u, and v—in that order and in a file having the extension V2D. Three-dimensional velocity vectors consist of x, y, z, u, v, and w—in that order and in a file having the extension V3D.

Layout

As mentioned before, Tecplot™ *requires* a layout file, which usually has the extension LAY. TP2 accepts an *optional* layout file, which has the extension TP2. With TP2, you can override any file extension (for example reading 2D velocity vectors from a file with extension VEC) by appending a minus followed by the intent, as in:

TP2 velocities.vec-v2d

Of course, this means that with TP2, you can't plot data from files that have a minus contained in the name, as this will be interpreted, truncating the file name.

Multiple Document Interface

Windows® recognizes what is called a *multiple document interface*, or MDI. TP2 is based around this concept, while Tecplot™ is not. Tecplot™ will only display a single context. TP2 will display up to 25 completely unrelated contexts, each in its own window. TP2 can be launched with wild cards:

TP2 *.v2d *.v3d *.2dv *.3dv

Animations

Tecplot™ will create animations—raster meta files (extension RM) for early versions and also audio visual interleave files (extension AVI) for recent versions. A utility, Framer, is provided with Tecplot™ to display the animations so created. AVI files can be displayed by various utilities. TP2 creates and also displays various animations in several formats, including GIF.

Examples

Tecplot™ comes with several excellent examples. These are separate files in a subfolder created during installation. TP2 comes with a variety of 2D and

3D examples, all of which are embedded inside the executable, so that you only need the EXE file with TP2. When you select a demo, TP2 creates the files and then displays the results. Both programs come with help files.

Data Processing

Both Tecplot™ and TP2 process data in a variety of ways, including interpolation, cutting, slicing, and translation from one form to another. TP2 has far more options for this because I added a feature every time I needed one for the work I was doing.

Drawings and Objects

TP2 will also read some AutoCAD™ files, including DXF and 3DS (3D Studio) as well as virtual reality markup language (VRML) files, which Tecplot™ will not import.

File Conversions

TP2 import many types of files, including several 3D formats. These may be written out to a different format, resulting in a file conversion. There are also many conversions available from the menu/convert.

Selecting Individual Elements

Individual elements may be selected by first setting *select 3D objects* from the options menu, then clicking on the desired elements. It will be useful to activate element borders, which can be done in the user options window, brought up from the menu/windows/user controls.

Appendix T: Compilers

If you don't have a C compiler, I suggest either Digital Mars® or Microsoft®. The former can be downloaded free from the following link:

http://www.digitalmars.com/

The Microsoft® C compiler is also available free of charge. Simply download and install the W7.1 SDK and DDK. While these developer kits are no longer available at the Microsoft@ Download Center, they can be found elsewhere on the web. After you install the two kits, combine the bin, include, and lib folders and put them in a folder called something like C:\VC32 or C:\VC64. There will be several folders with similar names. If you are targeting a system with an Intel™ processor, the folders you need will have either x86 or x64 in them. There are four combinations of the two architectures. These arise from the O/S you are running them on and the O/S you are targeting. For instance, you can create a 64-bit executable on a 32-bit machine and vise versa. Unless you need more than 2GB of memory in a single program, 64-bit is not necessary, as 32-bit executables will run on either O/S. You will, however, need to create the specific target when creating Add-Ins for Excel, as these are not interchangeable.

The Intel™ C compiler touts extended features and convenient access to unlock the full power of their processors. I used it extensively at one time, but now see no advantage to it. The early Microsoft® C compilers were a dreadful mess of bugs and would croak if you turned on any of the optimization options. Sometime around 2005 Microsoft® fixed their C compiler, eliminating any need for the Intel™ C compiler.

Code Profiling

The Intel® compilers provide runtime profiling (i.e., function calls and timing), though somewhat cumbersome and expensive. In over 40 years I've never seen anything that comes close to Walter Bright's C compilers (originally Zortech™, then Symantec™, and now Digital Mars™). Simply add –gt and recompile to get a list of who called what, when, how many times, and how long each took. The convenience and simplicity is in a league of it's own—plus it's free! Walter Bright is a genius!

Appendix U. Win3D by Leendert Ammeraal

This tool is an oldie, but a goodie. It's also free! I have included it in the archive as-is for your use. While you don't get the source code for this very useful tool, it provides an excellent illustration of several important concepts and can be used to create, import, and export 3D models. It recognizes several different file formats, including DXF. The following description of Win3D is provided in the help file:

> If you are interested in the mathematical principles and programming aspects on which this program is based, you can use the following books for further reference. They are by Leendert Ammeraal and published by John Wiley, Chichester, England. Some programs (in their executable form) and some data files discussed in the first two of these books are also on the Win3D distribution disk:
>
> *Programming Principles in Computer Graphics, 2nd Ed. (1992)
> *Interactive 3D Computer Graphics (1988)
> *Windows Wisdom for C and C++ Programmers (1993)
> *Programs and Data Structures in C, 2nd Ed. (1992)
> *C for Programmers, 2nd Ed. (1991)
> *C++ for Programmers (1991)
> *Graphics Programming in Turbo C (1989)
>
> If you have any comments on Win3D or on the above books, please write to the publisher (at the address given by File | About Win3D...), or to the author: Leendert Ammeraal, Reigerlaan 4, 1241 ED Kortenhoef, The Netherlands.

Perhaps the two most interesting aspects of Win3D are the implementation of hidden lines/surfaces and intersections between objects. Hidden lines are illustrated in the following figure:

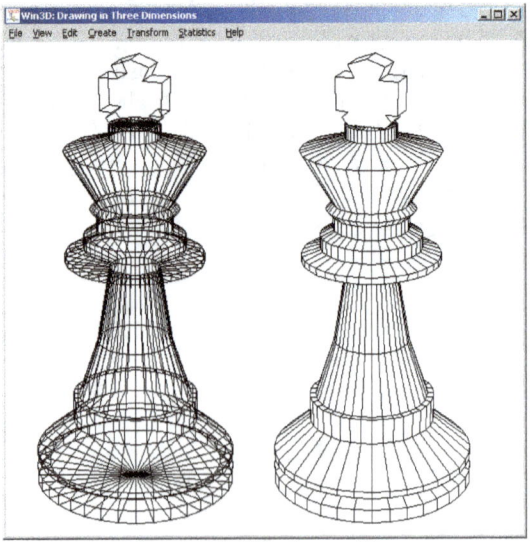

Figure 195. Wireframe View

The "solid" view of this same chess king is shown in the following figure:

Figure 196. Solid View

The facility of Win3D to find the intersection between two objects is illustrated in this next figure:

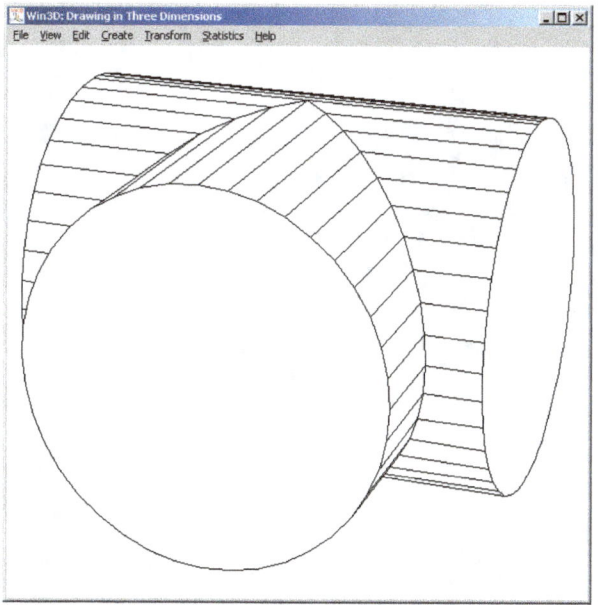

Figure 197. Intersecting Hidden Lines

The solid rendering is shown below:

Figure 198. Solid View of Intersecting Cylinders

also by D. James Benton

3D Articulation: Using OpenGL, ISBN-9798596362480, Amazon, 2021 (book 3 in the 3D series).

3D Models in Motion Using OpenGL, ISBN-9798652987701, Amazon, 2020 (book 2 in the 3D series).

3D Rendering in Windows: How to display three-dimensional objects in Windows with and without OpenGL, ISBN-9781520339610, Amazon, 2016 (book 1 in the 3D series).

A Synergy of Short Stories: The whole may be greater than the sum of the parts, ISBN-9781520340319, Amazon, 2016.

Azeotropes: Behavior and Application, ISBN-9798609748997, Amazon, 2020.

bat-Elohim: Book 3 in the Little Star Trilogy, ISBN-9781686148682, Amazon, 2019.

Boilers: Performance and Testing, ISBN: 9798789062517, Amazon 2021.

Complex Variables: Practical Applications, ISBN-9781794250437, Amazon, 2019.

Compression & Encryption: Algorithms & Software, ISBN-9781081008826, Amazon, 2019.

Computational Fluid Dynamics: an Overview of Methods, ISBN-9781672393775, Amazon, 2019.

Computer Simulation of Power Systems: Programming Strategies and Practical Examples, ISBN-9781696218184, Amazon, 2019.

Contaminant Transport: A Numerical Approach, ISBN-9798461733216, Amazon, 2021.

CPUnleashed! Tapping Processor Speed, ISBN-9798421420361, Amazon, 2022.

Curve-Fitting: The Science and Art of Approximation, ISBN-9781520339542, Amazon, 2016.

Death by Tie: It was the best of ties. It was the worst of ties. It's what got him killed., ISBN-9798398745931, Amazon, 2023.

Differential Equations: Numerical Methods for Solving, ISBN-9781983004162, Amazon, 2018.

Equations of State: A Graphical Comparison, ISBN-9798843139520, Amazon, 2022.

Evaporative Cooling: The Science of Beating the Heat, ISBN-9781520913346, Amazon, 2017.

Forecasting: Extrapolation and Projection, ISBN-9798394019494, Amazon 2023.

Heat Engines: Thermodynamics, Cycles, & Performance Curves, ISBN-9798486886836, Amazon, 2021.

Heat Exchangers: Performance Prediction & Evaluation, ISBN-9781973589327, Amazon, 2017.

Heat Recovery Steam Generators: Thermal Design and Testing, ISBN-9781691029365, Amazon, 2019.

Heat Transfer: Heat Exchangers, Heat Recovery Steam Generators, & Cooling Towers, ISBN-9798487417831, Amazon, 2021.
Heat Transfer Examples: Practical Problems Solved, ISBN-9798390610763, Amazon, 2023.
The Kick-Start Murders: Visualize revenge, ISBN-9798759083375, Amazon, 2021.
Jamie2: Innocence is easily lost and cannot be restored, ISBN-9781520339375, Amazon, 2016-18.
Kyle Cooper Mysteries: Kick Start, Monte Carlo, and Waterfront Murders, ISBN-9798829365943, Amazon, 2022.
The Last Seraph: Sequel to Little Star, ISBN-9781726802253, Amazon, 2018.
Little Star: God doesn't do things the way we expect Him to. He's better than that! ISBN-9781520338903, Amazon, 2015-17.
Living Math: Seeing mathematics in every day life (and appreciating it more too), ISBN-9781520336992, Amazon, 2016.
Lost Cause: If only history could be changed..., ISBN-9781521173770, Amazon, 2017.
Mass Transfer: Diffusion & Convection, ISBN-9798702403106, Amazon, 2021.
Mill Town Destiny: The Hand of Providence brought them together to rescue the mill, the town, and each other, ISBN-9781520864679, Amazon, 2017.
Monte Carlo Murders: Who Killed Who and Why, ISBN-9798829341848, Amazon, 2022.
Monte Carlo Simulation: The Art of Random Process Characterization, ISBN-9781980577874, Amazon, 2018.
Nonlinear Equations: Numerical Methods for Solving, ISBN-9781717767318, Amazon, 2018.
Numerical Calculus: Differentiation and Integration, ISBN-9781980680901, Amazon, 2018.
Numerical Methods: Nonlinear Equations, Numerical Calculus, & Differential Equations, ISBN-9798486246845, Amazon, 2021.
Orthogonal Functions: The Many Uses of, ISBN-9781719876162, Amazon, 2018.
Overwhelming Evidence: A Pilgrimage, ISBN-9798515642211, Amazon, 2021.
Particle Tracking: Computational Strategies and Diverse Examples, ISBN-9781692512651, Amazon, 2019.
Plumes: Delineation & Transport, ISBN-9781702292771, Amazon, 2019.
Power Plant Performance Curves: for Testing and Dispatch, ISBN-9798640192698, Amazon, 2020.
Practical Linear Algebra: Principles & Software, ISBN-9798860910584, Amazon, 2023.
Props, Fans, & Pumps: Design & Performance, ISBN-9798645391195, Amazon, 2020.
Remediation: Contaminant Transport, Particle Tracking, & Plumes, ISBN-9798485651190, Amazon, 2021.

ROFL: Rolling on the Floor Laughing, ISBN-9781973300007, Amazon, 2017.
Seminole Rain: You don't choose destiny. It chooses you, ISBN-9798668502196, Amazon, 2020.
Septillionth: 1 in 10^{24}, ISBN-9798410762472, Amazon, 2022.
Software Development: Targeted Applications, ISBN-9798850653989, Amazon, 2023.
Software Recipes: Proven Tools, ISBN-9798815229556, Amazon, 2022.
Steam 2020: to 150 GPa and 6000 K, ISBN-9798634643830, Amazon, 2020.
Thermochemical Reactions: Numerical Solutions, ISBN-9781073417872, Amazon, 2019.
Thermodynamic and Transport Properties of Fluids, ISBN-9781092120845, Amazon, 2019.
Thermodynamic Cycles: Effective Modeling Strategies for Software Development, ISBN-9781070934372, Amazon, 2019.
Thermodynamics - Theory & Practice: The science of energy and power, ISBN-9781520339795, Amazon, 2016.
Version-Independent Programming: Code Development Guidelines for the Windows® Operating System, ISBN-9781520339146, Amazon, 2016.
The Waterfront Murders: As you sow, so shall you reap, ISBN-9798611314500, Amazon, 2020.
Weather Data: Where To Get It and How To Process It, ISBN-9798868037894, Amazon, 2023.

www.ingramcontent.com/pod-product-compliance
Lightning Source LLC
Chambersburg PA
CBHW071445220526
45472CB00003B/680